The Legislative Veto

Westview Replica Editions

The concept of Westview Replica Editions is a response to the continuing crisis in academic and informational publishing. Library budgets for books have been severely curtailed. Ever larger portions of general library budgets are being diverted from the purchase of books and used for data banks, computers, micromedia, and other methods of information retrieval. Interlibrary loan structures further reduce the edition sizes required to satisfy the needs of the scholarly community. Economic pressures on the university presses and the few private scholarly publishing companies have severely limited the capacity of the industry to properly serve the academic and research communities. As a result, many manuscripts dealing with important subjects, often representing the highest level of scholarship, are no longer economically viable publishing projects--or, if accepted for publication, are typically subject to lead times ranging from one to three years.

Westview Replica Editions are our practical solution to the problem. We accept a manuscript in camera-ready form, typed according to our specifications, and move it immediately into the production process. As always, the selection criteria include the importance of the subject, the work's contribution to scholarship, and its insight, originality of thought, and excellence of exposition. The responsibility for editing and proofreading lies with the author or sponsoring institution. We prepare chapter headings and display pages, file for copyright, and obtain Library of Congress Cataloging in Publication Data. A detailed manual contains simple instructions for preparing the final typescript, and our editorial staff is always available to answer questions.

The end result is a book printed on acid-free paper and bound in sturdy library-quality soft covers. We manufacture these books ourselves using equipment that does not require a lengthy make-ready process and that allows us to publish first editions of 300 to 600 copies and to reprint even smaller quantities as needed. Thus, we can produce Replica Editions quickly and can keep even very specialized books in print as long as there is a demand for them.

About the Book and Author

The Legislative Veto:
Congressional Control of Regulation
Barbara Hinkson Craig

On June 23, 1983, the U.S. Supreme Court declared a legislative veto unconstitutional in the Immigration and Naturalization Service v. Chadha case, a ruling that seems to invalidate the legislative vetoes in more than two hundred laws. Two weeks later the court reaffirmed the principles of Chadha to invalidate the legislative veto in other acts. These epic cases, which are already being called the most important separation-of-powers rulings since the White House tapes cases, have generated debate over the implications of the loss of the legislative veto and the wisdom of the court's actions.

In this book the author argues that the legislative veto fell far short of its promise in actual operation over the regulatory process. Instead of promoting democratic congressional control over the actions of bureaucrats, legislative veto politics more often devolved to the politics of special interest protection, heavily influenced by unelected congressional staff. Moreover, the legislative veto allowed Congress to sidestep conflicts by issuing vague mandates that left agencies without the necessary congressional support to implement them.

Dr. Craig combines a historical perspective on the legislative veto with analyses of original case studies involving some of the most important policy issues of the 1980s--housing, education, energy, and consumer protection. Assessing all the cases available for research, she points to discrepancies between the legislative veto's intended effects and its actual results. In a final chapter she considers the impact of the Chadha case and discusses possible alternatives to the legislative veto for congressional control of regulation.

Barbara Hinkson Craig is assistant professor of government at Wesleyan University.

To the memory of my father
JAMES RICHARDS HINKSON

The Legislative Veto
Congressional Control
of Regulation

Barbara Hinkson Craig

Westview Press / Boulder, Colorado

A Westview Replica Edition

Copyright © 1983 by Westview Press, Inc.
Second printing 1984

Published in 1983 in the United States of America by
    Westview Press, Inc.
    5500 Central Avenue
    Boulder, Colorado 80301
    Frederick A. Praeger, President and Publisher

Library of Congress Cataloging in Publication Data
Craig, Barbara H. (Barbara Hinkson), 1942-
    The legislative veto.
    (A Westview replica edition)
    1. Legislative veto--United States. 2. Administrative procedure--
United States.   I. Title.
KF4944.C7   1983   328.73'0775   83-12371
ISBN 0-86531-998-7

Printed and bound in the United States of America

10 9 8 7 6 5 4 3 2

Contents

LIST OF TABLES ix
FOREWORD xi
ACKNOWLEDGMENTS. .xiii

INTRODUCTION 1

1   THE LEGISLATIVE VETO AND THE RULEMAKING
     PROCESS 7
          The Legislative Veto Defined 8
          Analytic Framework 11
          The Case Studies 16

2   HISTORICAL PERSPECTIVE ON THE LEGISLATIVE
     VETO: LEGAL AND ADMINISTRATIVE ISSUES . . . 23
          Early Historical Antecedents 23
          Expansion of the Legislative Veto . . . 26
          Constitutional Issues of the
               Legislative Veto 38
          Practical Considerations of the
               Legislative Veto in Rulemaking . . . 49

3   THE CASE OF THE HUD "CONSTITUTIONAL"
     VETOES 57
          Introduction 57
          The Department of Housing and Urban
               Development: 1965 to 1977 58
          The Department of Housing and Urban
               Development versus Congress:
               1978 61
          Thermal Standards Veto 64
          Spatial Deconcentration Veto 68
          Administrative Effects of the
               "Constitutional" Veto 74
          Policy Effects of the "Constitutional"
               Veto 76
          Summary 78

4   THE EDUCATION VETOES: CONFLICT AND
    ACCOMMODATION 83
        Introduction 83
        Education Policy: Local Control
            versus Federal Intrusion 86
        Education and the Legislative Veto,
            1972 to 1978:   Negotiation 90
        Education and the Legislative Veto,
            1979 to 1980:   Conflict 96
        The Department of Education versus
            Congress: The Face-off 107
        The Department of Education and
            Congress: Back to Negotiations . . . 112
        Summary 114

5   THE LEGISLATIVE VETO AS A MEANS FOR
    DECISION AVOIDANCE: TWO TARGETED VETOES   121
        Introduction 121
        Incremental Gas-Pricing Rule 122
        Passive Restraint Rule 138
        Targeted Use of the Veto: An
            Assessment 144

6   THE LEGISLATIVE VETO OF REGULATIONS:
    CONSEQUENCES FOR DEMOCRATIC
    POLICYMAKING 149
        The Legislative Veto and Democratic
            Control 150
        The Legislative Veto and Conflict
            Resolution 155
        The Legislative Veto and the
            Rulemaking Process 160
        Conclusion 163

EPILOGUE 169
        The Chadha Case: Summary and
            Analysis 169
        Picking up the Pieces: Life
            after the Veto 174

APPENDIX: EXCERPTS FROM THE EPIC CHADHA
            DECISION 183

INDEX 203

Tables

2.1 Legislative Vetoes Passed by Congress,
     by Decade 27

2.2 Legislative Vetoes Passed by Congress,
     1970s 28

2.3 Legislative Veto Authorities over
     Agency-Level Actions 31

5.1 Industrial and Residential Per-Unit
     Costs for Gas, 1978 to Third Quarter,
     1979 128

Foreword

Few recent Supreme Court decisions have been as widely debated, interpreted, and misinterpreted as the decision declaring the legislative veto unconstitutional. Some see the decision as a major defeat for the Congress and as a step toward return of the "Imperial Presidency." Others argue that the executive will be the loser because the Congress will be reluctant to grant discretionary powers without strings attached. But as Professor Barbara H. Craig's meticulously documented case studies conclusively demonstrate, it is highly misleading to reduce the complex and significant issues raised by the legislative veto to a simple contest for power between the executive branch and the Congress.

In analyzing the consequences of procedural change, Professor Craig is exploring a subject that up to now has received insufficient attention from administrators, lawmakers, and the scholarly community. Procedures may not attract headlines but they can have a critical influence on the formulation and execution of public policies. The ultimate test should be whether procedures contribute to more responsive and responsible government.

Procedural "reforms" such as the legislative veto may well produce results opposite from those intended by their advocates. While ostensibly designed to control the power of unelected bureaucrats, the legislative veto appears to have done the reverse. Professor Craig's research shows that instead of promoting more open government and effective control of bureaucratic power, the legislative veto in many instances has become a vehicle for secret negotiations and decision making by congressional and executive agency staff with minimal participation by elected members of the Congress.

Professor Craig's book should be required reading for lawmakers, administrators, and all those interested in understanding the intricacies of legislative politics, and executive-legislative relations. It underscores the need for substituting analysis for rhetoric in evaluating proposals for procedural reform.

Harold Seidman

Acknowledgments

The origins of this book go back several years--long before the legislative veto became a topic of general public interest. During this period, the unfailing support of colleagues who shared the vision of an issue whose time was yet to come made my efforts possible.

No one deserves more recognition for shaping my interest in the "veto" and my concern for intragovernmental relations than Harold Seidman and Robert S. Gilmour. The perspective I have gained from Harold Seidman's incomparable experience in Washington and in the world of academics has been matched in importance only by his friendship. The content and analysis of this book have been immeasurably improved by the time and expertise that Robert Gilmour so often and so enthusiastically provided.

Harold Bruff, George Cole, Phil Cooper, Lou Fisher, Alan Morrison, Terry McGinnis, Morton Rosenberg, and James Sundquist are all joint venturers in the trials and tribulations of the legislative veto who have provided valuable input into and comments on my research effort. The fact that some of us have not always shared the same views was to be expected and certainly added to the enjoyment of my studies.

I offer special thanks to the many people I interviewed during this undertaking from the congressional staffs, the White House, the executive departments, the independent agencies, and the special interest groups. Their willingness to share their time and experience with me clearly was the heart of the research.

Financial assistance for the expenses associated with my research was provided by the University of Connecticut. I gratefully acknowlege this aid, without which my many trips to Capitol Hill would have been impossible. I am equally indebted to Jennifer Dorn, who cheerfully provided bed and board in Washington, and also served as an informed guide around the congressional and executive staff offices to help me to locate the right people to interview.

Without Lee Messina's and Jan Bittner's word processing expertise and untiring patience in conquering

the intricacies of the new art of computer book publishing,
this book would not have been possible. Special thanks
also go to Betty Seaver--editor and friend extraordinaire,
to Helen Calabrese for cheerfully delivering numerous rush-
rush typing services, and to proofreaders Suzanne Chambers
and Linsley Craig.

    To my husband Bill, son Lathrop, and proofreading
daughter Linsley, take heart and do the rest of the dishes--
I'll soon be home again!

                              Barbara Hinkson Craig

Introduction

On June 23, 1983, just three weeks before this book was scheduled for print, the Supreme Court of the United States held the legislative veto unconstitutional in <u>Immigration and Naturalization Service</u> v. <u>Chadha</u>.* The chapters that follow have not been changed to reflect this far-reaching opinion. Instead, an epilogue has been added to assess the impact of this historical case and to review various veto replacements that have already been seriously proposed for adoption by Congress. As they stand, the case studies presented here lend practical support to the court's legal judgment, and provide evidence about the effects of congressional use of the legislative veto review power over agency regulations. Moreover, the case studies of the so-called constitutional veto (joint resolution of disapproval) applied in the Department of Housing and Urban Development cases (chapter 3) cast doubt on the wisdom of present congressional efforts to substitute constitutional veto devices for their now unconstitutional cousins.

The breadth of the court's ruling, which "appears to invalidate all legislative vetoes irrespective of form or subject" and which "strikes down in one fell swoop provisions in more laws enacted by Congress than the court has cumulatively invalidated in its history," came as a surprise to many.[1] In oral dissent from the bench (a rare departure from the norm), Justice White said that <u>Chadha</u> was "probably the most important case the Court has handed down in many years" and called the decision a "destructive action" that was "clearly wrong and unnecessarily broad." In an even more rare, and apparently extemporaneous reply, Chief Justice Burger—after noting the one point on which the court was in unanimous agreement, "that this is a very difficult and important case"—defended the majority position.[2] Two weeks later (July 6, 1983), without further comment, the court stood on the principles in <u>Chadha</u> to

---

*Excerpts from the majority opinion and dissents in <u>Chadha</u> are found in the Appendix.

1

invalidate the legislative veto in the Natural Gas Policy Act of 1978 and the Federal Trade Commission Improvements Act of 1980.

These epic cases, which are roundly described as the most important separation-of-powers rulings since the White House tapes cases, and which are among the Supreme Court's all-time most important decisions, have touched off a public debate over the implications of the loss of the legislative veto and the wisdom of the court's actions. Until these decisions, the legislative veto was an obscure, much ignored, and misunderstood creation--a fact that now means that the debate is being carried on with slogans and precious little concrete data or knowledge.

Pondering the effect of the Chadha decision on the effort of Congress to control delegated regulatory power, Representative Elliott H. Levitas (D, GA), the indefatigable champion of the legislative veto, has termed the court's holding a "train wreck of government"[3] that "opens the way for a true tyranny of the bureaucracy."[4] Others have charged the court with sounding the "death knell of direct congressional attempts to review executive and administrative action,"[5] and with throwing "shared power out the window."[6] Many observers see the president and the executive branch as the ultimate losers because Congress will be forced by its loss of the "flexible" veto device to circumscribe severely any delegations of authority by far narrower writing of legislation.[7] An editorial in the Atlanta Journal predicts even more dire consequences:

> The bottom line of the legislative veto decision is that the Supreme Court has approved a lawmaking process . . . in which the people and their representatives are left out entirely. The court has killed a method whereby Congress sought to find a remedy for this problem, but the problem remains--and we will not have a republic for very long unless another remedy is found.[8]

In decrying the loss of the legislative veto as a means of congressional control over the bureaucracy, commentators seem to have blindly accepted as fact the claim that exercise of the legislative veto has made, and could have continued to make, agency "lawmaking" more democratic. The assertion that the legislative veto has enabled the legislature to assume an effective role of supervisor of the executive, thereby assuring better protection of the public interest, is not supported by the evidence. In fact, the research presented in this book documents that the legislative veto never did what its proponents alleged it would do, and that in actual operation it fell far short of its promise.

Instead of promoting congressional control over the actions of bureaucrats, i.e., control by elected officeholders, legislative veto politics has more often devolved to the politics of special interest protection, typically operating in the secrecy of subcommittee anterooms, heavily influenced by unelected congressional staff. This is observed in veto reviews of the Department of Housing and Urban Development's fair housing regulations and thermal insulation standards (chapter 3); of the FTC's used-cars warranty rule (chapter 6) and of the National Highway Traffic Safety Administration's passive restraint (air-bags) rule (chapter 5); and in veto reviews of many federal education rules as well (chapter 4).

Rather than being a useful mechanism for conflict resolution within Congress, the legislative veto was used by Congress to paper over conflicts; installing the veto "in the wings" made possible imprecise and vague mandates that left agencies without the necessary support for implementation. The most common result was symbolic change and policy vacuum. Legislative vetoes included in Title IX of the Education Amendments of 1974 banning sex discrimination in programs receiving federal assistance, such as athletics (chapter 4), as well as those included in the FTC Improvements Act (chapter 6) and the Natural Gas Policy Act (chapter 5) offer apt examples of this.

When Congress chose to apply the legislative veto as a way to control regulation and the federal bureaucracy throughout the 1970s and 1980s, it put in peril a device that had seemed useful as a means of accommodation on issues of national moment between the president (as the president, distinct from an agency of the executive branch at several removes) and the Congress (as a voting body, not as a subcommittee and a few staffers negotiating behind closed doors). When Congress came very near to passing a generic veto as part of its regulatory reform bills in 1982, the spectre of universal application of congressional vetoes over all governmental regulations may have prompted the court to reach well beyond the facts in Chadha, when it could have ruled more narrowly.

No doubt Chadha does represent a "train wreck" of what looks to be a "highballing" new order: regulatory policymaking through veto-leveraged negotiation and negation. The following analysis of actual use of the legislative veto power over the regulatory process shows, however, that its loss is far from the catastrophe now bemoaned by so many commentators. In light of the evidence presented in chapters 3-6 concerning the effect of legislative veto politics on policy outcomes and the broad public interest, the current congressional scramble to replace the legislative veto with constitutionally acceptable (and often convoluted) surrogates needs to be viewed with some skepticism.

In the months and years ahead, Congress will be faced with finding suitable means of accommodation between itself, and the executive branch and the president, not only in regulatory matters but in foreign policy and other domestic issues as well. It is far too soon to make a final judgment on the efficacy of the alternatives now being offered, but it can be hoped that Congress will proceed with careful deliberation and a more realistic understanding of the disadvantages as well as the advantages of the now unconstitutional legislative veto in fashioning its successor mechanisms. It is to this end that the case studies in this book are now directed.

Notes

1. <u>INS</u> v. <u>Chadha</u> (80-1832, 80-2170, 80-2171--
Dissent), pp. 9, 38. As of the end of the last term (June
1982), the court had struck down as unconstitutional all or
part of 110 federal laws. See <u>Congressional Quarterly</u>,
June 25, 1983, p. 1263.
2. <u>New York Times</u>, June 24, 1983, p. B4.
3. <u>Congressional Quarterly</u>, June 25, 1983, p. 1264.
4. <u>Atlanta Journal</u>, June 27, 1983, p. 14-A.
5. Bernard Schwartz, "The 'Legislative Veto'--Now
That It's Gone," <u>New York Times</u>, June 30, 1983, Op-ed page.
6. <u>Congressional Quarterly</u>, June 25, 1983, p. 1264
(quoting Senator Carl Levin).
7. For example, see James L. Sundquist, "Without the
Legislative Veto . . . More Confrontation, Stalemate,
Deadlock," <u>Washington Post</u>, June 26, 1983, p. D-8, and <u>New
York Times</u>, June 25, 1983, p. 8 (quoting Norman Ornstein).
8. Robert Akerman, "Court Cuts the People Out of
Lawmaking Process," <u>Atlanta Journal</u>, June 27, 1983.

1
The Legislative Veto and the Rulemaking Process

Growing public disaffection with governmental regulation has directed the attention of lawmakers to the problem of control over administrative agencies and the bureaucrats who run them. One method of control that has been enjoying increasing popularity with many in Congress is the procedural device known as the "legislative veto" or "congressional veto." Major provisions that would subject every rule and regulation promulgated by executive and independent agencies to legislative veto scrutiny have been under consideration in both the House and Senate since 1976. Such agencies as the Federal Trade Commission, the Consumer Product Safety Commission, and the Department of Education already have their entire regulatory product subject to legislative veto review. Numerous other agencies must submit to Congress for review all regulations made under the authority of specific acts.

The congressional veto is a curious device that effectively stands the presidential veto on its head by requiring the agency to offer "legislation"--in this case in the form of agency-developed regulations--for congressional review and potential veto. Functional consequences for the governmental system of continued and expanded application of this device to the rulemaking process should receive far more notice and sustained analysis than obtain today. As the application of legislative veto controls becomes even more widespread, the need for the accumulation of information on experiences with veto-type oversight is imperative.

This book presents case studies of several currently operating legislative veto provisions over congressionally delegated rulemaking authority within a framework that allows for assessment of the veto's implications for the content and control of public policy within the regulatory process; for how Congress exercises its legislative and oversight functions; for the administrative system; and for what are understood to be the traditional guiding principles of administration and of our democratic process.

The Legislative Veto Defined

The legislative veto is an effort by Congress, by one house of Congress, or even by a single committee or chairman to retain control over the execution or interpretation of laws <u>after</u> enactment. The legislative veto has many variants but typically mandates that the executive branch notify Congress of an action proposed pursuant to statutory authority, and that it then wait for a specific time--usually thirty, sixty, or ninety days--before carrying out the action. Absent additional powers, congressional postenactment review of this sort is usually referred to as a "report-and-wait" or "advance-notification" require-ment. Reaction is limited under these circumstances to traditional legislative and budgetary channels. In this form, the procedure is safe from constitutional challenges, although some observers maintain that the resultant process is much the same as with other procedures, and they include review procedures such as these under the legislative veto rubric.[1]

If the review involves an inordinately long waiting period coupled with a procedure that allows a particular committee or its chairman to waive the waiting period, an executive official would have little choice but to come into agreement with a committee before acting. Under these conditions, the congressional review power is similar to the more controversial and constitutionally suspect legislative veto.[2] Included in this analysis is one case study involving application of a congressional postenactment review power of this design, the so-called constitutional veto.

A stronger form of postenactment review allows Congress to prevent implementation of proposed executive action by passing during the waiting period a concurrent resolution of disapproval (a majority vote in both houses, with no need for the president's signature; the so-called two-house veto); a resolution of disapproval by either house (a simple majority vote of one house, without the need of action by the other house or by the president; the so-called one-house veto); or even action of a single committee.[3] Another variant requires adoption of a resolution of approval by Congress or committees before the proposed executive action can go into effect.[4]

Proponents of the legislative veto assert that where regulations are involved, it provides a mechanism whereby Congress can respond more quickly than through the more protracted legislative process, and that it focuses the attention of Congress--or at least of some individual members or congressional staff--on potentially trouble-some aspects of regulations before they attain the force of law. Thus, Congress can protect the citizen from "bad law" before and not after damage is done.

Support for the legislative veto over regulations is also based on the veto's utility for resolving conflict within Congress. When the technology involved in policy considerations is complex or uncertain or when there is insufficient agreement among members to give specific policy direction, the legislative veto, it is argued, allows Congress to delegate the necessary flexibility to the executive to act, knowing that it can negate any delegation it deems improperly exercised.

The roots of the veto concept are found in the Legislative Appropriations Act for Fiscal Year 1933, which in Title IV (Reorganization of Executive Departments) authorized the president to transfer, to consolidate, and to redistribute by executive order any executive agencies or functions. An executive order issued under the act was transmitted to Congress to lie before it for sixty days. If either house passed a resolution disapproving the order within that time, it became null and void; if neither acted, the order became effective. This legislative veto concept, as applied to executive branch reorganizations, proved to be an ingenious way to enable Congress to transfer a time-consuming and politically sensitive legislative power to the president yet retain the right to negate its exercise.

Congress has increasingly employed veto-type controls in a variety of other efforts to oversee executive branch actions. According to the Congressional Research Service, between 1932 and February 1980 Congress approved at least 167 laws with one or more legislative veto provisions. Of these, more than half were enacted in the 1970s, forty-two during the Carter presidency.[5] More important than the surge in the veto's application, however, is the shift in target.

Prior to the 1970s, most of the provisions for veto review were in acts dealing with executive branch reorganization, conduct of foreign affairs and national defense, real estate transactions, and the administration of public works programs. Congressional control via the legislative veto in these instances has been exercised at the presidential-decision level or over pork-barrel, public-works-type project decisions. The Education Amendments of 1972, which included a legislative veto over the Office of Education's proposed family-contribution schedules for its program of basic grants for postsecondary education, signaled a dramatic alteration in the nature and scope of executive action that could be subject to the veto process. This broadened application to agency-level regulatory actions has been growing apace. Application of the legislative veto to executive agency and independent agency rules, regulations, plans, schedules, or guidelines is already a reality for many programs and is under consideration for many others.

Representative Elliott H. Levitas (D, GA), under the clarion call "Who Makes the Laws? Congress or Unelected Bureaucrats?" is continuing his crusade for application of the legislative veto to all rule-making procedures.[6] He is hardly alone in his efforts. Tabulations by Clark F. Norton of the Congressional Research Service show that twenty-three bills that provided for congressional review of agency rules and regulations in general--generic veto proposals--were introduced into the 96th Congress (1979-1980).[7] In 1981 Levitas again introduced his bill (H.R. 1776: Procedures for Congressional Review of Agency Rules), this time with more than two hundred cosponsors. By May 1981 at least seven other proposals to the same effect had been introduced in the 97th Congress.[8] In March 1982 the Senate voted 69 to 25 to make almost all agency regulations subject to a two-house veto procedure. Without the pressures of the FY 83 budget battle coupled with reelection demands, which precluded final action on regulatory reform during 1982, and given past House support for the veto, Congress undoubtedly would have enacted a generic veto in some form. Efforts are again under way in the 98th Congress (1983-84) toward this end.

In support of his bill Levitas argues, roughly: Agency regulations are tantamount to laws. Citizens must abide by them, often facing penalties for failure to do so. Therefore, a democratically elected legislature has not only the right but the <u>duty</u> to exercise control over their content. The best way to do this, in Levitas's opinion-- and in the opinion of many other members as well--is for Congress to have the opportunity to veto regulations before they go into effect.

Former Assistant Attorney General Robert G. Dixon, Jr., calls legislative veto provisions over regulatory matters "a significant attempt by Congress to move from vigorous oversight of the executive, through hearings, reports and revisions of statutes, to shared administration under existing statutory delegations."[9] By using the legislative veto device, Congress, as Harold Seidman points out, is able to "bypass the president and directly control subordinate executive branch officials."[10] Concern about legislative intrusion into the domain of the executive branch has prompted charges of unconstitutionality; indeed, such charges make up the bulk of current criticism of the veto device.

It is common for the political system to embrace simple-seeming procedural solutions for dealing with complex, often highly political, and conflicting policy problems. But, just as organizational arrangements are not neutral in their impact, structural and procedural arrangements are not neutral in theirs. Changes in procedures inevitably result in redistribution of political resources and, ultimately, of power to control outcomes of political processes. Reliance upon the legislative veto procedure has functional consequences-- for Congress, for the executive, and for the overall political and administrative process.

It has yet to be proved that the legislative veto insures that regulatory agencies will remain "true" to

congressional intent in carrying out the law, or that it
reduces abusive and excessive regulation. And although it
may, indeed, expeditiously resolve conflict, the policy
implications of this approach to lawmaking remain unclear.
It is essential that we know how the legislative veto
operates or is likely to operate in the reality of the
political process if we are to evaluate it as a "reform" for
regulatory problems. The analysis of the case studies in
chapters 3, 4, and 5 addresses three questions: (1) What
are the functional consequences for the political system of
the imposition of the legislative veto upon rulemaking? (2)
Who is advantaged? (3) Who loses in the redistribution of
power?

Analytic Framework

This study specially emphasizes the nature of the
interrelationships among various actors in the regulatory
process, the effect of the addition of the legislative veto
on the distribution of power within the interrelationships,
and the veto's impact upon rules and regulations, the
product of the regulatory process.

Because the character of each legislative decision-
making area is dependent upon the relationships that exist
among the participants (the agencies; the congressional
committee or individual member; the congressional staff;
the executive branch hierarchy--the president and Office of
Management and Budget or the secretary; the interest groups
or clienteles; and the public at large), analysis of the
interrelationships in areas where the veto is in place
offers the basis for understanding the impact of the veto[11]
upon each regulatory subsystem and its policy outputs.
Such a basis also helps to explain power distributions
within the interrelationships and alterations effected by
the addition of the legislative veto.[12]

Implicit in the analysis is the assumption that
structural or procedural changes within policy
subsystems--in this case regulatory processes--produce
functional changes in the nature of the procedure, the
product, or both. This assumed link between structural
change and resultant functional outcomes, either intended
(manifest) or unintended (latent), rests upon concepts of
structural functionalism as developed by contemporary
sociological theorists, particularly Robert K. Merton.[13]

The analytical framework is based on the conception of
"arenas of power," developed first by Harold Lasswell and
Abraham Kaplan, and later articulated by Theodore Lowi and
others.[14] The concept is used to analyze the nature of the
interrelationships among participants in policymaking
processes. Broadly categorized, policymaking relationships can be described by three variations: distributive,
pluralistic, and administrative arenas.

The accepted social science model of regulation used to be depicted as comfortably isolated coalitions of regulator and regulatee that were organized on an industry-by-industry basis, the so-called iron triangles of government policymaking. Typical of this would be the coalition of the television and radio industries, the Federal Communications Commission, and the Subcommittee on Communications of the House Interstate and Foreign Commerce Committee and the Subcommittee on Communications of the Senate Commerce, Science, and Transportation Committee. Regulatory decision making under this set of circumstances allows for protection and enhancement of the industry as well as regulation. Indeed, legislative intent in the creation of such regulatory agencies specifically spells out that kind of dual, if often conflicting, purpose. Lowi has referred to such relationships as distributive policymaking arenas that individualize conflict, provide the basis for highly stable coalitions, and allow for obscure piecemeal decision making.[15] Disagreements within distributive arenas rarely erupt in the public forum; rather, they are hammered out within the arenas. Under such an arrangement, the industry and the congressional oversight committee members enjoy a close and influential relationship with the regulatory agency.

Several things have happened to undermine the iron-triangle model for many regulatory areas. First, the governmental role has expanded, especially since the mid-sixties, beyond marketplace economic regulation into a broader regulation aimed at protecting the "public" by seeking to promote health, safety, a cleaner environment, and a more open political process. Second, the era of unlimited resources that had assured ever-expanding growth appeared to come to an abrupt though hardly unpredicted halt. The rise of the so-called public interest groups, such as Common Cause, the Sierra Club, Ralph Nader's Congressional Watch, and others, publicized and highlighted the effect of regulation on citizens. Finally, the cross-cutting nature of the problems that faced government--environmental protection versus energy needs versus jobs versus inflation versus defense needs versus social programs--made decision making in isolated, supportive enclaves difficult if not impossible.

In light of these realities, Congress has the politically problematic task of dealing with policymaking for governmental regulation in more visible and competitive pluralistic arenas. The current pervasiveness of regulation under these conditions should then mean that pluralistic arenas within the legislative process would abound, and that intergroup coalition building, bargaining, and compromise would dominate regulatory decision making in Congress. On the contrary, either because it is unable to deal with complex and highly technological issues, or because of the urgent need for a consensus to expedite enactment of legislation, or because it wants to avoid having to resolve open conflict among politically powerful groups--which is an essential part of the pluralistic politics of broad regulation-- Congress has increasingly transferred regulatory decision making to the administrative agencies.

Administrative arenas with broad mandates remove congressional actors from the center of decision making, replacing them with administrative "experts" whose decisions are expected to be the product of a "rational assessment" of a record that includes all relevant points of view, alternatives, and technical data. The procedure for the "rational assessment" combines some aspects that resemble the legislative process with others that are more akin to judicial procedures. Executive and independent agencies that promulgate regulations are subject to the Administrative Procedure Act. Section 553 of the act, which prescribes the informal rulemaking process, specifies that an agency publish a notice of intent to promulgate a rule, offer an opportunity for interested parties to comment, consider relevant matter presented to it, and publish the final rule at least thirty days before it becomes effective, together with a general statement on its purpose and the basis on which the agency has decided. This informal rulemaking process was designed to resemble the legislative model for holding hearings on proposed legislation as a method for allowing interested parties to make input into the decision-making process.

Since passage of the Administrative Procedure Act in 1946, and especially in the 1970s, both Congress and the federal courts have undertaken to formalize the rulemaking process. Much of the congressional motivation arises in the desire of Congress to insure that all interested parties have the opportunity and ability to participate fully in rulemaking. Many recent statutes reflect the trend toward formalization; the Federal Trade Commission Amendments of 1980 offer one example. Section 9(a) of the amendments provides that "no presiding officer [of a rulemaking proceeding] shall consult any person or party with respect to any fact in issue unless such officer gives notice and opportunity for all parties to participate. . . ." Section 10(a) provides for compensation for persons participating in rulemaking proceedings, and requires the Federal Trade Commission to "solicit public comment from small businesses whose views otherwise would not be adequately repre-sented. . . ."

At the same time that Congress has been forcing a more formalized rulemaking procedure by statute, court decisions, with a few notable exceptions,[16] have mandated the same thing. Among many examples is a 1977 ruling that held where "competing claims to a valuable privilege" are involved, ex parte contacts in informal rulemaking are illegal (Home Box Office v. FCC 567 F.2d9). There is also substantial case law encouraging more formalized

proceedings and demanding the construction of a complete
evidentiary record for judicial review (Dunlop v. Bachowski
421 U.S. 560 (1975); Overton Park 201 U.S. 402 (1971);
Environmental Defense Fund v. Ruckelshaus 439 F.2d 585
(D.C. Cir., 1971); Seacoast Anti-Pollution League v.
Costle 572 F.2d 872(1978)).

Rulemaking decisions, whether by members of Congress
or administrators, are political in nature. Few are the
decisions--especially in relation to the new social
regulation--that can be defended as clear, technologically
rational choices. One reason for this is the tendency of
Congress to pass laws directing administrators to act
before the technology to do so is fully developed or when
competing technological points of view would dictate
substantively differing actions.

The reality of administrative rulemaking under
Section 553 is a reality characterized as much by compromise
and bargaining as by technical expertise. In other words,
it is a pluralistic coalition-building process, which
inevitably means that it is essentially political. By
delegating broad powers to regulate "for the public good" to
the administrative agencies and then by formalizing and
judicializing the process, Congress has limited its own
informal participation in rulemaking. The capacity of the
individual member of the subcommittee to influence
regulations has thus been undercut.

It is obvious that the public is restive concerning
government regulation. "There is mounting evidence,"
former Representative John B. Anderson stated, "that
excessive government regulation is hamstringing our
economy, handcuffing our business enterprises and robbing
the consumer through increased inflation brought on by the
costs of complying with regulations and their stifling
impact on competition."[17] The disaffection permeates all
sectors: labor worries about jobs; big and small business
worry about compliance costs; consumers worry about higher
prices and the banning of products they perceive to be
relatively safe, such as saccharin and laetrile; academics
and journalists worry about the sheer bulk, complexity, and
conflict of the total regulatory output. Even the
regulators themselves, who in many cases are finding that,
without higher-level coordination, their efforts are often
thwarted or undone by others with conflicting or
overlapping mandates, worry.

It is at this juncture--heightened public concern
coupled with the lessened ability of the members of Congress
to influence the process--that the legislative veto has
emerged as a solution to the regulatory problem. The
legislative veto is usually described as a means for
Congress as an institution to regain control over the
uncontrollable bureaucracy. With few exceptions, however, power is vested not in the body as a whole but in its
committees and subcommittees and is exercised by committee
and subcommittee staffs.

Although most of the actual and proposed legislative
veto applications to rulemaking provide for participation
by the full Congress (concurrent resolution) or at least by
one house (simple resolution), all stipulate that after the
finally promulgated rule is transmitted to Congress it be
referred to the appropriate committee or, in some
instances, the appropriate committees. Congressional
procedure as it currently operates generally entails
referral of the rule immediately to the appropriate
subcommittee. It is at this level that the bulk of the
approximately ten thousand rules per year receives
attention, if they are acted upon at all. Given the
congressional workload, the obscurity of much of the
regulatory product, and the still-prevailing congressional tendency in most cases to "go along with the
subcommittee recommendation," it seems likely that it is
the subcommittees that control the outcome of the reviews.
Thus, in terms of arenas-of-power analysis,
regulatory decision-making power has increasingly been
moved by Congress from arenas that are distributive to
arenas that are designed to be administrative in nature.
Congress has chosen, at this point, to avoid defining
regulatory policy in statutes that would involve it in a
more pluralistic decision-making process. But decision
making within administrative arenas has not been based
merely on technological expertise; instead, it has more
often resembled a more pluralistic procedure. And, the
rulemaking procedures of the administrative arenas have
become less and less responsive to their oversight
subcommittees. This has occurred at the same time that
these subcommittees and their chairmen have won more power
within Congress. Since the 1974 Subcommittee Bill of
Rights, the disaggregation of power within Congress--with
the possible exception of the budget process--has further
diminished leadership and party control. If the
legislative veto power operates at the subcommittee and
subcommittee staff levels, as this analysis shows, the
resultant shift in power over regulations is unlikely to be
to a pluralistic review by the full Congress. More
probably it will signal a return to control over regulations
by the subcommittees (one of the major participants in the
policy subsystems or iron triangles). What this appears to
indicate is a shift of power from an increasingly
"pluralistic" administrative procedure to the more
distributive--and thus closed--procedure of the policy
subsystem, or iron triangle, where the subcommittee and
powerful interest groups exercise the major influence over
regulations and the rulemaking process. Experience under
existing legislative vetoes, as illustrated by the case
studies in chapters 3 and 4, demonstrated that this shift in
power has indeed occurred.
To be sure, the legislative veto speeds up the ability
of Congress to react to regulatory problems. But, when the
legislative veto is used as a lubricant to reduce the

friction inherent among today's difficult regulatory
policy choices (see chapter 5), it has not resolved
conflict; it has merely postponed resolution. This
"faster" route to lawmaking can result in a policy void.

To be effective, Congress often must move slowly
enough to allow for haggling and disagreement to bring out
all the needs and wants, weaknesses and strengths of
multiple points of view. Only then can the alliance
building, bargaining, and compromise of the legislative
process yield an outcome that is acceptable across a broad
constituency.

If we are at all concerned with preserving the Framers'
well-reasoned separation of the executive and legislative
powers as a protection for liberty, or their equally well-
reasoned constitutional design for legislative action as a
check on abuse of governmental power, the legislative veto
exercised over the rulemaking process in the cases
presented here shows that it is not a regulatory solution--
it is a misadventure.

The choice among regulatory areas to be studied was
limited, first, by existence of a legislative veto
provision, and, second, by congressional use of power.
Four regulatory areas met the criteria: the regulations of
the Department of Housing and Urban Development, the
Department of Education, the Federal Energy Regulatory
Commission, and the National Highway and Traffic Safety
Administration.

Information concerning the case studies is based in
part on a thorough analysis of the available legislative and
administrative documentation, as well as periodical and
newspaper coverage. The major source of information,
however, was interviews conducted with agency and
congressional participants in the legislative review
proceedings, with White House staff, with staff of the
Office of Management and Budget, with Justice Department
staff, and with members of involved interest groups.[18]

The Case Studies

The first case study (chapter 3) involves regulations
developed by the Department of Housing and Urban
Development (HUD) pursuant to its authority under the 1978
amendments to the Housing and Community Development Act,
which included a congressional review procedure. The
provision required that HUD semiannually submit an agenda
of proposed regulations to its oversight committees, the
Senate Committee on Banking, Housing, and Urban Affairs and
the House Committee on Banking, Finance, and Urban Affairs.
Either committee, within thirty days of continuous session
of Congress after the agenda was transmitted, could notify
HUD that it intended to review any of the regulations. The
department would then be required to transmit a copy of such
regulations to both committees at least fifteen calendar

days of continuous session before its being published for comment in the <u>Federal Register</u>. During that period either committee could vote to suspend the regulation for an additional ninety calendar days, a delay that would give Congress opportunity to pass a joint resolution or to amend legislation to overrule the regulation.

The provision further stipulated that both the submission of the regulation to the committees fifteen days prior to its being published for comment in the <u>Federal Register</u> and the twenty-day waiting period after the regulation had been published as final could be waived if requested by the secretary in writing and agreed to by the chairmen and ranking minority members of both committees. The fifteen-day "consultive period,"[19] the potential for a ninety-calendar-day delay,[20] and the waiver provision combine to make this review procedure substantially more powerful than a typical report-and-wait or advance-notification procedure. For this reason and because the House Committee on Banking, Finance, and Urban Affairs has exercised its power under this review procedure on several occasions, an analysis of its use is included in this study.

Chapter 4 presents an analysis of the regulations review procedure over rules issued by the Department of Education (formerly the Office of Education in the Department of Health, Education, and Welfare). Since 1974 all standards, rules, regulations, or general requirements developed by the commissioner of education have been subject to a procedure that allows Congress to veto any such items by adopting a concurrent resolution of disapproval stating that it would be inconsistent with the act from which the department derives its authority. When the Department of Education was created (May 4, 1980), the legislative veto provision was included in its enabling legislation. In May and June of 1980, the House Committee on Education and Labor, through Chairman Carl Perkins (D, KY), submitted three concurrent resolutions invalidating regulations of the department; and the Senate Committee on Labor and Human Resources, through the chairman of its Subcommittee on Education, Arts, and the Humanities, Claiborne Pell (D, RI), submitted a single concurrent resolution invalidating a department regulation. These instances of legislative vetoes of agency regulations, coupled with the analysis presented in a 1976 study done by Harold Bruff and Ernest Gelhorn of earlier use of this power by the education committees, provide the basis for this case study.

The final two case studies are presented together in chapter 5. One deals with a regulation developed by the Department of Transportation (DOT) pursuant to its authority under the Motor Vehicle and School Bus Safety Amendments of 1974. This legislation gave Congress the power to disapprove by concurrent resolution within sixty days of continuous congressional session any occupant-restraint standard developed by DOT. Legislative veto power in this instance was restricted to a single regulatory issue, not applied to all regulations of the department. Although the congressional attempt to veto the final regulation failed, the study of this case provides additional insights into the veto process.

The other case study in chapter 5 involves a similarly restricted legislative veto power over the incremental pricing rule that the 1978 Natural Gas Policy Act directed the Federal Energy Regulatory Commission (FERC) to issue by May 1, 1980. A provision gave either house the power to veto the final rule within thirty calendar days, which, on May 20, 1980, the House of Representatives did.

Although congressional veto action under provisions of the 1980 Federal Trade Commission Act came too late to be included as a full case study, a brief analysis of the two-house veto of the FTC's used-cars rule in May 1982 is included in chapter 6, which also integrates the findings of the separate cases studied and assesses the validity of the legislative veto's alleged advantages.

The aim of this research, then, is to identify and analyze rulemaking arenas that operate under legislative veto scrutiny, and to assess the functional implications of exercise of the legislative veto power for the content and control of public policy. Before turning to this task, however, we focus in chapter 2 on the historical development of the legislative veto concept, the constitutional questions raised by its use, and the varied perceptions that participants and observers have of its reform value for the rulemaking process.

Notes

1. Clark F. Norton, the Congressional Research Service expert on the legislative veto, has consistently included review procedures such as these in his tabulations of veto control devices. His rationale for doing so rests in "the presumption that Congress would be able to disallow the contemplated action if it so willed." Norton, Congressional Review, Deferral and Disapproval of Executive Actions: A Summary and an Inventory of Statutory Authority, Report No. 76-88G (Washington, DC: Library of Congress, Congressional Research Service, April 30, 1976). Hereafter cited as Norton 1976.

Another observer who includes this type of postenactment review within the legislative veto category is H. Lee Watson, who argues: "Often the mere existence of the procedures is sufficient to force the executive to respond to congressional will. . . . In theory disapproval of the proposed actions could only be effectuated by legislation, but in practice there is little doubt that this provision [report and wait] gave the committee veto power over acquisitions even without formal control power." Watson, "Congress Steps Out: A Look at Congressional Control of the Executive," 63 California Law Review 983 (1975).

Like Watson and Norton, Joseph Cooper and Ann Cooper refer to this type of review as a legislative veto, and classify it as a "deliberative" form of the veto power. In assessing the power of this type of procedure, the Coopers note that "theoretically the actual disallowance of the proposal must take the form of regular legislation. However, in reality many of the committees of Congress are so strong that the mere hint of their disapproval often is sufficient to convince the executive not to take the proposed step." Cooper and Cooper, "The Legislative Veto and the Constitution," 30 George Washington Law Review 467 (1962), p. 468.

2. A 1964 Bureau of the Budget paper, "Legislative Encroachment" (Papers of Harold Seidman), p. 6, included a statement to this effect: "However, when a waiting period is combined with an option to waive the waiting period, constitutional questions do arise. The delegation of that power by Congress to a committee or committees is a violation of the principle that neither Congress nor a committee of Congress may exercise executive powers (since the practical effect may be to require an executive official to come into agreement with a committee) or legislative powers which are only properly vested in the whole Congress. The constitutional problem becomes clear if an inordinately long waiting period is assumed coupled with a waiver option."

3. Examples of these legislative veto forms are: Concurrent Resolutions of Disapproval. Education Amendments of 1974 (88 Stat. 484-613; P.L. 93-380; approved August 21, 1974). The act provides that a copy of any standard, rule, regulation, or general requirement be sent to Congress (concurrently with publication in the Federal Register) and that it not become effective for forty-five days; during that time Congress could adopt a concurrent resolution of disapproval.

Single-House Resolution of Disapproval. Energy Policy and Conservation Act (89 Stat. 871-969; P.L. 94-163; approved December 22, 1975). The act defines sixteen situations (including development of plans and amendments to various regulations)in which proposed action must be transmitted to Congress. Fourteen of these proposed actions were subjected to a procedure permitting a resolution of disapproval by either the Senate or the House.

Committee Disapproval. Energy Interim Consumer Product Safety Standard Act of 1978 (92 Stat. 386; P.L. 95-319; approved July 11, 1978). The act provides for committee disapproval within fifteen days of a proposed extension of time for any provision superseding requirements for the cellulose insulation safety standard mandated by the act.

For further examples, see Norton 1976.

4. Joint Resolution of Approval. Public Utility Regulatory Policies Act of 1978 (92 Stat. 3117; P.L. 95-617; approved November 9, 1978). The president was authorized to waive provisions of federal law to facilitate the construction or operation of any crude oil transportation system that he has approved. Such waiver would not become effective unless approved by adoption of a joint resolution by both houses within a period of sixty calendar days of continuous session.

Concurrent Resolution of Approval. Petroleum Marketing Practices Act (92 Stat. 322; P.L. 95-297; approved June 19, 1978). Interim rules for the subsidization of motor fuel marketing prescribed by the president must be transmitted to Congress. The interim rules could not become effective unless approved by adoption of an affirmative resolution by both houses within ninety calendar days of continuous session.

Single-House Resolution of Approval. There has been no instance of this.

Committee Approval. Energy Research and Development Administration Authorization Act of 1976 (89 Stat. 1063; P.L. 94-187). The administrator of ERDA was required to submit any proposed use of funds in excess of the amount authorized by this act for nonnuclear energy development programs to the Senate Committee on Interior and Insular Affairs and the House Committee on Science and Technology. If the committees had not transmitted notice of approval for the intended use within thirty days, the proposed use would be prevented.

5.   Irwin B. Arieff, "Legislative Vetoes Multi-plying as Congress Seeks New Limits on Executive Branch Actions," Congressional Quarterly, March 8, 1980, p. 662.

6.   For a more complete description of Levitas's position, see 127 Cong. Rec. H427-430 (daily ed.), February 6, 1981.

7.   Clark F. Norton, Congressional Veto Provisions and Amendments: 96th Congress, Issue Brief 79044 (Washington, DC: Library of Congress, Congressional Research Service, March 2, 1982), pp. 2-11. Hereafter cited as Norton 96th Congress.

8.   See Library of Congress, Congressional Research Service, "Congressional Veto of Executive Actions," Issue Brief 76006 (Washington, DC, May 1, 1981), pp. 8-9.

9.   Robert G. Dixon, Jr., "The Congressional Veto and Separation of Powers: The Executive on a Leash," 56 North Carolina Law Review 427 (1978).

10.   Harold Seidman, Politics, Position, and Power, 3d ed. (New York: Oxford University Press, 1980), p. 56.

11.   For further elaboration of the importance of these interrelationships within policy subsystems, see: J. Leiper Freeman, The Political Process: Executive Bureau-Legislative Committee Relationships (New York: Random House, 1955, 1965), especially pp. 66-118; Theodore J. Lowi, "American Business, Public Policy Case Studies and Political Theory," World Politics 16 (1964):677-715; Douglas Cater, Power in Washington, 2d ed. (New York: Random House, 1964).

12.   For discussions of power distribution and its effect on democratic politics, see: Robert Dahl, Who Governs?: Democracy and Power in an American City (New Haven: Yale University Press, 1961); Robert Dahl, A Preface to Democratic Theory (Chicago: University of Chicago Press, 1956); Harold D. Lasswell, Power and Personality (New York: W. W. Norton and Company, 1940); Harold D. Lasswell and Abraham Kaplan, Power and Society (New Haven: Yale University Press, 1950); Theodore J. Lowi, The End of Liberalism, 2d ed. (New York: W. W. Norton and Company, 1979).

13.   Robert K. Merton, Social Theory and Social Structure (Glencoe, IL: Free Press, 1964). See also Robert T. Holt, "A Proposed Structural-Functional Framework for Political Science," in Functionalism in Social Science, ed. Don Martindale, Monograph 5 (Philadelphia: American Academy for Political and Social Sciences, 1965).

14.   Lasswell and Kaplan, Power and Society; Lowi, "American Business, Public Policy Case Studies and Political Theory"; Theodore J. Lowi, "Four Systems of Policy, Politics and Choice," Public Administration Review 32 (1972):298-310; Robert S. Gilmour, "Environmental Preservation and Politics," Political Science Quarterly 90 (1975):719-38; Randall Ripley and Grace Franklin, Congress, the Bureaucracy and Public Policy (Homewood,

IL: Dorsey Press, 1976).

15.   Lowi, "Four Systems of Policy, Politics and Choice"; Lowi, "American Business, Public Policy Case Studies and Political Theory."

16.   See Florida East Coast Railway Company v. United States (410 U.S. 224 (1973) and Vermont Yankee Nuclear Power Corporation v. Natural Resources Defense Council, Inc. (435 U.S. 519 (1978)).

17.   Congressional Quarterly Weekly Report, March 31, 1979, p. 560.

18.   Interviews were begun in the spring of 1979. During nine sessions of approximately five days each between then and May 1981 more than eighty interviews were completed.

19.   The Conference Committee Report to P.L. 95-557 states, "Since the 15 day consultive period is designed to provide an opportunity for misinterpretations to be resolved . . ." (p. 84).

20.   Calendar days run only during continuous days of Congress.   By definition of 7(6)(B) of the 1978 amendments, "the days on which either house is not in session because of an adjournment of more than three days to a day certain are excluded in the computation of continuous session of Congress."   Thus long weekend adjournment and vacation breaks do not count in the twenty- or ninety-day deferral periods.   Given the numerous long recess breaks, the deferral period would necessarily often be far in excess of the stated ninety-day period.   Considering that HUD is subject to annual appropriations and that much of its regulatory effort is directed toward annual grant requirements, the pressures of such a review period should be obvious.

2
Historical Perspective on the Legislative Veto: Legal and Administrative Issues

Early Historical Antecedents

Supporters of the legislative veto and some scholars trace the roots of the legislative veto to the nineteenth-century British practice of "laying" and to a 1789 United States statute that created the office of Secretary of the Treasury. It is of interest here to look briefly at each.

The British Experience

To maintain control over delegated legislative powers, Parliament, as early as 1800, often provided within an enabling statute the requirement that any instruments made under the statute be laid before Parliament. Statutes mandated "formal delivery of the statutory instrument to the appropriate office in the House before which it had been laid, and publication of the title in the formal proceedings of the House."[1] Older statutes often provided no further procedures, but the laying requirement is more usually accompanied by the power to approve or annul by resolution the instrument in question.

There are many significant differences between the laying procedure and its American cousin, the legislative veto. One important difference is the centralized process for review that has developed in the British model. In 1924 the House of Lords provided for a single committee to review laid items.[2] By 1973, Parliament had established the Joint Committee on Statutory Instruments to do away with the duplicative work of separate committees in each house. Congress, contrariwise, had decentralized its review procedure by parceling out responsibility to standing committees and subcommittees--creatures renowned for their jealously guarded and overlapping jurisdictions.

Institutional dissimilarities also confound efforts to rely upon the British experience as a precedent. Parliament not only is considerably larger (635 members in the House of Commons alone) than Congress but acts far more as a forum for debate than as a decision-making body. Parliament has limited its veto review to rules and regulations; Congress has expanded its veto review to a wide array of executive actions.

The most significant differences, however, are to be found in the power and control of parties and in the relationship between the legislative and executive branches. In Britain, the prime minister and those in the cabinet are members of the majority party or coalition and are drawn from and responsible to Parliament. The American political system, on the other hand, is so constructed that Congress and the president represent different constituencies (often this means that the majority in Congress represents a party other than that of the president). This difference in perspective and accountability coupled with the absence of strong national parties has resulted in a far more antagonistic relationship between the American executive and legislative branches. Congressional review of executive actions in these circumstances is more likely to be a struggle between the branches than would be the case where strong parties and like perspective and responsibility act as coordinating mechanisms.

In light of these differences, reliance upon the British laying experience as a model or compelling rationale for development of a congressional veto is, at the very least, of doubtful utility.

American Origins

Attempts to legitimize the legislative veto have included tracing its American origins to the very first session of Congress. In an act of September 1, 1789, that created the office of Secretary of the Treasury, Congress ordered the secretary to provide information about his office when required to do so by a resolution of either house. H. Lee Watson describes this as "the first manifestation of congressional desire to step out of its legislative role and directly control executive action."[3]

The concept lay dormant until the late 1800s, when Congress once again attempted to enact statutory provisions for congressional control of executive action by committee-level action or by concurrent or simple resolutions. These early efforts were restricted to information gathering, agency printing of documents, and directives or requests for surveys and reports on river and harbor improvements. One exception to this limited use is found in the Senate version of the treaty provisions for United States membership in the League of Nations, which authorized Congress to declare United States withdrawal from the organization by concurrent resolution. The United States failed to join the League, however, so this attempt to apply the control mechanism to the area of foreign affairs came to nought.[4]

As the interest of Congress in concurrent and simple resolutions as a form of control over executive actions increased, presidential opposition--especially from President Wilson--became an important limiting influence.[5] But soon presidential objections were tempered by desires for added grants of authority from Congress; often the congressional veto--in the form of a concurrent or simple resolution, or committee-level veto power--was the price Congress exacted in return for the transfer of additional power to the executive branch. As early as 1932 this trend was evident in President Hoover's acceptance of a legislative veto in exchange for the power to reorganize the executive branch.

The continued reluctance of Congress to act on reorganization proposals prompted President Hoover to ask for reorganization authority. By the time Congress responded to his request in June 1932, the Democrats had gained control of the House. There was considerable opposition by then to granting a Republican president the discretion to reshuffle and consolidate government agencies. And yet, there was the reality that Congress itself had proved unequal to the task. This political stalemate was resolved by the Legislative Appropriations Act of 1932, which provided for presidential authority to consolidate executive agencies and functions by executive order but included as well a procedure for congressional veto of the president's action. The executive order was to be ineffective for sixty days, during which period <u>either</u> chamber was empowered to "pass a resolution disapproving of such Executive order, or any part thereof," in which case the order was to be "null and void to the extent of such disapproval."[6]

The following year, however, upon the advice of Attorney General William D. Mitchell, Hoover vetoed a bill containing a committee-level veto provision. In his opinion, Mitchell also questioned the constitutionality of the legislative veto in the 1932 Reorganization Act, which would "give to either House of Congress, by action which is not legislative, the power to disapprove administrative actions."[7] This constitutional concern was sufficiently shared by Congress to cause it to delete the legislative veto provision when reorganization authority was extended for a period of two years in 1933.[8] Congress did, however, restrict presidential authority in the act by not permitting the abolishment or transfer of an executive department or all its functions. It was not until passage of the Reorganization Act of 1939 that Congress again subordinated a delegation of reorganization authority to the president to congressional review power--this time in the form of a two-house legislative veto.[9]

Ever since initiation of the legislative veto as a form of congressional postenactment review authority,

presidents have raised questions about its constitutionality. Opposition to the veto on constitutional grounds
has come from legal scholars and from many members of
Congress as well. Issues involved in the legislative
veto's constitutionality are addressed below, but the next
section summarizes the growth and expansion of the veto over
the years since its politically expedient birth in 1932.

Expansion of the Legislative Veto

Reluctance within Congress about further use of the
legislative veto, which had surfaced in the wake of Hoover's
constitutional challenge, was short lived. In the decades
since the 1930s, legislation has included a steadily
increasing number of legislative veto provisions at a rate
that has come close to or exceeded an exponential growth
rate for each succeeding decade of its existence (Table
2.1). In fact, more than three times as many legislative
veto provisions were added in the 1970s than had been
enacted in the preceding thirty-eight years that followed
upon its initial application in the 1932 Reorganization Act
(Table 2.2).

Legislative architects in Congress and the executive
have been inventive in their efforts to adapt the
legislative veto to fit an ever-increasing variety of
subject matter and purposes. From its application to
grants-of-power to reorganize the executive branch, the
legislative veto quickly spread into the areas of foreign
affairs and national security. During World War II,
national security needs forced Congress to transfer
extraordinary powers to the president. Since legislative
action by Congress to repeal a statutory grant of such power
would be subject to presidential veto, it could mean that a
two-thirds majority would be necessary to recall the broad
grants-of-power made in response to the wartime emergency.
Rather than providing for a scheduled termination date, and
in some cases an addition to such a termination date,
Congress chose, in more than thirty laws enacted between
1941 and 1945, to include the power to terminate such
statutory power by concurrent resolution.[10] Often the
president actively promoted such legislative veto
provisions as an inducement to Congress to assent to the
desired grant-of-power.[11] Although this use of a
concurrent resolution to terminate a law is quite different
from legislative veto provisions used to restrain executive
actions made pursuant to statutory authority, most scholars
include these termination provisions under the legislative
veto rubric.

In subsequent years, as the complexity of the world
situation has mandated increasing presidential initiative
in matters relating to national security and foreign
affairs, Congress has continued to use the legislative veto
as a means to terminate or restrain presidential activity in

Table 2.1

Legislative Vetoes Passed by Congress, by Decade

Decade	Number of Acts	Number of Provisions	Percentage Increase in Provisions over Preceding Decade
1932–1939*	5	6	–
1940–1949*	19	20	230
1950–1959*	34	36	80
1960–1969*	49	70	94
1970–1980+	248	423	507

*Derived from Clark F. Norton, Congressional Review, Deferral and Disapproval of Executive Actions: A Summary and an Inventory of Statutory Authority, Report 76-88G (Washington, DC: Library of Congress, Congressional Research Service, 1976), p. 8. Cited below as Norton 1976.

+Figures for 1970–1975 derived from Norton 1976; figures for 1976–1977 derived from Clark F. Norton, 1976-1977 Congressional Acts Authorizing Prior Review, Approval or Disapproval of Proposed Executive Actions, Report 78-117 (Gov) (Washington, DC: Library of Congress, Congressional Research Service, 1979), pp. 1–41. Figures for 1979–1980 derived from Clark F. Norton, Congressional Veto Provisions and Amendments: 96th Congress, Issue Brief 79044 (Washington, DC: Library of Congress, Congressional Research Service, 1981), pp. 2–76.

Note: It should be noted that Norton includes postenactment reviews of the report-and-wait, advanced-notification, and joint-resolution-of-disapproval varieties within his tabulations of congressional veto review provisions. By Norton's count, approximately half (228) of the 466 review provisions enacted between 1932 and 1978 were of the more powerful legislative veto format (disapproval or approval by committee, single-house resolution, or two-house resolution). The rest (238) were of the report-and-wait or advanced-notification type of review. Norton does not break these figures down by year of application, however, making separation of these categories difficult. See Clark F. Norton, Data on Congressional Veto Legislation (1932-1978) and on Extent of Usage (1960-July 31, 1978) (Washington, DC: Library of Congress, Congressional Research Service, 1979), p. 1.

Table 2.2

Legislative Vetoes Passed by Congress, 1970s

Decade	Number of Acts	Number of Provisions	Percentage Increase in Provisions over Preceding Decade
1970-1975*	89	163	--
1976-1960+	159	260	60

*Figures for 1970-1975 derived from Clark F. Norton, Congressional Review, Deferral and Disapproval of Executive Actions: A Summary and an Inventory of Statutory Authority, Report 76-88G (Washington, DC: Library of Congress, Congressional Research Service, 1976), p. 8.

+Figures for 1976-1977 derived from Clark F. Norton, 1976-1977 Congressional Acts Authorizing Prior Review, Approval or Disapproval of Proposed Executive Actions, Report 78-117 (Gov) (Washington, DC: Library of Congress, Congressional Research Service, 1979), pp. 1-41. Figures for 1979-1980 derived from Clark F. Norton, Congressional Veto Provisions and Amendments: 96th Congress, Issue Brief 79044 (Washington, DC: Library of Congress, Congressional Research Service, 1981), pp. 2-76.

these areas. The Foreign Assistance Act of 1961, for example, provided that Congress could terminate assistance under any provision of the act by adoption of a concurrent resolution. By the 1970s, as congressional concern over the Vietnam situation intensified, Congress moved to curb presidential actions that might prolong United States involvement in the war or actions that might inject United States forces into new hostile situations. The 1973 War Powers Resolution included a provision for congressional termination of the use of armed forces in hostile or potentially hostile situations by concurrent resolution. Legislative veto authority was also included over proposed sales of defense articles in excess of $25 million in the Foreign Assistance Act of 1974. Similar provisions are also in the International Security Assistance Act of 1978, and the International Security Development Authorization Act of 1980.

Termination or restraint of executive authority in the areas of national security and foreign affairs were not the only examples of ingenuity in adapting the legislative veto. In 1940 Congress also imposed legislative veto power over authority it had delegated to the attorney general to suspend deportation of certain aliens. In the Alien Registration Act of 1940, Congress retained for itself, as a condition attached to the original grant of authority, the power to overturn by concurrent resolution the attorney general's ruling that a deportation proceeding be suspended. In this case the legislative veto was applied to a delegated quasi-judicial function of a subordinate-level executive officer, not to presidential-level executive action, as was the case in the reorganization and termination statutes. In the 1952 Immigration and Naturalization Act, Congress authorized single-house veto power over the attorney general's ruling that a deportation proceeding be suspended. This statutory provision, which has remained in effect, was the subject of a 1980 decision by the U.S. Court of Appeals for the Ninth Circuit that found the legislative veto under these circumstances to be unconstitutional.[12] The case Chadha v. Immigration and Naturalization Service is discussed in the next section.

Another subject area was soon added to the growing list of those that were found to be suitable for legislative veto review; it involved decisions relating to real estate transactions and public works building programs. Often the review power was lodged at the committee level by mandating that the department secretary "come into agreement" with a specific congressional committee or committees. Review powers of this sort provide members of Congress with the opportunity to protect or enhance their district and constituency interests. The first instance having to do with committee-level veto power is found in the 1944 Navy Public Works Construction Authorizations. The secretary of the navy was required by the act, prior to acquisition of land for naval use or disposal of such land, to come into agreement with the Naval Affairs Committees of the Senate and House with respect to the terms of prospective acquisitions or disposals. Military and naval construction projects were soon subject to similar review by Congress, followed in quick order by construction and real estate transactions of such domestic agencies as the General Services Administration, the Department of Agriculture, and the Department of the Interior.[13] Congress has continued to include committee-level veto power in numerous acts, and has extended the actions that are subject to review to include a wide variety of matters, such as: changes in the boundaries of Forestry Service regions, changes in route service on the national systems of intercity rail passenger service, construction of major facilities by the National Aeronautics and Space Administration, and plans for the relocation of Navajo and Hopi households.[14]

At least 64 of the 101 acts, or close to two-thirds of the acts, passed between 1932 and 1968 that contained veto-type control provisions fall within the following broad categories: (1) executive reorganization authority--13 acts; (2) foreign affairs and national defense issues--22 acts; and (3) real estate transactions and public works construction projects--29 acts.[15]

Throughout the 1970s, Congress attached legislative veto provisions to legislation in the above categories and at the same time also found new subject matter and uses for the veto. In some cases it added controls to regain powers it believed to have been usurped by the "imperial presidency" in general and by the excesses of the Nixon presidency in particular. Prime examples are the single-house veto over budget deferrals found in the Congressional Budget and Impoundment Control Act of 1974 and the single-house veto over disposal of presidential papers found in the Presidential Recording and Materials Preservation Act of 1974. In other cases Congress used the veto as an ultimate control device when it chose to transfer politically sensitive tasks to the president, such as federal salary recommendations and motor fuel rationing plans.[16]

Of even more significance, was the surge in application of the legislative veto to actions of officials of independent agencies and of subordinate-level officials of executive agencies. The 1972 Education Amendments, which include a congressional veto over the Office of Education's proposed family contribution schedules for its program of basic grants for postsecondary education, mark the first effort to apply the legislative veto to executive agency and independent agency rules, regulations, plans, schedules, forms, or guidelines. From this beginning, Congress has expanded legislative veto review power over an increasing number of programs and agencies (Table 2.3).

Congressional Research Service documentation for 1979-1980 reveals that of the 183 bills introduced that provided for legislative veto authority, 82 (60 percent) involved application of the veto to agency-level-developed rules, regulations, plans, schedules, forms, or guide-lines. Although only about 20 (15 percent) were enacted into law, congressional interest in expanding the legislative veto in this manner is evident.[17]

Congressional initiative for the imposition of the veto control device has come from all quarters--from the Senate, the House, from both Democrats and Republicans, and from committee action, as well as from individual-member action. There have been some instances, especially those involving issues of foreign affairs and national security, in which legislation has been the subject of Senate-initiated congressional provisions. The Department of Defense Authorization Act of 1980 (S. 428) and the International Security Assistance Act of 1979 (S. 584), as respectively reported by the Senate Armed Services Committee and the Senate Foreign Relations Committee and as passed by the Senate, included congressional veto provisions. In both instances the House companion bills did not provide for any congressional veto authority; and in

Table 2.3

Legislative Veto Authorities over Agency-Level Actions

Agency	Act	Type of Veto	Action Subject to Veto Control
Office of Education	Education Amendments of 1974 (88 Stat. 484)	Two house	Standards, regulations, or general requirements issued by commissioner.
Department of Education	Department of Education Organization Act of 1979 (93 Stat. 668)	Two house	Extended power provided in 1974 act to new department.
Department of Labor	Employees Retirement Income Security Act of 1974 (88 Stat. 829)	One house	Rules to protect pension rights/benefits of personnel under federal contracts/grants.
	Airline Deregulation Act of 1978 (92 Stat. 1705)	One house	Rules for monthly assistance payments to eligible employees affected by act.
Department of Transportation	Motor Vehicle and School Bus Safety Amendments of 1974 (88 Stat. 1470)	Two house	Passive restraint regulations issued by National Highway and Traffic Safety Administration.
	Amtrak Improvement Act of 1975 (89 Stat. 90)	One house	Plans to add or discontinue service made by National Railroad Passenger Corp.

Agency	Act	Type of Veto	Action Subject to Veto Control
	Amtrak Improvement Act of 1978 (92 Stat. 923)	One house	Recommendations of secretary for design of basic route system.
Department of Commerce	Act to Improve Coastal Management, 1980 (94 Stat. 2060)	Two house	Final rules promulgated under Coastal Zone Management Act.
Department of Health, Education, and Welfare	Amendment to Social Security Act Child Support Provisions, 1975 (89 Stat. 433)	One house	Standards to protect best interests of children affected by child-support provisions of Social Security Act.
Department of Justice	Act Concerning the Deprivations of Rights of Institutionalized Persons, 1980 (94 Stat. 349)	One house	Minimum standards set by attorney general for implementation of system to resolve grievances of persons confined in correctional facilities.
Department of Interior	Alaska National Interest Lands Conservation Act of 1979 (94 Stat. 2371)	One house	Regulations issued under the act.
	National Historic Preservation Act Amendments, 1979 (94 Stat. 2987)	Two house	Rules promulgated under act.

Agency	Act	Type	Description
Environmental Protection Agency	Extension of Federal Insecticide, Fungicide, and Rodenticide Act, 1980 (94 Stat. 3194)	Two house	Rules issued under the act.
	Comprehensive Environmental Response Compensation, and Liability Act, 1980 (94 Stat. 2767)	One and a half house*	Rules or regulations promulgated under Title I of act.
Federal Trade Commission	Federal Trade Commission Amendments, 1980 (94 Stat. 374)	Two house	Rules and regulations of commission.
Veterans Administration	Veterans Administration Health Resource and Program Extension Act of 1979 (93 Stat. 1092)	Staff-Agency	Directed V.A. to make study of effects of "Agent Orange" on Vietnam veterans but required Office of Technology Assessment, a congressional staff agency, to review and approve protocol for study.
Federal Elections Commission	Federal Elections Commission Act Amendments of 1974 (88 Stat. 1263)	One house	Rules on filing or reporting financial statements.
	Federal Elections Commission Amendments, 1976 (90 Stat. 475)	One house	Extended to all rules or regulations of commission.

Agency	Act	Type of Veto	Action Subject to Veto Control
	Federal Elections Commission Amendments, 1980 (94 Stat. 1339)	One house	Extended veto power to cover forms developed by commission.
Federal Energy Regulatory Commission	Energy Policy and Conservation Act 1975 (89 Stat. 871)	One house	Four provisions subject various commission actions to veto, including plan developed for strategic petroleum reserve and amendments to existing allocation/pricing rules.
	Energy Conservation and Protection Act 1976 (90 Stat. 1125)	Two house	Energy conservation performance standards regulating new building construction.
	Natural Gas Policy Act 1978 (92 Stat. 3350)	One house	Rules for pass-through of certain natural gas costs, including an incremental pricing regulation.
Synthetic Fuels Corporation	Energy Security Act Extension Amendments of 1980 (94 Stat. 611)	Committee, one and two house	Veto provisions over actions proposed by corporation.
Consumer Product Safety Commission	Omnibus Budget Reconciliation Act of 1981 (95 Stat. 357)	One and a half house*	All rules and regulations of the commission.

Source: Information on acts that are subject to legislative veto review power over agency rules, regulations, plans, schedules, forms, guidelines, etc. was derived from Clark F. Norton, _Congressional Review, Deferral and Disapproval of Executive Actions: A Summary and Inventory of Statutory Authority_, Report 76-88G (Washington, DC: Library of Congress, Congressional Research Service, 1976); Clark F. Norton, _1976-1977 Congressional Acts Authorizing Prior Review, Approval or Disapproval of Proposed Executive Actions_, Report 78-117 (Gov) (Washington, DC: Library of Congress, Congressional Research Service, 1979); Clark F. Norton, _Congressional Veto Provisions and Amendments_: 96th Congress, Issue Brief 79044 (Washington, DC: Library of Congress, Congressional Research Service, 1981).

*These are the first instances of the so-called one-and-a-half-house veto, which provides for disapproval of a final rule by concurrent resolutions within ninety days or by single resolution within sixty days if not disapproved by the other house within the subsequent thirty days.

both instances the veto provision did not survive in the final acts as passed by Congress.[18]

In other instances the House has included a the Senate Foreign Relations Committee and as passed by the Senate, included congressional veto provisions. In both instances the House companion bills did not legislative veto provision and the companion Senate bill has not. It appears to be more typical for the House to originate proposals for veto review over individual agency rulemaking authority, although the Senate has on occasion initiated such proposals.[19] The recently passed Coastal Zone Management Act of 1980 and the extension of the Federal Insecticide, Fungicide, and Rodenticide Act are examples of House-initiated legislative veto authority.

Of the more than one hundred fifty bills or amendments, as well as two joint resolutions, that were introduced, reported, or offered in the 96th Congress for the purpose of extending or modifying congressional authority to approve or disapprove executive branch proposals, a majority were House measures. At least fifty of these provisions, however, were submitted in the Senate.[20]

It is evident in the sponsorship of generic-veto proposals that members of both political parties have supported and continue to support legislative vetoes. The major generic-veto provisions introduced in the House in the 94th to 96th sessions of Congress (1975-1980) have been sponsored by Democrat Elliott Levitas (D, GA); in the Senate, by Harrison Schmitt (R, NM). In addition to the Levitas and Schmitt bills, there were twenty-eight other bills introduced in the 96th Congress that proposed some form of legislative veto over all agency rulemaking: of the twenty-four House bills, seven were sponsored by Democrats and seventeen by Republicans; of the five Senate bills, three were sponsored by Democrats and two by Republicans.[21] The proposals introduced in the 97th Congress (1981) reflect a similar mix of sponsors' party affiliations.[22]

Although presidents of both parties typically have been opposed to the legislative veto, they have been willing on occasion to accept, even to suggest, legislative veto provisions in order to acquire desired additional authority. Franklin Roosevelt, for example, signed without objection numerous bills containing legislative veto termination authority.[23] It was later revealed, however, through publication of a hitherto secret presidential legal opinion that he had constitutional reservations about the veto device.[24] More recently, Carter defended the constitutionality of the veto in the narrow context of a reorganization statute when it became apparent that his desire for a reinstatement of presidential reorganization authority would depend upon his acquiescence to congressional veto control.[25]   (Later in his term Carter delivered the first presidential message to Congress specifically attacking the legislative veto as both an unconstitutional and an unwise mechanism.)[26] Agency- level officials have been equally willing to accept and to seek legislative veto constraints in order to obtain desired legislation.[27]

A myriad of factors, then, appears to have been influential in the expansion of legislative vetoes. The following listing summarizes the predominate trends in the veto's history.

1. Since its birth in the Reorganization Act of 1932, the legislative veto has been applied relatively consistently over reorganization authority.

2. The world turmoil that led to World War II occasioned the need to transfer greater authority to the president in the areas of foreign affairs and national security. The legislative veto was included in statutes conferring additional authority to constrain presidential initiative and/or to allow Congress to withdraw the authority more easily. Congressional grants of authority over national security and foreign affairs have continued to be the subject of similar legislative veto control up to and including the present.

3. Military and domestic public works projects involving real estate transactions and construc- tion projects were also targeted for legislative veto review during World War II, but in these instances the review power was lodged at the committee level. Similar legislative veto power over public works projects has been added in subsequent decades up to and including the present.

4. During the 1970s, legislative veto scrutiny was extended to presidential initiatives in the domestic arena in reaction to the "imperial presidency."

5. The major surge in new legislative veto provisions during the seventies was in the area of agency- level action, i.e., agency-developed rules, regulations, plans, schedules, forms, and guidelines.

While constitutional concerns have not served so far to inhibit the spread of legislative veto provisions, it is nonetheless important to address the substance of the constitutional challenges. Such an assessment is especially critical in light of the number of court cases that are currently winding their way through the courts.

also pg. 26

Constitutional Issues of the Legislative Veto

In fashioning a government intended to preserve and protect the liberty of its citizens, the Founding Fathers relied on the principle of separation of powers and the countervailing principle of checks and balances. Power was to be divided among the executive, the legislative, and the judicial branches, and as a check against its misuse, each branch was given some power over the others.

The Constitution of the United States vests legislative power in the Congress (Article 1, Section 1), the power to execute the laws passed by Congress in the executive (Article 2, Sections 1, 4), and judicial power in the judiciary (Article 3, Sections 1, 2). Each of these grants of power is limited by other constitutional requirements. Provisions of the so-called Presentation Clause (Article 1, Section 7) make the legislative power subject to the restraint of a presidential veto—a power that is in turn restrained by allowing for two-thirds of both houses of Congress to override a presidential veto. A requirement for the advice and consent of the Senate (Article 2, Section 2) restrains the constitutional authority of the president to appoint ambassadors, other public ministers and consuls, justices of the Supreme Court, and all other officers of the United States (Article 2, Section 2). The president's role in presenting measures for legislative consideration is constitutionally assured as well (Article 2, Section 3).

Opponents of the legislative veto argue that it upsets this carefully designed constitutional balance of powers. The challenge of unconstitutionality involves several constitutional issues:

1. The legislative veto violates the Presentation Clause by denying the president the opportunity to exercise his veto power.
2. The legislative veto gives Congress an extralegislative role in administering substantive statutory programs that impinges on the president's constitutional duty to see that the laws are faithfully executed and involves members of Congress in the executive branch in derogation of the Incompatibility Clause (Article 1, Section 6), which separates members of Congress from administrative functions.
3. The legislative veto arrogates to Congress power reserved by a firmly developed principle in the constitutional system (judicial review) for the nonpolitical judicial branch.
4. The one-house legislative veto violates the constitutional concept of bicameralism that requires action by both houses.

Answering these constitutional charges, supporters of the legislative veto maintain that:

1. Because the president signed the original legislation containing the legislative veto provision (or had his veto overridden by a two-thirds vote of Congress), the Presentation Clause has been complied with.

2. Congress has the power to constrain grants of power to the president by placing controls within a statute, and the elastic clause that provides Congress with the power "to make all laws which shall be necessary and proper" (Article 1, Section 8) gives Congress sufficient power to pass laws with legislative vetoes in them.

3. Because Congress has the power to delegate quasi-judicial functions to the executive, it can restrain the exercise of that power in the same manner that it can restrain grants of quasi-legislative powers, i.e., presidential acquiescence through signing the original legislation containing the veto provision coupled with congressional power through the elastic clause to constrain granted power by the legislative veto mechanism.

4. Because both houses agreed to the original legislation providing for a single-house veto and because the veto provided a congressional review of "executive legislation," which could be blocked by one house in the normal legislative process, the requirements of bicameralism are met.

Throughout the course of the legislative veto's history, governmental and legal scholars have been divided in their assessment of the veto's constitutionality. In 1941 John Millett and Lindsay Rodgers, scholars in the field of public administration, defended the legislative veto in the Reorganization Act of 1939 and argued that it should be expanded to other situations "where Congress cannot or should not determine details."[28] By including the legislative veto in acts that delegated power to either the executive or judiciary, Congress would allay fears about "unlimited delegations" and would thereby be encouraged to strengthen the executive position by increased delegations of power, thus ensuring a better balance of power between the branches.

Unlike Millett and Rodgers, Department of Justice attorney Robert W. Ginnane in 1953 was apprehensive lest legislative veto provisions--to the extent that administration of statutes was vested in congressional committees or made subject to approval or disapproval by congressional resolutions or committees--would create an undue concentration of power in Congress, thus upsetting the traditional balance of power between the branches. Ginnane expressed "grave doubts" as to the constitutionality of all the then-existing statutory provisions for congressional resolutions--including the reorganization statutes. He argued:

> That the President cannot be excluded from the legislative process by the simple expedient of embodying policy decisions having the force of law in the form of "resolutions" not presented to him is made clear by the second paragraph of Section 7, providing that "Every order, resolution, or vote requiring the concurrence of Senate and House, except on a question of adjournment must be presented to the President as in the case of bills"--a provision added for the express purpose of preventing evasion of the President's veto.[29]

In a 1962 law review article, political scientist Joseph Cooper and attorney Ann Cooper defended the constitutionality of the legislative veto. Because the veto provision constitutes an integral part of the original legislation that the president would have had the opportunity to veto, it cannot be attacked as an attempt to avoid the president's constitutionally granted veto power. For the same reason, action under the veto, unlike a new legislative act, is merely a condition upon which the powers delegated are made to depend; thus, since it was contemplated in the enabling act, exercise of the veto represents no inherent change in policy. Therefore, the Coopers concluded, because exercise of the veto is not a legislative act, it cannot be considered to be constitutionally improper legislation.[30]

The Coopers also defended the delegation of the legislative veto review process to one house or to committees. "If the legislative veto can be said to be ancillary to legislation, and not legislation per se, and if therefore the veto can be accepted as properly exercisable by the Congress as a whole"--both conditions accepted by Cooper and Cooper--"then it would seem to be permissible for it to delegate the power to some part of Congress."[31] Although supportive of the constitutionality of such a delegation, the Coopers raised doubts as to the political desirability of giving this power to a committee or its chairman.

If the features of submission through the president and nonamendability, which are essential to protect the president, are coupled with the features of privilege, cloture, and decision by the whole of one or both houses, which are essential to protect the principle of majority rule, then in the Coopers' view the veto represented a new, effective, and vitally needed oversight weapon to supplement the traditional congressional arsenal. In addition, they argued, "The veto provides a mechanism for inducing Congress to give the executive needed flexibility in areas where Congress otherwise might restrict discretion or authority to such an extent as to hamstring or at least impair the ability of administrators to achieve the objectives prescribed for them."[32]

In a statement before the Senate Special Subcommittee on Separation of Powers in 1967, Yale law professor Alexander M. Bickel disagreed with the contention that presidential acquiescence to the original legislation containing the legislative veto provision would be sufficient to meet the requirements of the Presentation Clause.

> The Constitutional separation of powers is not ordained for the convenience of the separate branches of government . . . but is intended to ensure observance of certain principles which the Framers believed would conduce to effective and responsible government, consistent with the liberties of the people. Hence, neither the Congress nor the President may choose to suspend these principles when convenient.[33]

By this reasoning, the president cannot relinquish his constitutional veto power by the mere expedient of signing a statute. In Bickel's judgment, Congress ought to do more reviewing and rewriting of its laws in light of their administration rather than attempt to reshape and redirect their administration. The problem is not that executive and independent agencies are "disregarding legislative policy, but that at many of the most important junctures in their activities they have no legislative policy available to disregard."[34] Relying on Watkins v. United States (354 U.S. 178, 1957), which curbed in some respects the powers of the House Un-American Activities Committee by holding that Congress cannot constitutionally delegate, without standards, as much power as was delegated to that committee, Bickel further reasoned that delegation of congressional veto power to congressional committees was necessarily invalid.

In an appearance before the same subcommittee hearings, Harvard professor of government Arthur A. Maass testified that he could find "nothing unconstitutional in the legislative veto."[35] Maass urged its application in situations where the president and Congress are not able to define standards clearly in the authorizing legislation, as was the case in the disposition of government-owned rubber firms after World War II; and in situations where executive proposals are, for technical or quasi-technical reasons, so delicately balanced that they should be either accepted by Congress or presented or rejected entirely, as is the case with reorganization proposals. Although supportive of the constitutionality of the committee veto, Maass assailed it as "probably unwise for the reason that it denies to the whole Congress the opportunity to review the decision of its committees."[36]

In his appraisal of the legislative veto, attorney H. Lee Watson found in 1975 two potentially valid categories of control by resolution. The first, congressional response by resolution to presidential reorganization proposals, was, he felt, both confinable and constitutionally innocuous. The second, use of resolutions to control <u>nonstatutory</u> actions by the administration--such as exercise of the war power--might prove to be potentially useful, confinable, and not in conflict with the constitutional criteria.[37] But, in general, Watson remained concerned that reliance on the legislative veto controls might on the one hand tempt Congress to create powers in excess of those it would otherwise allow the president, resulting in an aggrandizement of federal power, while on the other hand it might shift the balance of power toward the legislature by allowing Congress to act outside the presidential veto power or the bicameral check.[38] Watson's heaviest attack was aimed at the committee-level veto, which he argued should be considered per se invalid.

After a lengthy presentation of the constitutional consideration raised by the legislative veto, Washington attorney John R. Bolton in 1977 concluded that "although the goals sought through the use of the device are commendable, the device itself is almost necessarily unconstitutional."[39] Bolton's objection to the legislative veto in the reorganization acts was couched in less "constitutional" terms. He could find no convincing reasons that reorganization of the executive branch should not be treated in the same way as more substantive legislation. This position was later supported by Congressional Research Service specialists Ronald Moe and Louis Fisher. They contended that the cost is too great, and preferred that reorganization be done through the regular bill process, in large part to make Congress act positively instead of react negatively.[40]

Three years earlier, in 1978, Fisher had expressed "sympathy" with the effort of Congress to use the legislative veto to control power that belongs to Congress (reorganization authority, federal employee paysetting) and to monitor activities that represent a mix of legislative and executive functions (impoundment, war powers, executive agreements with foreign powers). Yet, he found "objectionable" efforts to make all departmental regulations subject to legislative veto.[41]

Bernard Schwartz, a professor at the New York University School of Law, charged in 1978 that the logic of the claim of unconstitutionality of the legislative veto "rests upon a perverted construction of the separation-of-powers doctrine."[42] The veto could be of particular significance as a tool to control delegated rulemaking authority. In this era of expanding administrative authority it would be "most unfortunate if specious construction of a constitutional doctrine should bar use of one of the most promising methods of control of executive and administrative action."[43]

One final article that must be included in any overview of scholarly discourse on the subject of the legislative veto's constitutionality was written in 1978 by a former assistant attorney general, Robert G. Dixon, Jr. Dixon found the veto to be generally both unwise and unconstitutional. In his analysis, even the veto in the reorganization acts and the War Powers Resolution raised potential constitutional problems. He concluded:

> The difficulty with use of the congressional veto as a general congressional control device over the administration of the government is that it goes beyond the oversight function per se and becomes an intermeddling activity with serious implications for responsible government and orderly policy development. Pushed to its extreme, it would make the Congress not *primus inter pares,* but simply *primus.*[44]

Although the foregoing presentation of scholarly opinion concerning the legislative veto's constitutionality in no way exhausts the voluminous writing on the subject, it serves to underscore the diversity in conclusions reached by observers throughout the veto's existence.

Over the course of the legislative veto's history, appraisal of its constitutionality by members of Congress has also been mixed. Clearly, a majority of the members have accepted the veto on numerous occasions--after all, at least 355 acts containing over 500 legislative veto provisions have been passed since 1932. But the legislative veto has not been without its congressional detractors. As mentioned above, Attorney General Mitchell's constitutional challenge to the veto in the 1932 Reorganization Act met with sufficient support in Congress to cause the veto provision to be deleted from the 1933 Reorganization Act. During floor debate on the 1933 act, Senator James Byrnes (D, SC; later a Supreme Court justice) commented: "I concur that his [the attorney general's] statement of the law is correct, and because of that, I think it would be exceedingly unwise to include in this bill a provision which undoubtedly would result in his advising the President . . . and bring about the veto of the bill."[45]

Although the committee-level legislative veto over public works programs has flourished, it too has been called into question by members of Congress. In 1954 Senator Everett Dirksen (R, IL) raised the constitutional issue concerning a come-into-agreement amendment added by the Senate Public Works Committee to H.R. 6342, the 1954

Amendments to the Public Building Act of 1949. "The fact is," he pointed out, "that the Chief Executive has constantly and consistently resisted this kind of encroachment on the executive power. . . . What this measure, in its present form, would do is vest in two Committees of Congress a function which the Constitution does not sanction."[46] His attempt to convert the come-into-agreement provision into a report-and-wait procedure by floor amendment was, however, soundly defeated by a vote of 60-8.

Questions about the constitutionality of the one-house and two-house forms of the legislative veto have also been voiced by members of Congress. In debate over the War Powers Resolution, Representative Dave Martin (R, NB) argued that provisions in its own rules prevented Congress from using a concurrent resolution in the manner contemplated by the bill. Citing <u>Jefferson's Manual of Parliamentary Procedure</u>, which was adopted by the Senate in 1801 and by the House in 1837, he declared: "A concurrent resolution is binding on neither House until agreed to by both. Since not legislative in nature it is not sent to the President for approval." <u>Cannon's Precedents of the House of Representatives</u> further supported this point: "A concurrent resolution is without force and effect beyond the confines of the Capitol."[47] These internal congressional rules combined with the second paragraph of the Presentation Clause appear to make the War Powers Resolution legislative veto not only constitutionally invalid but counter to Congress's own rules as well. Senator Sam Ervin (D, NC), one of the foremost constitutional authorities in Congress, corroborated this reasoning:

> It is because it [the concurrent resolution] has legislative effect. That is what it is designed to have. You cannot pass a resolution which is not subject to the Presidential veto which has legislative effect. This certainly has legislative effect.[48]

Senator Jacob Javits (R, NY) disagreed with this interpretation. As a major architect of the War Powers Resolution, he was a strong supporter of the legislative veto applied in this manner. In testimony Javits stated: "I would like to make clear that where executive branch decisions involve broad policy, such as the Reorganization Act, the War Powers Resolution or sales of military equipment or nuclear technology to foreign nations, I support the legislative veto."[49] Javits's support for the veto did not include support for the generic veto over rulemaking, although his objection was not based on constitutionality: "Extension of the legislative veto procedure from broad questions of national policy to all agency regulations . . . creates more problems than it solves."[50] Concern about the effect of the generic veto was also voiced by Rules Committee Chairman Richard Bolling (D, MO): "If you once start accepting a legislative veto, you end up with a legislative veto in practical fact by the committee chairman. . . . And that makes absolutely no sense in terms of government of laws and a government that concerns itself with the country as a whole."[51]

The inconsistent attitude of many members of Congress toward the veto is perhaps best illustrated by a statement of Representative Bob Eckhardt (D, TX):

> I am not a true believer or a true disbeliever with respect to the legislative veto. I voted for a good number of legislative vetoes and I have very strongly fought a good number of others. . . . But I believe when Congress in effect attaches a yo-yo string to the grant of authority [a reference to the generic veto over rulemaking], and says we as a body will look at it later and possibly change our policy, it seems to me when Congress acts in such a way that there is no escaping the very clear and express language of Article I, Section 7, the second clause. . . .[52]

The judiciary has not cleared up the confusion surrounding the constitutionality of the legislative veto. In spite of the fact that several cases involving the veto have come under the scrutiny of the courts, no Supreme Court decision has yet reached the question of the veto's constitutionality. In Clark v. Valeo (559 F.2d 642, DC Circuit, 1977), the court declined to reach the merits of the constitutionality of the veto issue on ripeness grounds, because the veto power has not as yet been exercised by Congress over the Federal Elections Commission.

In Buckley v. Valeo (424 U.S. 1, 1976), the Supreme Court found the method of appointment of the Federal Elections Commission (two presidential appointees, two House appointees, and two Senate appointees) to be violative of the appointments clause of the Constitution but refused to reach the legislative veto question raised by the plaintiffs. Some analysts have relied on the strongly worded dicta in Justice White's concurring opinion that indicated that if the commission were constitutionally appointed, the congressional veto device would be constitutional, as proof of judicial support for the device. But White's lone opinion is not binding nor equivalent to a court ruling on the issue.

In Atkins v. United States (556 F.2d 1028, Ct. Cl. 1977), which deals with a one-house veto of judicial pay raises, the Court of Claims, split 4-3, allowed the exercise of this one-house veto (S. Res. 293) that disapproved the whole of the president's salary increase recommendation proposal. The majority opinion, however, specifically states: "We are not to consider and do not consider, the general question of whether a one-house veto is valid as an abstract proposition, in all instances, across-the-board, or even in most cases" (556 F.2d 1059). In January 1978, the Supreme Court denied the petition for review of <u>Atkins</u>, the effect of which was to let stand the lower court disposition.

<u>McCorkle</u> v. <u>United States</u> (559 F.2d 1258, 4th Cir. 1978) dealt with a similar issue. In this case, suit was brought by a high-level civil servant on behalf of federal employees in grades 15 through 18 of the General Schedule who had been denied a salary increase recommended by the president because the Senate in March 1974 exercised a legislative veto over the presidential recommendation. The Fourth Circuit Court of Appeals affirmed a district court dismissal of the suit. McCorkle had asked the court to declare unconstitutional the one-house veto provision of the Federal Salary Act of 1967 (U.S.C. 359, (1) (B)) on the ground that it abridged bicameralism, separation of powers, and the presidential veto. The court refused to reach the question of the constitutionality of the veto provision because it found that the one-house veto was inseparable from parts of the statute that empowered the president to make potentially binding recommendations. Because the court found that Congress would not have passed the act without retaining authority to veto the presidential recommendation, the salary increase recommended could not stand in isolation from the veto power. The Supreme Court also denied the petition to review the case, which left the lower court decision in effect.

More recently, a three-judge panel of the U.S. Court of Appeals for the Ninth Circuit has ruled unanimously that a provision permitting one house of Congress to override the attorney general's decision to suspend deportation of aliens violated the separation of powers doctrine (<u>Chadha</u> v. <u>Immigration and Naturalization Service</u>; 634 F.2d 408, 9th Cir. 1980). The congressional veto following administrative proceedings to suspend deportation was deemed, by the court, to be an impermissible intrusion on functions constitutionally granted to the executive and judicial branches. The court defined a violation of the separation of powers doctrine as an assumption by one branch of powers that are central or essential to the operation of a coordinate branch, provided that the assumption is disruptive and is unnecessary to implement a legitimate governmental policy. The court concluded that the single-house disapproval scheme rendered meaningless the executive's duty to execute the law faithfully, and rendered equally nugatory the role of judicial review in determining the procedural or substantive fairness of administrative action. This marked the first time that a federal court invalidated a legislative veto. The Supreme Court accepted <u>Chadha</u> for review during its 1981-82 term. Oral argument on the case was heard on February 22, 1982. Unable to reach a decision in the 1982 term, the court reheard oral argument in the case on December 7, 1982. If the Supreme Court upholds the lower court decision, it would be its first ruling overturning a legislative veto as unconstitutional. Even so, it would probably restrict the ruling to the case at hand, as did the Ninth Circuit Court in its decision, and not address the general issue of the veto's constitutionality in other situations.

In the latest cases involving the legislative veto question a three-judge panel of the Circuit Court of Appeals for the District of Columbia held unconstitutional a one-house legislative veto provision contained in the Natural Gas Policy Act (NGPA) that was used by the House of Representatives to veto an incremental gas-pricing rule developed by the Federal Energy Regulatory Commission (FERC) (Consumer Energy Council of America et al. v. Federal Energy Regulatory Commission et al. (673 F.2d 425, January 29, 1982)). And in a per curiam opinion that simply relied on the FERC court analysis, a unanimous eight-judge panel of the same court held unconstitutional a two-house legislative veto provision contained in the Federal Trade Commission Ammendments of 1980 that was used by Congress to veto a used-cars rule developed by the Federal Trade Commission (FTC) (Consumers Union of U.S., Inc. v. Federal Trade Commission (691 F.2d 575, October 22, 1982)).

Brought by several consumer groups, the FERC case challenged the one-house veto provision in the NGPA on four constitutional grounds: (1) that it violated the constitutional doctrine of separation of powers; (2) that it deprived the president of his veto power under Article 1, Section 7, of the Constitution; (3) that it violated Article 1, Section 7's requirement of bicamerialism; and (4) that it delegated legislative authority without standards (673 F.2d 448). Rallying behind the consumer group petitioners and the respondent FERC was a rather bizarre lineup of intervenors. The Department of Justice, which might normally be expected to represent the commission, filed an amicus curiae brief in support of petitioners' constitutional challenges. Counsel for FERC avoided the constitutional issues by arguing instead that the case was moot because the commission had subsequently withdrawn the rule. Intervenors on behalf of several natural gas industry groups defended the legislative veto's constitutionality, as did the U.S. Senate and House of Representatives in amici curiae briefs.

The primary basis of the court's holding in the FERC case was that the one-house veto violates Article 1, Section 7 both by preventing the president from exercising his veto power and by permitting legislative action by only one house of Congress. In addition the court found that the one-house veto contravened the separation of powers principle implicit in Articles 1, 2, and 3 "because it authorizes the legislature to share powers properly exercised by the other two branches." Because it found these grounds to be sufficient basis for resolving the issue, the court declined to reach the undue delegation of power issue (673 F.2d 448).

The sweeping 104-page opinion addresses and agrees with almost every constitutional issue raised by constitutional scholars against the legislative veto. Only in the case of reorganization and foreign affairs did the court leave open any question of its opinion on the veto's constitutionality. Stating that the apparent accommodation between the executive and Congress on the use of the veto in reorganization statutes "might be relevant to a challenge to those statutes," the court firmly dismissed respondent's contention that such accommodation would have any bearing on the constitutionality of the veto in rule-making or other contexts. In sidestepping the veto's constitutionality when applied to foreign affairs, the opinion noted that foreign affairs vetoes present unique problems "since in that context there is the additional question whether Congress or the President or both have the inherent power to act" (673 F.2d 458, 459).

Showing little sympathy for the request made by congressional amici that the court approve the legislative veto under the principles of flexibility and practicality in constitutional adjudication, the court declared that "congressional unwillingness to use its constitutional powers cannot be deemed a sufficient reason for inventing new ways for it to act" (673 F.2d 477). If Congress is concerned that it has given away too much power, the court pointed out, it may by statute take it back or it may in the future enact more specific delegations. The fundamental problem with the one-house veto, according to the court's decision, is that it represents an "attempt by Congress to retain direct control over delegated administrative power" and that it "effectively changes the law" without following the constitutional process for doing so (673 F.2d 474).

In conclusion, the opinion recognized that the decision of the court in this case could have "far reaching effects on the operation of the National Government" but nevertheless defended the actions by noting that the preservation of the constitutional system of government depends on "the steadfastness with which its basic principles and requirements are observed" (673 F.2d 478). Otherwise, its critical protections against governmental tyranny would quickly become meaningless, because the government in power could shape it to suit whatever purposes seem sound at the present. Since the legislative veto provision in the NGPA attempts to evade the constitutional restrictions on the exercise of the legislative power and the principle of separation of powers that are fundamental to the constitutional scheme, it is necessarily unconstitutional.

Counsel for the natural gas companies as well as attorneys for the Senate and House of Representatives have appealed the FERC decision to the Supreme Court. If the Supreme Court were to uphold the lower court's ruling in its entirety, the broadness of such a ruling would probably outlaw most of the committee-level and two-house veto provisions as well. The Supreme Court could, on the other hand, restrict its finding of unconstitutionality to the bicameralism issue alone, leaving open the question of the two-house veto's constitutionality. Whatever the Supreme Court decides, resolution of the veto issue may not come for some time.

It is clear, then, that the question of the legislative veto's constitutionality remains both controversial and unresolved. Congress, meanwhile, continues to extend legislative veto controls over the rulemaking authority of an increasing number of programs, agencies, and even complete departments. The implications of this trend, which have been raised by scholars and members of Congress alike, are discussed in the next section.

Practical Considerations of the Legislative Veto in Rulemaking

The first presidential message on the legislative veto was delivered, as mentioned above, by President Carter on June 21, 1978. His purpose was "to underscore and explain" his concern about the legislative veto as recently employed to "inject Congress into the details of administering substantive programs and laws."[53] Although the message began by raising the constitutional problems associated with the legislative veto, the bulk of it was addressed to the serious practical policy and administrative problems raised by its aplication to the regulatory process.

For Congress to act responsibly under a legislative veto review of agency rules, which are often adopted after months or years of hearings and are based on many volumes of evidence, Carter emphasized, it would have to examine all of the evidence, hold its own hearings, and make its decision all within a few weeks' time. This would add a tremendous burden to Congress's legislative agenda. The implication was clear: If Congress were to exercise a legislative veto power without such steps, it would not be acting responsibly.

The legislative veto would also greatly compound delay and uncertainty in a regulatory process already criticized for being slow and for creating a problematic climate for business and for state and local government planning. Carter also pointed out that indefinite deadlock could result if the House and Senate disagreed with the agency or each other on the specifics of a desired regulation; the veto could only reject a regulation, not develop an alternative.

Carter also asserted that legislative vetoes could seriously harm the regulatory process. The perceived political power of affected groups might carry more weight than would their substantive arguments with a regulator who was anxious to avoid a legislative veto. "Many regulations would be evolved in negotiations between agency officials and congressional staff members, subverting requirements in present law for public notice and comment and for decisions based on the record."[54] Regulators might also reverse the constructive trend toward adopting uniform rules by reverting to case-by-case action, because legislative vetoes cannot be applied to such decisions. This would reduce both the clarity and certainty provided by uniform rules.

In Carter's opinion, however, the most vexatious aspect of the legislative veto is that it "treats symptoms not causes."[55] He was concerned that the vast effort required to second-guess individual regulatory decisions could impede the crucial task of revising the statutes at issue. Only through regulatory reform can Congress deal with the underlying problems caused by a multitude of individual legislative mandates.

Concern about the effect of the legislative veto when applied to agency-level action, such as rulemaking, has come from other quarters as well. Professor Harold Seidman recently charged that as it is currently employed the legislative veto tends:

1. To confer authority without responsibility by providing a continuous process of consultation that may entail off-the-record negotiations and clandestine deals.
2. To blur accountability for executive actions by involving Congress in agency decision making.
3. To compromise the independence of Congress and to impair its ability to oversee executive operations by further institutionalizing the ad hoc approach to oversight that relies on constituent or special interest pressures for its stimulus.
4. To divert limited time and staff resources from legislation of greater importance if the process is to be more than simply a pro forma approval by default.
5. To cause delays and possibly to produce stalemates.[56]

The late Judge Harold Leventhal of the District of Columbia Circuit Court of Appeals raised another troubling prospect: "Even assuming they [the veto provisions] are upheld, I do think it likely that legislative veto provisions will tend to reduce the rigor of judicial scrutiny over agency rules and decisions."[57] Although he recognized that all the legislative veto bills provided that "congressional inaction on or rejection of a resolution of disapproval or of a resolution for consideration shall not be deemed an expression of approval of such a rule," he suggested that as a matter of "judicial inclination" courts cannot help but be "influenced by that in conducting judicial review."[58] Courts would not be oblivious, Leventhal thought, to the veto review process and would use it as an indication of at least congressional acquiescence in and validity for the rule, if not outright approval.

Many members of Congress have also voiced serious misgivings about the efficacy of the legislative veto as a congressional reform of the regulatory process. In recent testimony before the Subcommittee on Administrative Law and Government Relations, Representative John J. Moakley (D, MA), chairman of the Subcommittee on Rules of the House of the House Rules Committee, which held extensive hearings on the generic-veto proposals during the 96th Congress, stated:

> I strongly believe that the legitimacy of the legislative veto is not a function of its constitutionality. . . . I do, however, have serious problems with the veto. To my mind, it will not enhance the ability of Congress to conduct effective oversight of the regulatory agencies. I think that the traditional legislative veto will simply set up a procedure to formalize an impasse between Congress and the agency. A yes or no vote on a resolution of disapproval does not provide any congressional guidance to the agenies. Moreover, the resolution of disapproval would be referred to standing committees having jurisdiction over the agency issuing the rule, and thus the veto would be subject to the same institutional weaknesses which now preclude the consideration of overall regulatory policy.
>
> The legislative veto, as an oversight tool available to House and Senate committees, might serve to strengthen the "Iron Triangle" or "Subsystem Politics" which presently exist among legislative subcommittees, regulatory agencies, and the regulated community. The relationship among the members of this trilogy is cultivated by close cooperation on policy matters from which an inevitable single perspective emerges. The veto power wielded by a subcommittee would make that "cooperation" a practical necessity, thereby insuring the mainte-nance of the status quo in our regulatory policies.[59]

Representative Anthony C. Beilenson (D, CA) carried this argument further by raising the problem of the potential relationship between campaign contributions and regulated interest groups. He commented that the members of the committees looking at these regulations are the very members who in some instances accept and receive thousands of dollars from political action committees of the very interests who are petitioning them to review the regulations that those interests do not like. When Senator Carl Levin (D, MI) countered that the same problem exists in regard to legislation, Beilenson replied: "But this is even more so. The people that gave $1,500 last November are all of a sudden affected, they think, adversely by a rule being promulgated by an agency that regulated their interest, and they come to you and say take a look at this regulation, maybe you people can overturn it. It is such an obvious and clear relationship."[60]

In their 1976 study of five programs that operated under legislative veto controls, Harold H. Bruff and Ernest Gelhorn found many of the above concerns corroborated by their data. For example, they found negotiations and compromises between the agency and the congressional oversight committee to be significant in the five programs, and in some cases the low visibility or secretive nature of the negotiations made pinpointing accountability for the final regulation difficult if not impossible. The congressional time constraints resulted in the review's being an attempt to second guess the agency without the benefit of all the facts that the agency had developed in most of the cases. Workloads of both congressional and agency staff were greatly increased. Delay was significant, especially in the case of the Federal Elections Commission rules, which lapsed because of the adjournment of Congress before the review period expired. Most of the review of the regulations studied was based on disagreement with policy questions, not on the agencies' conformity to statutory purpose. "Indeed," Bruff and Gelhorn noted, "the chief effect of the veto power seems to be an increase in the power of congressional committees and in the practice of negotiating over the substance of rules."[61]

The Bruff and Gelhorn study is the only major study of the operative effects of the addition of legislative veto power over the regulation process published prior to this effort. Since their work, Congress has added legislative veto provisions over the rulemaking authority of numerous programs and agencies (see Table 2.3), and on several occasions since then has also exercised veto power over regulations promulgated under statutory legislative veto provisions. The case studies in chapters 3, 4, and 5 are an effort to build on the existing information about the actual operative effect of the legislative veto over rulemaking. All the case studies to be presented involve either legislative veto provisions added since the Bruff-Gelhorn 1976 research or congressional exercise of already existing legislative veto power in the years after that study.

Notes

1. Quoted in U.S. Congress, House, Committee on Rules, Recommendations on Establishment of Procedures for Congressional Review of Agency Rules, 96th Cong., 2d sess., 1980, p. 20. Hereafter cited as Rules Report.
2. Ibid., p. 23. In 1944 the House of Commons followed suit by establishing a similar committee.
3. H. Lee Watson, "Congress Steps Out: A Look at Congressional Control of the Executive," 63 California Law Review 996 (1975).
4. Ibid., pp. 998, 999, 1004.
5. Ibid., p. 1015.
6. Legislative Appropriations Act of 1932 (47 Stat. 414). Watson points out that this power amounted to an item-veto power for Congress over presidential actions. Hoover's reorganization efforts under this authority were all vetoed by Congress. Watson, "Congress Steps Out," p. 1010.
7. Watson, "Congress Steps Out," p. 1010.
8. Ibid., p. 1013. Congressional debate at the time indicated an acceptance of the attorney general's proposition that such power was properly exercised only with the concurrence of both houses and opportunity for presidential veto.
9. Reorganization Act of 1939 (53 Stat. 561; P.L. 76-19). In this case presidential reorganization authority was subject to disapproval by a concurrent resolution if passed within sixty calendar days.
10. Clark F. Norton, Congressional Review, Deferral and Disapproval of Executive Actions: A Summary and an Inventory of Statutory Authority, Report 76-88G (Washington, DC: Library of Congress, Congressional Research Service, 1976). Hereafter cited as Norton 1976. Examples of acts with legislative veto termination authority include: Act to Promote Defense of the United States (55 Stat. 32); Emergency Price Control Act (1942) (56 Stat. 24); War Labor Disputes Act (1943) (57 Stat. 168).
11. See Watson, "Congress Steps Out," p. 1016.
12. 634 F.2d 408, 9th Cir. 1980.
13. Military and Naval Construction Authorization Act of 1952, Public Building Purchase Contract Act of 1954, Watershed, Protection and Flood Prevention Act of 1954, and Small Reclamation Projects Act, 1956.
14. Department of Interior and Related Agencies Appropriations for FY 1979, Amtrak Improvement Act of 1975, National Aeronautics and Space Administration Authorization for FY 1976, Hopi and Navajo Tribe Act, 1974.
15. Norton 1976, pp. 117-27. Of the twenty-nine acts in the public works category: space project construction programs, six; watershed projects, five; reclamation and irrigation projects, three; building

54

construction or acquisition programs, fifteen.

16. Emergency Unemployment Compensation Extension
Act of 1977 includes a provision for a concurrent resolution
of approval on each of the salary recommendations submitted
by the president under the Salary Act of 1967; the Energy
Policy and Conservation Act of 1975 provides for a one-house
veto over a rationing contingency plan that Congress
directed the president to submit. The Emergency Energy
Conservation Act of 1979 requires the president to submit a
new rationing plan subject once again to a one-house veto.

17. The compilation is based on descriptive accounts
of the legislative veto provisions in Clark F. Norton, Data
on Congressional Veto Legislation (1932-1978) and on
Extent of Usage (1960-July 31, 1978) (Washington, DC:
Library of Congress, Congressional Research Service,
1979). Hereafter cited as Norton, 96th Congress. In
addition to the 138 bills here tabulated, there were 30
bills containing some form of generic-veto proposals.

18. For a complete account, see Norton, 96th
Congress, pp. 19, 25.

19. The Comprehensive Environmental Response,
Compensation, and Liability Act (P.L. 96-510) is an example
of a Senate-initiated legislative veto that originated in
the Senate version of the bill (S. 1480). See Norton, 96th
Congress, pp. 49-50.

20. Norton, 96th Congress, p. 2.

21. Ibid., pp. 2-11.

22. Thomas J. Nicola, Clark F. Norton, and John T.
Melsheimer, Congressional Veto of Executive Actions,
Issue Brief 76006 (Washington, DC: Library of Congress,
Congressional Research Service, 1981), pp. 8-9.

23. For examples of veto termination authority bills
signed by Roosevelt, see note 10, above.

24. Robert H. Jackson, "A Presidential Legal
Opinion," 66 Harvard Law Review 1353 (1953). Jackson
took the occasion of publication of an article by Robert
Ginnane to reveal a hitherto secret legal opinion signed by
Roosevelt, which in Roosevelt's words placed him "on the
record in regard to the unconstitutionality of that
provision of Section 3(c) of the Lend-Lease Act, Public Law
No. 11, 77th Congress, which authorized repeal by a
concurrent resolution of the Congress" (p. 1359).

25. Opinion of the Attorney General of the United
States to the President (January 31, 1977) in H.R. Rep. No.
105, 95th Cong., 1st sess., pp. 10-11. By Attorney General
Griffin B. Bell's reasoning, which was supported by Carter,
the president would scarcely submit a plan of which he
disapproved, and because he would retain the "ultimate veto
power" in his decision not to submit a plan at all, his powers
would be protected under the procedures. The opinion
further argued that because reorganization deals only with
the internal organization of the executive branch and does
not affect the substantive rights of the people, it was
merely legislation in reverse. Thus, both the people's

rights and the president's authority were preserved.

26. President Jimmy Carter, Message to Congress, June 21, 1978, reprinted in Congressional Quarterly, June 24, 1978, pp. 1623-24.

27. Federal Trade Commission Chairman Michael Pertschuk stated that he did not consider the congressional veto included in the 1980 FTC authorization act to be "much of a problem" for the FTC; far less a problem, in fact, than the Senate proposal for restricting FTC authority to regulate in certain areas. Interview with Pertschuk, June 12, 1980.

28. John D. Millett and Lindsay Rodgers, "The Legislative Veto and the Reorganization Act of 1939," Public Administration Review 1 (1941):188.

29. Robert W. Ginnane, "The Control of Federal Administration by Congressional Resolutions," 66 Harvard Law Review 584 (1953), p. 611.

30. Joseph Cooper and Ann Cooper, "The Legislative Veto and the Constitution," 30 George Washington Law Review 467 (1962), p. 476.

31. Ibid., p. 477.

32. Ibid., p. 514.

33. U.S. Congress, Senate, Committee on the Judiciary, Subcommittee on Separation of Powers, Hearings on Separation of Powers, 90th Cong., 1st sess., 1967, p. 247.

34. Ibid., p. 248.

35. Ibid., p. 187.

36. Ibid., p. 190.

37. Watson, "Congress Steps Out," pp. 1077, 1084.

38. Ibid., p. 996.

39. John R. Bolton, The Legislative Veto: Unseparating the Powers (Washington, DC: American Enterprise Institute, 1977), p. 49.

40. Louis Fisher and Ronald C. Moe, "Reorganization Authority: Is It Worth the Cost?" Political Science Quarterly 96 (1981):301.

41. Louis Fisher, "A Political Context for Legislative Vetoes," paper presented at the White Burkett Miller Center of Public Affairs, University of Virginia, Charlottesville, February 10-11, 1978, p. 7.

42. Bernard Schwartz, "The Legislative Veto and the Constitution--A Reexamination," 46 George Washington Law Review 351 (1978), p. 374.

43. Ibid., p. 375.

44. Robert G. Dixon, Jr., "The Congressional Veto and Separation of Powers: The Executive on a Leash?" 56 North Carolina Law Review 427 (1978), p. 494.

45. 76 Cong. Rec. 3539 (1933).

46. Quoted in Virginia A. McMurty, "Legislative Vetoes Relating to Public Works and Buildings," in U.S. Congress, House, Committee on Rules, Studies on the Legislative Veto (committee print prepared by the Congressional Research Service), 96th Cong., 2d sess.,

1980, pp. 446-47.

47.   119 Cong. Rec. 20206 (June 25, 1973) (floor debate on War Powers Resolution).

48.   Ibid.

49.   125 Cong. Rec. S15167 (daily ed.), October 25, 1979.

50.   Ibid.

51.   Rules Report, p. 439.

52.   Ibid., p. 19.

53.   President Jimmy Carter, Message to Congress, June 21, 1978, p. 1623.

54.   Ibid.

55.   Ibid.

56.   Harold Seidman, "Legislative Veto: Two Views-- One 'Yea," One 'Nay,'" Staff: Congressional Staff Journal (Washington, DC: Committee on House Administration, Office of Management Services, September/October 1980), p. 23.

57.   Rules Report, p. 1121.

58.   Ibid.

59.   U.S. Congress, Senate, Committee on the Judiciary, Subcommittee on Administrative Practice and Procedure, Hearings, 97th Cong., 1st sess., 1981, July 13, 18, 20, 25, 26--from copy of testimony in author's files.

60.   Rules Report, pp. 1333-34.

61.   Harold H. Bruff and Ernest Gelhorn, "Congressional Control of Administrative Regulation: A Study of Legislative   Vetoes,"   90 Harvard Law Review 1369 (1976), p. 1420. Also see pp. 1409-23.

3
The Case of the HUD "Constitutional" Vetoes

Introduction

On June 9, 1978, the ranking minority member of the Housing and Community Development Subcommittee of the House Committee on Banking, Finance, and Urban Affairs, Garry Brown (R, MI), offered a floor amendment to the 1978 Housing and Community Development Act that one-house veto power be included over all rulemaking of the Department of Housing and Urban Development (HUD). In introducing his proposal, Brown commented:

> The executive branch has used its regulation writing authority not to flesh out the law but to undermine the law. It has used its authority to thwart the will of Congress. . . . Of all the executive branch departments, I believe HUD is one of the worst offenders.[1]

Brown was hardly alone in his opinion of HUD; the amendment passed that day by a vote of 244 to 140. It passed despite the opposition throughout a lengthy and heated debate by the Democratic chairman of HUD's oversight subcommittee--the Housing and Community Development Subcommittee, the same committee of which Brown was ranking minority member.

Although the Senate version of the legislation embodied no congressional review authority over HUD's rulemaking, the conference committee compromise that was enacted contained a complex congressional review procedure to cover all rulemaking by HUD.[2] the compromise was an attempt to design a procedure that would not raise the constitutional questions associated with the one-house and two-house legislative veto procedures. Only by avoiding the constitutional issue was the compromise acceptable to the Senate conferees and, ultimately, to the full Senate.

The provision, as enacted, required that HUD semiannually submit an agenda of proposed regulations to its oversight committees, the Senate Committee on Banking, Housing, and Urban Affairs, and the House Committee on

Banking, Finance, and Urban Affairs. Either committee, within thirty days of continuous session of Congress after the agenda was transmitted, could notify HUD that it intended to review any of the regulations. The department would then be required to transmit a copy of such a regulation or regulations to both committees at least fifteen calendar days of continuous session before its publication for comment in the Federal Register. HUD was also required to forward all final regulations (at the time of publication in the Federal Register as final) to the same committees and to delay implementation for twenty calendar days of continuous session. (The delay period was extended to thirty calendar days by the Housing and Community Development Act of 1980.) During that period either committee could vote to suspend the regulations for an additional ninety calendar days, a delay that would give Congress the opportunity to pass a joint resolution or to attach a rider amendment to an existing bill (similar to the appropriations bills' riders) to overrule the regulation.

It was also provided that both the submission of the rule or regulation to the committees fifteen days prior to publication for comment in the Federal Register and the twenty-day waiting period after the rule or regulation had been published as final could be waived if a written request by the secretary to that effect were agreed to by the chairmen and ranking minority members of both committees.

To understand why Congress passed this rather convoluted review procedure--the so-called constitutional veto, because the president was to be included in the process--it is necessary to look briefly at HUD's thirteen-year preceding history. It is a history that can help to explain the antagonism that has developed between the department and Congress.

The Department of Housing and Urban Development: 1965 to 1977

On September 9, 1965, President Lyndon Johnson signed into law legislation establishing the Department of Housing and Urban Development. At the ceremony that day he said, "In less than a lifetime America has become a highly urbanized nation. We must face the many meanings of this new America."[3] The primary reason for creating the department, according to its sponsors, had been "to secure a seat at the bargaining table in the White House where the federal pie is cut up and divided. . . . In Washington, influence is largely measured by prestige, payrolls, and budgets and only a cabinet officer commanding ample amounts of these can represent the people."[4]

Five years of legislative effort spanning both the Kennedy and Johnson administrations as well as more than three decades of federal involvement in urban development and housing matters had preceded the formation of a

department devoted to our cities and our new urban age.
Although earlier versions of the departmental legislation
had reflected the need for wider powers to cope with the
immensity of the urban problem, provisions of the final act
bespoke the reality of the legislative process. To gain
sufficient votes for passage, compromises must be
incorporated in legislation to satisfy diverse vested
interests.[5]

Tension and conflict among the potential clientele and
interest groups were evident from the beginning of the
legislative effort. On one side was the housing industry--
home builders, mortgage lenders, building-materials
manufacturers, realtors, labor unions. On the other side
were mayors, represented by the United States Conference of
Mayors and the National League of Cities, minority groups,
and housing consumers.

The president of the National Association of Home
Builders (NAHB) testified in 1961 before House and Senate
committees that the organization could support the bill to
create a Department of Urban Affairs and Housing (H.R. 6433)
only if it were amended to change the name to Department of
Housing and Urban Affairs. He also demanded as
prerequisite to industry support inclusion of language that
made encouragment of a prosperous and efficient
construction industry a stated purpose. At the same time,
mayors stressed giving city people an advocate in
Washington so big cities would have an adequate voice in the
highest councils of government. They favored a department
that in both name and mission would press their interests.
Organizations representing the poor and minorities
similarly articulated hopes for a department devoted to the
concerns of cities, where their numbers were so
disproportionately found.

The strength of the housing industry should not be
underestimated. It is a highly fragmented industry, with
members in most congressional districts and states. Its
thousands of small entrepreneurs are not only dispersed but
numerous. They have in the NAHB an effective and strong
political presence. Numerous other trade orgnizations,
such as the American Institute of Planners and the American
Institute of Architects, reinforce the lobbying power of
the housing industry. The name chosen for the new
department, and the inclusion as one of its major mandates
"to support, through mortgage financing and otherwise, the
stable production of needed homes in good neighborhoods for
all urban Americans" (emphasis added) attest only partially
the influence of the industry on Congress.[6]

Congress was also responsive to the plight of the
cities, and in enabling legislation directed the department
to address that plight, especially the needs of the urban
and minority poor. Development of viable urban
communities through efforts to solve critical social,
economic, and environmental problems was made a notable part
of the HUD mandate. The originating act and subsequent

legislation (Model Cities Program, Section 8 Housing, Community Development Block Grants, Urban Development Action Grants, etc.) underscore the importance Congress has accorded cities.

The conflicting desires of the interest groups involved are very much reflected in the charges Congress has given HUD in various enabling acts. HUD's encouragement of slum clearance and economic development, for example, often results in compounding other aspects of its mission, such as insuring adequate housing for the poor. Demands with built-in contradictions have brought significant tension among HUD, its oversight committees, and its interest groups. The policymaking arena involved could hardly be referred to as the cozy iron triangle characterized by subsystem policymaking; rather, it is characterized by pluralistic bargaining and compromise both in Congress and the department. Prior to the 1978 amendments that added the legislative review procedure described above, HUD's relation with its oversight committees--especially the House committee--was, as one participant commented, cantankerous.[7]

Through the Nixon and Ford presidencies (1969-1976), a period that represents over half the department's existence and that began only four years after its formation, leadership at HUD paralleled the conservatism of Republican administrations. This was even more the case after the resignation in 1972 of Secretary George Romney, whose deep concern saved the Model Cities Program for a time before increasing hostility between him and the White House undermined his efforts. During most of Romney's tenure, the department's primary mission reflected his highest priority: production of housing. This meant that the housing industry was HUD's foremost interest group. Fierce pressure was exerted by the department on the industry to increase production. Large subsidies were approved, and the largest volume of housing in history was built. The Federal Housing Authority (FHA) processing system for dealing with applications, however, faltered and then collapsed. The public and Congress became aware at that point "of inexcusable program abuses, scandals and even numerous acts of criminal collusion between FHA officials and private promoters."[8] HUD's credibility was much tarnished, and thus it became easier for the White House to press for a lessening of HUD's role.

Romney's successor, James Lynn (1972-1974), saw no merit in many HUD programs, and appeared to be in complete agreement with the Republican philosophy of the time in its sharp turn against federal social programs. His efforts were directed toward reducing expenditures and limiting the department's programs. Carla Hills, who was appointed by Ford to replace Lynn, also appeared to act in line with the conservative Republican philosophy.

Congressional unhappiness with HUD often led to charges--most often from liberal Democratic members--that

it was subverting the intent of Congress: it moved too
slowly, it failed to act, it inhibited or prevented goals
from being realized.   One example had to do with the
Emergency Homeowners Relief Act of 1975, which provided for
HUD coinsured mortgage loans or temporary payments (for up
to twenty-four months) of up to $250 to persons unable to
meet mortgage payments because they became unemployed in
the recession of 1974-1975.   HUD regulations to implement
the act, according to Senator Carl Levin (D, MI), "destroyed
what Congress had passed by adopting a nationwide trigger
for the program so high that the program was never
implemented."[9]   Impoundment was another strategy used by
the Nixon and Ford administrations to cut back at HUD.
        Jimmy Carter's election and his appointment of
Patricia Harris as secretary of HUD marked a return to a more
aggressive role for the department.   Congressional
complaints no longer concerned departmental footdragging
but centered on overzealousness, haste, and exceeding the
mandate--and the complainers were more often from the
conservative side of the aisle.   An example is one of HUD's
early actions under Harris.   On May 9, 1977, the department
in a regulation defined family groups eligible for public
housing.   The definition of "stable family relationship"
was not only broad enough to include unmarried couples, as
HUD had intended, but also ambiguous enough to include
homosexual couples, which HUD had not intended.   Congress
reacted by passing an amendment to nullify the regulation,
which was quickly enacted into law.[10]

The Department of Housing and Urban Development
versus Congress: 1978

        In their study of legislative vetoes over agency
rulemaking, Harold H. Bruff and Ernest Gelhorn found that
the congressional motivation for adopting such veto power
was often mistrust of agency intentions or displeasure with
agency decisions in politically sensitive areas.[11]   The
HUD case certainly fits neatly into their analysis.
        Many HUD actions angered members of Congress.   Some
members objected, for example, to HUD's definition of
"expected to reside" for the purpose of the Community
Development Block Grant (CDBG) Housing Assistance Plans,
but the incident that precipitated passage of a legislative
review procedure to cover all HUD rulemaking involved
Harris and CDBG funding.   She first announced that several
communities would be denied block grants under the Housing
and Community Development Act unless their plans were
modified to provide housing for a diversity of income
levels.   The 1977 Housing and Community Development
Amendments had appeared to make it clear that Congress
intended its monies to benefit those of low and moderate
income.   Congressmen whose districts faced possible fund
cutoffs were, understandably, unhappy with the secretary's

action. But when Harris next proposed a regulation that would require all communities to use the CDBG funds for the benefit of low- and moderate-income families, she created what might best be described as an uproar on Capitol Hill.

Harris claimed that the proposal was congruent with the clear statement of purpose of the original Housing and Community Development Act of 1974: "The primary objective of this title is the development of viable urban communities, by providing decent housing and a suitable living environment and expanding economic opportunities, principally <u>for persons of low or moderate income</u>"[12] (emphasis added). The need for the new regulation was substantiated by two studies of the block grant programs that had recently been released. The "Community Development Monitoring Report," issued under contract to HUD by the National Association of Housing and Redevelopment Officials (NAHRO), found a notable shift of housing construction activities from lower-income to middle-income sections of cities. The other study, by the Southern Regional Council, a nonprofit public interest group, concluded that "local diversions from the national purpose are not just occasional abuses, but rather form a pattern inherent in the implementation of the act; decisions are made by politicians who often have little regard for concerns of low and moderate income citizens."[13] One abuse widely reported by the news media at the time was the use of $150,000 in block grant funds for a tennis court complex in an affluent section of Little Rock, Arkansas. The city program director was quoted as saying, "You can't divorce politics from that much money . . . we must remember the needs of the people who vote . . . and poor people don't vote."[14]

The real controversy was over what many felt was HUD's arbitrary choice of a 75-percent rule, which required that unless a community was specifically exempted by HUD, it must spend at least three-quarters of its CDBG money to benefit low- and moderate-income persons. The act as amended, Harris's congressional opponents argued, allowed for the alternative priorities of (1) benefiting low- and moderate-income persons or (2) preventing or eliminating slums and blight;[15] thus, Harris had exceeded the legal mandate and acted contrary to legislative intent. As the <u>New York Times</u> editorialized, however, Harris was the one hewing to the original intent of Congress to help the poor:

> She is resisted by big-city Mayors, who are under pressure to use more of the money for sewers and parks in well-to-do neighborhoods, and by suburban officials, who are reluctant to use the funds for low-income housing. Once Congress takes a hand in writing HUD rules the unorganized poor are bound to fare even worse.[16]

Members of Congress are inevitably responsive to constituent pressures. When both city and suburban officials are united in vociferous opposition to government action, change or reversal can be expected in the House. Senators, with their larger and more diverse constituencies, and in consideration of their longer terms, are often more resistant to pressures from home but are not always above the fray. Not too surprisingly, then, congressional reaction was swift and clear. In addition to the legislative review procedure over future regulations described above, the 1978 amendments included a provision that prohibited the secretary from disapproving an application because it stressed one of the priorities more than the other.[17] The unorganized nonvoting poor stood little chance in the battle over the single issue posed by one HUD regulation, especially because Harris's 75-percent rule was arguably arbitrary and foolish.

The normal legislative process proved equal, in this case, to curbing Harris. Would it have been sufficient to prohibit a secretary from enforcing a far less controversial 51-percent rule that would have met the "principally benefit" criterion? Although answers to questions about such a nonevent are at best educated guesses, it is perhaps fair to note that the Senate housing committee and the Senate as a whole were more sympathetic in 1978 than the House to the need for low-income and low-income minority housing. There was, for example, no provision in S. 2084 (the 1978 Senate HUD bill) to restrict the secretary's authority to disapprove applications. The final amendment was a watered-down version of H.R. 12533's provision based on a compromise reached by the conference committee.

It is also possible that mayors might have found a 51-percent rule difficult to oppose in light of their own reelection strategies. With only the normal legislative process through which to respond, and with both Congress and the affected interest group at odds, rejection of a more reasonable 51-percent rule would have been less likely. But, the one-house veto proposed by Representative Brown would have provided the House, even in these hypothetical circumstances, with the ability to act alone to negate the rule. This suggests the possibility that when substantial differences between the Senate and the House over substantive policy issues have been resolved through the legislative process and enacted into law, the legislative veto power exercised by one house could undermine the interest of Congress as a whole.

The two case studies that follow deal with the exercise of the congressional review power enacted as Section 7(o) of the Housing and Community Development Amendments of 1978. Even though this procedure falls short of actual congressional veto power, the examples illustrate how the "constitutional veto"--given the reality of the congressional process, the influence of special interest groups, and the importance to the department of its relationship with Congress as it pursues its mandate--can be, in fact, as strong as the one-house veto.

Thermal Standards Veto

In April of 1979, the House Committee on Banking, Finance, and Urban Affairs attempted to use the newly enacted (October 1978) congressional review authority to overrule a HUD regulation dealing with thermal insulation standards for HUD-financed single- and two-family dwellings. The controversy originated in the Energy Policy and Conservation Act of 1975 (88 Stat. 871, Section 381(a)(2)), which mandated, among other things, that the Department of Energy (DOE) promulgate energy efficiency standards for new residential and commercial construction (the responsibility was first given to HUD, but passed to DOE in 1977). When it became apparent that the DOE standards would not be ready until 1980 or 1981, Congress directed the secretary of HUD to devise interim thermal standards for the HUD housing programs.[18] By this action Congress indicated its intention to insure that at least federally financed new construction of this type would meet some energy-conservation criteria. In part, the reason for the DOE delay was that the National Bureau of Standards (NBS) had not completed its technical analysis of the thermal properties of various building materials.

HUD proposed amendments to the Minimum Property Standards that established thermal requirements for FHA-financed, new one- and two-family buildings by creating maximum values ("U-values") for the coefficient of thermal conductance of walls.[19] In the simplest terms, the lower the U-value, the more insulation needed. Generally, the new standards meant that all currently accepted types of construction would have to be thermally improved in all but the milder climates. During the rulemaking process following publication of the proposed amendment in the Federal Register, the masonry industry voiced to the department its opposition to the amendment as it applied to masonry construction, claiming that the thicker masonry wall requires less insulation. HUD listened but did not agree. Harris explained in a letter to Chairman Henry S. Reuss (D, WI) of the Banking, Finance, and Urban Affairs Committee:

> We do not consider the mass effect of solid walls in calculating heat losses at this time, as there is no agreement in the housing industries and in the scientific or academic communities as to the effect of mass on energy use or values to be used in calculating heating loads. When some degree of consensus is

reached and substantiating technical data are provided, we will consider them.[20]

In order to get the regulations out in time for the 1979 building season, as the department believed it was under congressional direction to do, it was forced to rely on the currently available technical data.[21] At the time the NBS cost-benefit analysis for thermal insulation was based on the most common construction of HUD's single-family building program, the so-called board or stick-built wooden construction; masonry construction under HUD programs was estimated to be as low as one percent by one department spokesman.[22] Harris also explained to Reuss that a variance for masonry construction was provided for within the standards for those areas where the amount of such construction is significant, and that it would be continued until the NBS study was completed, probably in July or August 1979. The department would consider modifications then, if appropriate.

The masonry industry was not satisfied, and took its case to the Hill through Representative Richard Kelly (R, FL), mounting what one observer described as one of the most intense lobbying efforts he had seen.[23] Significantly, in Kelly's district masonry was the preferred building material, and a local-standards exception was already in effect for Florida. On April 30, Kelly entered a joint resolution of disapproval (H.J. Res. 310) to invalidate the requirements. After amendment by Representative Stewart McKinney (R, CT), which confined the disapproval of masonry construction (in effect, exempting such construction from the new regulations), the committee voted 22-6 to support the resolution. The action delayed for ninety calendar days implementation of the regulations as applied to masonry construction, thus giving the full Congress time to act on the resolution and allowing most of the 1979 building season to pass with masonry construction exempted from the thermal insulation requirement.

At the time, Chairman Thomas Ashley (D, OH) of the House subcommittee on housing, one of the six representatives opposed to the resolution, pointed out that the committee itself was ignoring the intent of the legislative review procedure: to insure that regulations were consistent with congressional intent, not to provide a way to disagree with how an executive department carried out that intent.[24] Without hearings or any apparent attempt to assess the potential damage to the masonry industry and, for that matter, to alternative building materials industries if masonry were exempted, and without independent evaluation of the masonry industry's claims of the benefit of mass in energy savings, the committee accepted Kelly's and the industry's say-so.

Harris chose to fight for HUD's thermal standards, a battle she was destined to lose. Although the committee vote had occurred on the eighteenth day of the initial twenty-day review period, the committee did not deliver documentation of the vote to the clerk of the House until the twenty-third day. HUD claimed that the failure to meet the deadline meant that the thermal regulations would go into effect on May 16. A headline in the <u>Legal Times of Washington</u> proclaimed, "Harris Snubs Congressional Order to Delay Housing Regs."[25]

When the masonry industry sought an injunction from the Federal District Court of the District of Columbia, Judge Oliver Gasch agreed with HUD's interpretation of "reporting out," overturning the committee's delay of the effective date for the thermal regulations.[26] During the floor debate in the House on the masonry exemption amendment, Ashley defended Harris's actions: "We have a Secretary of HUD who is really being mandated by Congress in two different directions, being mandated to promulgate and to implement thermal efficiency standards pursuant to the legislation passed by this body last year on the one hand, and being mandated to renege on and tear up the proposed regulations as far as masonry construction is concerned on the other."[27] Other members of the housing committee of the House did not take the rebuff so lightly. Two amendments were added to the 1979 housing amendments: one invalidated the current thermal standards for masonry construction and required the department to issue a new rule based on the more recent NBS analysis within one month of passage of the act; the other defined "reported out" to mean the vote of either committee to report out a bill or resolution. Neither amendment appeared in the Senate version of the bill, but when the bill emerged from the conference committee in December, both were included.

Whether the lobbying efforts of the masonry industry, even with its allies among the bricklayer unions, would have been successful enough to survive the conference compromise without what McKinney called HUD's "direct slap . . . made to the face of Congress"[28] is debatable. The costs incurred and time consumed by HUD, Congress, and the courts compared to the special benefit afforded masonry over competitive building materials is similarly debatable. More disconcerting here is the evident tendency for members of Congress to accept the word of industry lobbyists without serious question. One senator's testimony underscores this:

> Technical problems inherent in attempting to measure the thermal qualities of masonry construction materials and wood frame products . . . are not within the expertise of members of the Subcommittee. . . . Nor do I think the Subcommittee should hire thermal standards specialists.[29]

It was not until September 1980, eight months—and another building season—after the 1979 Housing and Community Development Amendments' "within one month" directive, that HUD issued new insulation standards covering the masonry industry. Based on the NBS "Economic Analysis of Insulation in Selected Masonry and Wood-Frame Walls," masonry walls performed only slightly better than wood-frame walls (.5 percent to 1.3 percent better for heating; .7 percent to 4.9 percent better for cooling). Because the difference was so small, HUD did not establish separate standards for masonry.[30]

It is interesting to note the apparent effect of congressional timetables on HUD's actions. Using the data from the NBS study that had been completed by early winter 1980, HUD representatives, as directed by Congress, met with personnel from DOE and the Farmers Home Administration to resolve differences in the thermal standards developed by the three agencies. Although no one at HUD will say as much, it appears that the final rule for masonry was ready to be issued at least by the end of May 1980. Why, then, the three-month delay? In an interview on June 10, 1980, a professional staff member of the House Committee on Banking, Finance, and Urban Affairs predicted that the final thermal regulation for masonry would appear "shortly after the House completes action on the Housing and Community Development Amendments of 1980." The prediction proved accurate. House action on the 1980 amendments was completed by the end of August 1980. HUD issued the new final masonry regulation on September 11. The major reason for the delay was department concern that, despite its substantiating technical data, the House might still reject the new standard because it was not a modification of the previous standard. Since the HUD congressional review provision allows for rejection by a joint resolution (which the president could easily veto) or by amendment to a piece of legislation, the annual authorization bill would have provided a "presidential-veto-proof" vehicle for overturning the masonry standard. New complexities in agency and congressional strategies have thus been introduced by this congressional review process, strategies that in this case caused significant delays in the promulgation of an agency regulation.

Several concerns raised in the Bruff and Gelhorn study are also illustrated by the thermal insulation case: "If interest groups can lobby Congress during the review period, their influence might render currently required public procedures for rulemaking ineffective."[31] The success of the masonry industry, after it had lost in the agency rulemaking procedure, demonstrates the validity of this concern. The wood products groups, apparently unaware of the masonry industry's push until after the twenty-day committee review period, did not mobilize their lobby until after the committee voted to defer the regulation for masonry construction for ninety days, too late to affect the decision process. The decision of Congress thus was based on only one side of a story--a side that it had unquestioningly accepted from the most concerned party.

Although the legislative history accompanying the HUD congressional review authority stated precisely, "The conferees also expect that the 90 day deferral provision will only be followed where either committee believes that the proposed regulations violate the intent of Congress,"[32] the deferral in this case was based on substantive disagreement with the regulation. In all the cases studied by Bruff and Gelhorn except the Federal Elections Commission, the congressional role was limited by statute to reviewing the legality of the agency's rule, that is, its conformity with statutory purpose. They found, nevertheless, that in all their cases the congressional review was also primarily based on policy.[33] Such discrepancy between what is said and what is done may create a significant problem. If Congress implies that all congressional review is to be directed simply at making sure that the conditions of statutory delegations are met, while in actuality the review process becomes one of policy review, the public and some members of Congress may not give the attention they otherwise would to such activity. The case studied here received considerable publicity because of Harris's actions, but the publicity was all after the fact. It did not serve to notify other interested parties that a policy decision that they had thought was complete when the final rule was published was, in fact, being altered by congressional moves.

Spatial Deconcentration Veto

The second instance involving congressional exercise of its veto power over HUD regulations is even more illustrative of the problem of low public visibility and its potential for undermining political accountability.

On June 12, 1979, while HUD was still under Harris's leadership, a proposed revision of the Section 8 new construction program regulation in its entirety was published in the <u>Federal Register</u> for public comment.[34] Interested parties were given until August 13 for submissions. A small portion of the revision attempted to put teeth into the congressional mandate of fair housing for the poor. The issue at question--fair housing--is fraught with controversy in Congress and in HUD as well. Whether there is an underlying public consensus on the subject is also debatable. But federal law on the issue is clear: the Section 8 Housing Assistance Payments Program for New Construction is, by congressional mandate, subject to equal opportunity requirements and must comply with Title VI of the Civil Rights Act of 1965 and Title VIII of the Civil Rights Act of 1968, which together proscribe discrimination in any federally funded project.[35] Section 8 housing programs, therefore, must not only benefit the poor but also provide equal opportunities for poor minority-group members to participate.

HUD's regulations have since the early 1970s required Section 8 recipients to include an affirmative fair housing marketing plan based on the Housing Assistance Plan (HAP) as developed by the community. In other words, the developer must provide goals--HUD officials carefully emphasize that these are goals, not quotas--for minority representation in the eventual rental population. Since 1972 the department has also had advertising guidelines for fair housing that prohibit advertising or sales tactics with respect to HUD-aided housing that are in any way discriminatory, define these practices, and require each applicant to submit a marketing plan showing how minority families will be informed that housing is to become available.[36] All this was already on the books.

HUD was attempting with its new so-called spatial deconcentration rules to see to it that the projects under Section 8 would give equal residential opportunities to minorities. If there were not enough poor minority-group members within the community, then the developer would be required to provide advance marketing, at least ninety days prior to occupancy, in areas where minorities were most likely to be found; by HUD definition such areas would be economically impacted areas within the same Standard Metropolitan Statistical Area (SMSA) as the project. The new regulations also prohibited residency requirements as a condition of occupancy--which would have clearly prevented minorities from occupying new housing if the community were "lily white," thus mocking the affirmative fair-housing plan from the start--but permitted residency preference if it were not inconsistent with the affirmative marketing plan for the project. Morton S. Baruch, deputy assistant secretary for housing and deputy federal housing commissioner of HUD, explained by example:

> The sponsor of a project and HUD agree that renting 15 percent of the units to minority persons is a realistic goal and this is stated in the plan. [Later Baruch stated that the breakdown would relate to the population demographics and the economics of the SMSA in question.] However, the sponsor wishes to apply a residency preference to selecting applicants. For 85 percent of the units there is no potential conflict. For the remaining 15 percent of the units--the preference may be applied in selecting tenants among minority applicants if there are minority applicants who are residents of the community.
>
> In addition, if the sponsor does not attract a sufficient number of minority applicants to meet the affirmative marketing goal and must consider other applicants in renting the remaining units, the sponsor may apply the preference in selecting among those applicants.[37]

The regulations concerning advance marketing and local-residency prohibition were a part of a complete reworking of the Section 8 construction requirements. When published as final on October 15, 1979, the revised regulations covered twenty pages in the Federal Register.[38] They represented an effort by HUD--based on more than a year of study, review, and substantial public comment. More than 230 individuals and organizations made submissions that reflected the varied perspectives of groups affected by the Section 8 construction program. The two sections of the revised regulations to which some members of Congress reacted negatively accounted for less than a page of the changes. The narrative that follows describes the congressional review process as it was applied to the regulations.

About a month after the proposed regulations had been published in the Federal Register (June 12, 1979), a constituent of Representative Millicent Fenwick's (R, NJ) who was director of a senior citizen housing project told her that he feared that the regulations would apply to such projects. Fenwick asked all the mayors of her district to comment on the regulations; those who answered were opposed, and she sent copies of their responses to HUD.[39]

On September 20, Fenwick and twenty-two colleagues wrote HUD of their dissatisfaction with the proposed regulations. Significantly, the letter addressed the issue as if the new regulations would eliminmate the preference for local residents,[40] whereas they allowed preference to the "extent that . . . [it is] not inconsistent with the affirmative fair housing market objectives." The real concern appeared to be that if a residency requirement were disallowed, no new low-income housing would be built-- especially in the suburbs. On October 16, HUD issued its final Section 8 regulations, modified somewhat in response to the congressional comments, and including assurances that the advance-marketing requirement would not apply to housing for the elderly, whose displacement had been the major concern of mayors who had responded to Fenwick's letter. The regulations were duly transmitted to Congress and for publication in the Federal Register.

On October 17, Fenwick introduced H.J. Res. 424 for the purpose of invalidating and disapproving HUD's final regulations. At the subcommittee hearing on October 30, which was attended by eleven of the twenty-seven members, Baruch and Fenwick were the only persons to testify. Chairman Ashley carefully defined the subcommittee's purpose under the legislative review procedure of the 1978 amendments: a review of the regulations to determine whether they had been properly promulgated in accord with specific statutory direction. "But if the complaint is directed toward unhappiness or disagreement with the direction of the proposed regulations," he admonished, "then I would feel constrained to object to further committee proceedings."[41]

The hearing record indicates that "unhappiness" and "disagreement," mixed with a considerable uncertainty over the regulations' wording, were at the heart of the review attempt.[42] Members did not question either the department's statutory authority or the concept of equal opportunity. Charles L. Edson, counsel for the National Leased Housing Association, presented in a letter to Chairman Reuss of the Banking, Finance, and Urban Affairs Committee several legalistic arguments to prove that the regulations exceeded congressional authorization. As Edson later noted, "The Committee, however, paid scant attention to these technical arguments primarily because the members had no real policy objection to the challenged requirements."[43]

As an ideal, equal opportunity housing appears to enjoy considerable support in Congress. Its translation into operative enforcement seems to be an entirely different matter. One Senate staffer commented, "Equal opportunity housing is a mandate Congress makes with the understanding 'We don't mean to do it with teeth. Just use a mild-mannered surface treatment approach.'"[44] Implementation is resisted under the guise of localism (local housing for local residents) or pragmatism (fears that enforcement of equal opportunity would bring an end to Section 8 building altogether).

The hearings closed with a "consensus" that confusion more than disagreement was the problem. The secretary was directed to send to the subcommittee clarification of the guidelines that the department would use to implement residency preference and advance-marketing requirements, especially the operating instructions to the field offices. The clarification was to be delivered by the close of business on the following day so that the subcommittee could act on the motion to defer within its time constraint.

On November 2, the subcommittee received a letter from Assistant Secretary Lawrence B. Simons in which the department agreed to suspend enforcement of the part of the Section 8 regulations in question pending issuance of a clarification. The rest of the regulations would go into effect on November 5. Simons expected "to issue a clarification within thirty days," but none has ever been issued. The matter was quietly dropped.[45] In effect, a "consensus"--not even a recorded vote--of eleven committee members of one subcommittee of one house of Congress negated a part of a finally promulgated rule of an executive department. This happened under a review procedure that was to have assured that such action would need a majority approval of the full Congress and the signature of the president.

Part of the reason the department dropped the offending regulations can be attributed to timing. The Section 8 construction program was at the start of another year of operation. Much of the revision of the regulations had been aimed at simplifying and streamlining the paperwork of application and management processes. To let these important changes fall along with the spatial deconcentration regulation--a favorable committee vote on H.J. Res. 424 would have deferred the entire package of Section 8 revisions for an additional ninety calendar days--would have caused significant confusion and delay in the entire program. In addition, there were many within the department who looked favorably upon the opportunity to withdraw the spatial deconcentration regulations. Considerable conflict existed within HUD over the use of its housing programs to further fair housing goals. With the possibility of losing the entire revision effort, the departmental faction opposed to the fair housing regulations was in a far stronger position to force a compromise in its favor.[46] The appointment of Moon Landrieu to replace Harris in August 1979, during the comment period on the proposed regulations, may also have contributed to a more conciliatory stance on the part of the departmental hierarchy.

Clearly, HUD, in developing the Section 8 regulations, had the difficult task of coordinating and balancing the constitutional and statutory mandates of equal opportunity concerns, which fell under the jurisdiction of the judiciary committees, with the conflicting concerns of local community housing needs, for which the Banking, Finance, and Urban Affairs Committee of the House and the Banking, Housing, and Urban Affairs Committee of the Senate were responsible. Moreover, at the time of the hearing before the housing subcommittee of the House, the Subcommittee on Civil and Constitutional Rights of the House Judiciary Committee had just completed action on the Fair Housing Act of 1979, which indicated a strong congressional concern about discrimination in housing. Spokespersons for this viewpoint were conspicuously absent at the legislative review hearing. As the chairman of the Senate housing subcommittee later pointed out, "Unless in the process of legislative review, hearings are required so that all segments of the affected Congress, agencies and public are permitted to participate, such a process is inconsistent with our concern for an open and fair process."[47]

By narrowing the scope of the conflict to a single regulation within a housing program and reducing the number of participants to a handful of members of Congress, the subcommittee was able to deal with a highly controversial issue with little public exposure of its actions. It is questionable whether its actions were visible to other members of Congress. The result might have been different if the judiciary committees of the House and Senate had taken part. Certainly the intensity and visibility of the debate would have been heightened. Newspaper coverage of the event at the time of the congressional review hearing appears to have been nonexistent. So lacking was general awareness that six months later in the Washington Post

Senators Carl Levin and David L. Boren (D, OK) commented on the spatial deconcentration case in a manner that might be described as a colossal misstatement of the facts. Their letter, entitled "The Case for Legislative Veto," said, in part: "When HUD issued regulations that discouraged people from moving into senior citizen projects by locating them far from their old neighborhoods, we were glad that there was a legislative veto mechanism in place to say, 'No, that's not what senior citizen housing is all about.'"[48] No mention was made of the issue of minority housing opportunities; rather, the controversy was recast as a "motherhood-and-apple-pie" issue.

Whatever the merits of the controversy, the very process of utilizing legislative veto power (even a nonuse, as in this instance) suggests that there are serious implications in the adoption of congressional veto review for such regulatory arenas as energy planning or environmental and consumer protection. The regulatory means of implementing broad social goals, it seems, can be quietly de-fanged in nearly sub rosa settings involving only a handful of members of Congress and articulate, narrowly interested claimants. Powerful organized specialized interests are likely to fare well under such a structure.

The late E. E. Schattschneider warned that "since the contestants in private conflicts are apt to be unequal in strength, it follows that the most powerful special interests want private settlements because they are able to dictate the outcome as long as the conflict remains private. . . . It is the weak who want to socialize conflict, i.e., to involve more and more people in the conflict until the balance of forces is changed."[49] As the legislative veto is described by its proponents, by purpose and design it is supposed to accomplish the latter. By involving Congress it would broaden participation and render rulemaking more democratic. Yet, in the spatial deconcentration case, the legislative veto did just the opposite: it narrowed participation and excluded the weaker minority voice from the process.

As in the thermal insulation case, congressional review of the spatial deconcentration regulation was clearly an example of the disagreement of Congress with the substance of an agency rule, not with the rule's conformity to statutory intent. Through use of the congressional review power, Congress, in this case, as Bruff and Gelhorn put it, was able to "hide behind the structure it has created."[50] Congress can use the provisions of law to prove its commitment to fair housing and at the same time use the congressional review process to protect suburbanites from being forced to accept minority tenants in federally funded housing.

Administrative Effects of the
"Constitutional" Veto

The Department of Housing and Urban Development is not generally thought of as a major regulatory agency. HUD does, however, issue a large number of regulations dealing with grants, subsidies, housing standards, insurance mortgage loans, and related matters; on the average, from 100 to 250 newly proposed, revised, and final regulations annually, some of which run to 300 pages. Since 1976, most HUD programs have been subject to an annual authorization process, which typically makes many changes in, additions to, and deletions from the programs. Final action on the bill by Congress rarely comes until near the end of the session. It was October 3, 1978, just days before Congress adjourned <u>sine die</u> for elections, that it completed action on that year's annual authorization bill, the same bill that added the congressional review procedure over HUD rulemaking (in 1979, it was December 26; in 1980, September 26). HUD is thus often under tight time constraints if it is to get out new and revised regulations reflecting congressionally mandated changes in its many grant programs sufficiently early for local and state governments or private groups to prepare and submit applications for funding. The department must also allow an adequate period for review, approval, and allocation of funds before the end of the fiscal year.

According to HUD officials, the congressional review procedure has significantly added to the department's already heavy workload and caused considerable delays in already tight scheduling. All the delay periods required by Section 7(o)--the fifteen-day delay prior to publication of a proposed rule, the thirty-day delay after publication of a final rule, and the ninety-day delay if a committee reports out a joint resolution of disapproval--are expressed in days of continuous session. Session days depend on the ebb and flow of congressional business, not on the calendar. Congressional recesses can in this way extend delay periods noticeably. For example, if Congress adjourns on November 1 (which would be typical in an election year), any regulation published after October 2, whatever its merits, could not take effect until at least thirty session days following the return of Congress in January; this means probably late February or even March-- as much as five months' delay. Donna E. Shalala, former assistant secretary for policy development and research at HUD, in testimony before Congress stated that "the necessity of working HUD's development and issuance of regulations around congressional recesses and adjourn- ments, some of which occur on very short notice, has greatly complicated the task of carrying out the objective of orderly internal management of this Department's regulations process."[51] To monitor the process requires "some very tricky scheduling and a lot of staff work and a lot of paperwork."[52]

Delay is a very prominent source of public criticism of the regulatory process, esecially when it results in confusion and uncertainty. Under present requirements of the Administrative Procedure Act, agencies must state, at the time of publication of a final rule, a clearly ascertainable date upon which the rule is to become effective. This enables the private sector as well as state and local governments to prepare for compliance with the rule. HUD has had problems, however, estimating the actual span of time that will be involved in the thirty-day deferral period, and predictions of effective dates of regulations have gone awry. Planning the department's regulatory process around congressional recesses and adjournments thus can be problematic for the department's clientele as well as for itself. Confusion caused by the congressional review procedure's delays can be particularly troublesome when a new regulation alters requirements for grant applications. Jane McGrew, HUD's former general counsel, testified that in 1979 "the process significantly delayed the implementation of programs for Tenant Participation in Multifamily Housing Projects and Flexible Subsidies for Multifamily Housing Projects. . . ."[53]

The "waiver" system provided for in Section 7(o)(4) was designed to alleviate some of the delay problems. In the first year under the review procedure, 1979, HUD requested waivers for forty-five, or approximately 35 to 40 percent of its regulations; of these, about thirty-five were granted. After the first year, the department has almost never relied on the waiver system. One reason may be what one HUD spokesperson referred to as the waiver's potential for "blackmail." Because the secretary has to have the signatures of both chairmen and both ranking minority members, each would have the opportunity to press for favors as a quid pro quo. One staffer admitted that his member of Congress had "traded" his signature on a waiver request for changes in the rule in question or other pending regulations at least six times.[54]

McGrew also claimed that the review procedure had "required HUD to prepare and publish more material, including semiannual regulation waiver requests, and Federal Register notices of such transmittal and of changed effective date for interim or final regulations."[55]

It is not just the increased workload, the confusion, the uncertainty, and the delay that are created as a result of this review procedure that have been attacked by HUD officials. Of more importance is the apparent reluctance to alter existing rules that the procedure engenders in HUD regulators. According to McGrew, "Congressional review impacts on HUD's consideration of public comments by inducing some hesitancy to change rules which previously have been reviewed by Congress."[56] If this is indeed the case, as more and more rules run the congressional review gauntlet, there may result an inflexible status quo preserving regulatory strategy at HUD.

According to some observers, there have been beneficial effects for HUD's regulatory process as a result of the congressional review procedure. One Hill source claimed, "They [HUD] seem to have developed a real respect for the process, with the result that their relations with the Hill may actually be improving."[57] Others claimed that it has compelled HUD "to take an organized approach to its regulatory process."[58] In answer to this, McGrew admitted that HUD's system to clear regulations in the department had become increasingly orderly and well managed since the congressional review procedure was imposed, but she pointed out that Carter's contemporaneous Executive Order 12044 would have accomplished the same thing in equal time.[59] Another HUD official who was more approving of the congressional review procedure mentioned as a benefit "the chilling effect the review procedure has had on HUD's overaggressive pursuit of its mandates."[60] Clearly, there are at least some HUD personnel who were relieved to have the secretary reined in a bit.

Policy Effects of the "Constitutional" Veto

The report that accompanied the Housing and Community Development Amendments of 1978 makes quite clear what Congress sought by imposing a congressional review procedure on HUD. As stated in the report, "The amendment formalizes a procedure designed to assure a constructive consultative relationship between Congress and the executive branch. The intent is to encourage cooperation and to develop a spirit of comity."[61] By "spirit of comity" Congress--or, to be more accurate, the oversight subcommittees--appeared really to mean that it wished a role in deciding the content of regulations developed by HUD. While Section 7(2)(A) does not confer upon Congress the formal power to veto HUD regulations, it does provide an opportunity for Congress to exercise a significant and perhaps decisive influence. The section provides a fifteen-calendar-day review period for Congress before a proposed rule can be published for comment if either oversight committee notifies the secretary in writing that it intends to review the rule or any portion of it that appears on the agency's semiannual agenda mandated by Section 7(o)(1). The housing subcommittees have not been reluctant to use this pwer. For example, in 1980 the committees notified the department that they "wished to review" all thirteen pending regulations involving equal opportunity.[62]

Senator Jake Garn (R, UT), ranking minority member of the Senate Subcommittee on Housing and Urban Affairs, claimed that the minority staff of the committee reviewed "every regulation" on the HUD semiannual agenda. He further stated that in the first year under the review procedure, "the Minority has asked for copies of about 30 regulations."[63] There had been, according to Garn, "much more consultation between HUD and the Minority Members of the Subcommittee."[64] (They seemed to be much more interested in the review procedure than the majority members.) For example, HUD held several legislative briefings for subcommittee staff prior to formal submission of regulations under the review procedure. In assessing the value of the "comment period," Garn said, "I can think of only one formal comment submitted. However, there have been numerous informal comments and the comment period has been very helpful."[65]

According to one report, "Seldom does a major regulation leave the department that has not already been subject to revision at the bidding of some concerned legislator. . . . Several regulations have been revised and rewritten because of objections raised by individual lawmakers."[66] The report mentions specific instances of such revision, including HUD contractor debarment regulations, the flexible subsidy regulations, and the Section 8 regulations discussed in this study. It appears, then, that the department, in an effort to avoid additional delays, has been willing to negotiate and compromise with individual members of Congress over the content of its proposed and in some cases its final regulations. For some reason, minority members have vigorously exercised this potential power. This may mean that the minority viewpoint has had undue influence over HUD regulations since the congressional review power was enacted. But even if it were predominantly majority members who press the department for change, there would be cause for concern. When informal comment by individual members becomes in reality departmental directives, two problems are raised. First, such action may undermine the intent of the whole Congress by allowing individual members to "nibble away" at legislative mandates by altering one rule at a time. And second, it may intrude on the department's administrative functioning in accordance with the law.

One of HUD's clientele groups, the Mortgage Bankers Association of America, explained the problem with the congressional review procedure in this way:

When proposing a new regulation, the present administration at HUD has made it a consistent practice actively to seek the input of a wide range of affected groups. . . . Final regulations reflect the many compromises necessary to reconcile the competing needs and interests of HUD's extremely diverse constituency. To impose yet an additional layer of review could seriously undercut the input of affected groups. Individual Members of Congress will be faced with increasing constituent pressure to amend regulations to respond to individual as opposed to consumer and industry concerns.[67]

The HUD congressional review procedure appears, then, to allow members of Congress and congressional subcommittees to evaluate individual regulations on an ad hoc basis. This kind of review fails to take into account that HUD must reconcile legislative mandates that are often at odds with one another when it acts through its rulemaking process. Alteration and rejection of isolated rules may jeopardize the department's ability to coordinate its legislative mandates, thereby preventing the department from carrying out the intent of the laws for which it is reponsible.

Summary

In both of the case studies presented in this chapter, Congress exercised its authority under Section 7(o) of the Housing and Community Development Amendments Act of 1978, not as the conference report directed ("the 90 day deferral provision will only be followed where either committee believes that the proposed regulations violate the intent of Congress") but as a means of altering the substantive policy of the offending regulation. In both the "thermal insulation case" and the "spatial deconcentration case" Congress was responding to the pressure of only one of many interests affected by the regulation at issue. Without the Harris "snub" it is unlikely that the thermal standards review would have received any publicity; the spatial deconcentration case was completely obscured at the time and, for the most part, has remained so. The full Congress was indeed involved in the thermal insulation case, although to what extent it was a minor tradeoff in the larger conference committee compromise over other issues of the 1978 amendments remains unknown. In the spatial deconcentration case, it is unlikely that many members of Congress other than those involved in the Fenwick letter and the subcommittee hearing were aware of the process. The legislative review power over the Department of Education, discussed in chapter 4, is substantially different from the HUD "constitutional veto," but the number of similarities between the cases is striking.

Notes

1. 124 Cong. Rec. H6204 (daily ed.), June 29, 1978.
2. See Housing and Community Development Amendments of 1978 (92 Stat. 2080, Section 7(o)).
3. Quoted, M. Carter McFarland, Federal Government and Urban Problems. HUD: Successes, Failures, and the Fate of Our Cities (Boulder, CO: Westview Press, 1978), p. 16.
4. Ibid., p. 19.
5. For a complete description of the events leading to the establishment of HUD and the legislative history of the act, see: Emmette S. Redford and Marlan Blissett, Organizing the Executive Branch: The Johnson Presidency (Chicago: University of Chicago Press, 1981); Frederick N. Cleveland, Congress and Urban Problems (Washington, DC: Brookings Institution, 1969); Mark I. Gelfand, A Nation of Cities (New York: Oxford University Press, 1975), John B. Willmann, The Department of Housing and Urban Development (New York: Frederick A. Praeger, 1967).
6. McFarland, Federal Government and Urban Problems, p. 24.
7. Interview with personnel, HUD Office of Congressional Relations, May 28, 1980.
8. McFarland, Federal Government and Urban Problems, p. 43. For a further assessment of Romney's administration at HUD, see pp. 42-45.
9. U.S. Congress, Senate, Committee on Governmental Affairs, Congressional Review of Federal Agencies Rules and Regulations, Hearings on S. 1945, 96th Cong., 1st sess., December 6, 1979, p. 2. Hereafter cited as S. 1945 Hearings.
10. Louis Fisher, The Constitution Between Friends: Congress, the President, and the Law (New York: St. Martin's Press, 1978), p. 138.
11. Harold H. Bruff and Ernest Gelhorn, "Congressional Control of Administrative Regulation: A Study of Legislative Vetoes," 90 Harvard Law Review 1369 (1976), p. 1381.
12. Housing and Community Development Act of 1974, 88 Stat. 633, Section 101(c).
13. McFarland, Federal Government and Urban Problems, p. 74.
14. Ibid., p. 75.
15. 88 Stat. 633. Section 191(c) describes in addition to the primary objective seven "specific objectives" of the act. Some members of Congress stress that the list including the "primary objective" should be read as an "either-or" catalog, not as a priority ranking of objectives. In 1977 Congress added an eighth objective: "The alleviation of physical and economic distress through

80

the stimulation of private investment and community revitalization in areas with population outmigration or a stagnating or declining tax base" (91 Stat. 1111).

16. New York Times, July 10, 1978, p. 18.

17. Legislative History of PL 95-557, S. Rept. 95-871, 95th Cong., 2d sess., p. 61.

18. National Energy Conservation Policy Act (925 Stat. 3206; approved November 9, 1978), Section 252: "Such standards shall establish energy performance requirements . . . until such time as the energy conservation performance standards required under the Energy Conservation Standards for New Building Act of 1976 become effective. Such requirements shall be implemented as soon as practicable after the date of enactment of this sentence." The DOE Building Energy Performance Standards (BEPS) have not as yet been issued; in fact, with DOE blessing, they have been postponed by Congress until at least 1983.

19. On April 16, 1979, HUD published "Increases in Thermal Requirements for HUD Minimum Property Standards," 44 Federal Register 22444. Interested persons were given until June 15, 1979, to comment.

20. Patricia Harris to Henry S. Reuss, April 19, 1979.

21. Interview, HUD personnel, May 28, 1980.

22. Ibid.

23. Interview, staff, Housing and Community Development Subcommittee, May 29, 1980.

24. U.S. Congress, House, Conference Rept. 95-1792 to Accompany S. 3084, Housing and Community Development Amendments, 1978, p. 84: "The 90 day deferral provision will only be followed where either committee believes that the proposed regulations violate the intent of Congress."

25. Legal Times of Washington, June 4, 1979, p. 1.

26. S. 1945 Hearings, pp. 112-13, citing Gasch memorandum, July 23, 1979.

27. 125 Cong. Rec. H41501 (daily ed.), June 6, 1979.

28. Legal Times of Washington, June 4, 1979, p. 6.

29. S. 1945 Hearings, p. 127.

30. 45 Federal Register 59857-59 (September 11, 1980).

31. Bruff and Gelhorn, "Congressional Control of Administrative Regulation," p. 1378.

32. See note 23, above.

33. Bruff and Gelhorn, "Congressional Control of Administrative Regulation," p. 1419.

34. 44 Federal Register 33804.

35. Morton S. Baruch cites this as HUD's statutory basis for the spatial deconcentration's "affirmative marketing provision." U.S. Congress, House, Committee on Banking, Finance, and Urban Affairs, Hearing on H.J. Res. 424 Disapproving and Invalidating HUD Regulations Concerning Section 8, 96th Cong., 1st sess., October 30, 1979, p. 48. Hereafter cited as Section 8 Hearing.

36. 37 Federal Register 75-76 (January 5, 1972).

37. Section 8 Hearing, p. 35.
38. 44 Federal Register 59048-28.
39. S. 1945 Hearings, p. 69.
40. Ibid., pp. 100-101. The letter states: "We think that senior citizen housing, for example, should be for people of the locality. . . . Further, in many cases, housing centers funded by Section 8 receive favorable tax treatment from their localities which would be jeopardized if preferential treatment were no longer accorded residents of those localities."
41. Section 8 Hearing, p. 27.
42. Ibid., esp. pp. 60-70. Interviews with members of the staff of the House of Representatives Housing and Community Development Subcommittee, May 27, 28, 29, 1980, corroborate this.
43. S. 1945 Hearings, p. 39.
44. Interview with staff member, Senate Committee on Banking, Housing, and Urban Affairs, May 27, 1980.
45. Interviews as late as December 1980 indicate that no further action has occurred in this area. A HUD spokesman interviewed on June 10, 1980, stated that the matter "has been dropped."
46. This point was made by a department spokesman in an interview, May 28, 1980.
47. S. 1945 Hearings, p. 128.
48. Washington Post, May 23, 1980.
49. E. E. Schattschneider, The Semi-sovereign People (Hinsdale, IL: Dryden Press, 1975), pp. 39-40.
50. Bruff and Gelhorn, "Congressional Control of Administrative Regulation," p. 1047.
51. U.S. Congress, Senate, Committee on Government Affairs, Subcommittee on Oversight of Government Management, Hearings on Oversight of Agency Compliance with Executive Order 12044, "Improving Government Regulations," 96th Cong., 1st sess., October 10, 1979, p. 43.
52. Jane McGrew, "Legislative Veto: 'Statutory Infill' Fails On All Accounts," Legal Times of Washington, March 2, 1981, p. 16.
53. S. 1945 Hearings, p. 32.
54. Interview with staff, Housing and Community Development Subcommittee, May 29, 1980.
55. S. 1945 Hearings, p. 31.
56. Ibid., p. 29.
57. Tim Pryor, "Congressional Review Succeeds in Inhibiting HUD," Legal Times of Washington, November 12, 1980, p. 3. Hereafter cited as Pryor article.
58. Ibid.
59. McGrew, "Legislative Veto."
60. Interview, HUD personnel, June 10, 1980.
61. U.S. Congress, House, Conference Rept. 95-1792, p. 84.
62. Interview, HUD personnel, May 28, 1980.
63. Letter, Garn to Senator Carl Levin, S. 945 Hearings, p. 129.

64. Ibid.
65. Ibid.
66. <u>Pryor article</u>.
67. 124 <u>Cong. Rec.</u> S11278 (daily ed.), July 20, 1978; letter from Mortgage Bankers Association placed in the <u>Congressional Record</u> by Senator William Proxmire (D, WI).

4
The Education Vetoes:
Conflict and Accommodation

Introduction

To the Office of Education (OE) goes the dubious distinction of being the first federal agency to have its rulemaking authority subject to the legislative veto. It was in 1972 that Congress attached a one-house legislative veto over "expected family contribution schedules," a necessary component of OE's new program for postsecondary education, the Basic Educational Opportunity Grants Program. The action resulted from growing congressional mistrust of OE's handling of aid to students, as well as from substantial disagreement between the House and Senate conferees regarding who should qualify for grants under the program and how the program should be administered.[1]

The basic grants program pays up to half of an undergraduate's educational costs remaining after subtraction of the expected family contribution for the year. To determine eligibility for a grant, the 1972 amendments directed OE to develop a schedule of "expected family contributions" and to publish the schedule in the Federal Register not later than February 1 of each academic year. At the same time that the schedule was published, the commissioner of education was to submit a copy to the president of the Senate and to the speaker of the House of Representatives. If either the Senate or House adopted a resolution disapproving the schedule before May 1, the commissioner was to publish a new schedule in the Federal Register not more than fifteen days later. The revised schedule was expected to take into consideration the recommendations made in the resolution of disapproval.

Since passage of the 1972 amendments, staff of the House Subcommittee on Postsecondary Education and the Senate Subcommittee on Education have been involved in extensive negotiations with OE over which assets must be included in calculating the expected family contribution. Numerous hearings have been held on the subject by the subcommittees. But, to date, there has been no serious attempt to veto an OE proposed schedule. Instead of making recourse to the formal veto procedure provided for by the act, the subcommittees have relied on staff negotiations and hearings to modify the annual schedules. Pressed by constituents, the subcommittees have urged OE to structure the schedules to increase the number of persons eligible for the grants. In their 1976 study, Bruff and Gelhorn found that pressure from the subcommittees may have resulted in such a broadening of the number of eligible participants that it is the original legislation itself that has been modified.[2] Although Congress has never actually resorted to the veto power it enacted, the level of bargaining between the subcommittees and OE may be directly attributed to the potential power of the veto.

Higher education grant programs were not the only source of congressional frustration with OE in the early 1970s. Efforts by the Republican administration at OE to consolidate administration and funding for several programs for which there were independent authorizations and appropriations, to reallocate funds within such consolidated programs, and to transfer decisionmaking responsibility to regional offices were viewed by the Democratic-controlled Congress as actions to thwart congressional intent.[3] As a result, relations between OE and its oversight committees, the House Committee on Education and Labor, and the Senate Committee on Labor and Public Welfare (which in 1976 became the Senate Committee on Labor and Human Resouces), were becoming increasingly fractious. By 1974 the relations had deteriorated to the point that the House Committee on Education and Labor proposed to amend the General Education Provisions Act (GEPA) to extend legislative veto controls over all standards, rules, regulations, and requirements of general applicability prescribed by the commissioner. Representative William D. Ford (D, MI) later commented about the committee's motives:

> In 1974 we amended the law in this committee because this committee was having trouble with HEW which at that time had a new Secretary every few months. He took the attitude that since the executive branch was headed by a different party that they really were elected to run the country and then started changing the direction of the laws this committee had written.[4]

The 1974 Education Amendments as enacted include the House committee's proposed provision, which has remained in effect. In 1979 the legislative veto provision was transferred to cover all regulations of the newly created Department of Education (ED).

Concurrently with publication in the Federal Register of any final regulation, the 1974 Education Amendments direct that a copy of the regulation be transmitted to the president of the Senate and to the speaker of the House of Representatives. Such final regulation is to "become effective not less than forty-five days after such transmission" unless Congress adopts a concurrent resolution stating that the regulation is "inconsistent with the Act from which it derives its authority" and disapproves it.[5]   "The problem which this amendment seeks to meet," according to its House Report, "is the steady escalation of agency quasi-legislative power, and the corresponding attrition in the ability of Congress to make the law."[6] The report underscores the circumstances in which the new legislative veto procedure applies:

> The "standards, rules, regulations, and requirements of general applicability" to which the new procedure has reference should be understood to mean any administrative document of general applicability which the agency intends to govern the administration of applicable programs. . . .   If an agency piece of paper is intended to be binding on the public, it should be issued under the procedures set forth in the new subsection. . . .[7]

The responsibility of Congress under the statute to make an "explicit finding that a proposed rule is not consistent with the legislation from which it derives its authority" and to set forth that finding "in detail in the concurrent resolution itself" is also clearly stated in the report.

In the event that a regulation is disapproved under the procedure, the agency that issues the offending regulation is required to issue a modified regulation to govern the same situation and to publish that regulation in the Federal Register together with an explanation of how it differs from the disapproved rule and how the modification meets the objections raised in the disapproval.   The modified rule is not, however, subject to the forty-five-day delay and the legislative veto procedure.

From 1974 until 1980, when the four vetoes of education rules that are the subject of the case studies in this chapter occurred, there was only one effort to veto an education regulation.   The regulation dealt with Title IX of the Education Amendments of 1972, which prohibits sex discrimination in educational programs receiving federal financial assistance. After a one-day hearing and a subcommittee recommendation against passage of the veto resolution, it died in subcommittee.

Although formal use of the veto has been limited, its informal effect on negotiating power has been evident.   The review process for the most part has consisted of "negotiations between the agency and the members and staff of congressional subcommittees."[8]   But by 1980, circumstances had changed sufficiently to cause Congress to veto within one month four education regulations.   To understand this sudden spate of vetoes, one must look at the national climate and mood regarding the larger question of federal involvement in education.

Education Policy: Local Control versus Federal Intrusion

Federal involvement in education has long been controversial, with the pros and cons remaining relatively constant throughout the nation's history. Those who favor a federal role maintain that education is the "greatest instrument for establishing and perpetuating our form of government"; therefore, they argue, the interests of the nation dictate a role for the federal government.[9] Fear of federal encroachment and of federal domination over academic freedom and education policy, which have "historically, traditionally, and wisely . . . been left to local institutions, state institutions, and private institutions," is the taproot of the opposite position.[10]

The earliest federal aid to education was the land grants to the states, the Morrill Act of 1862, and in 1867 the first federal agency concerned with education was created. Its role was closely defined as fact finder, statistics gatherer, and information disseminator. Just one year later, the independent education agency was downgraded to the status of an "office" within the Department of the Interior; two years later, to a "bureau." The specter of federal encroachment on local control of education was the reason given for both changes.[11]

The next major thrust to give education a more prominent national standing came in 1928 when Representative Daniel Reed and Senator Charles Curtis introduced a bill to create a department of education. Although heatedly debated, the proposal did not succeed. Throughout the next half-century Congress considered but failed to pass numerous similar pieces of legislation. During the same period there were also many recommendations for a greater national emphasis on and commitment to education, especially from presidentially appointed task forces and commissions. It was not until President Carter's successful effort to create a new department, however, that education gained the status of a cabinet department.

During the 1976 presidential campaign, in response to a written question from the National Education Association (NEA), candidate Jimmy Carter promised that if elected he would create a cabinet-level department of education. As a result, the 1.8 million-member NEA endorsed Carter, an historical first. The clout with the new administration that accrued to NEA was soon evident. (It should be noted that the membership of NEA was larger than the margin of Carter's victory over Gerald Ford.) A few months into his first year in office, Carter directed the Office of Management and Budget and the Department of Health,

Education, and Welfare to undertake a broad study of the organization of federal education activities. By November 1977, results of the study, which recommended against creating such a narrow constituency-oriented department, were presented to the president.

Carter's 1979 State of the Union Message, however, made clear his intention to fulfill his earlier commitment, and on April 14, 1978, his formal proposal for a department of education was made to Congress. Although Congress failed to pass legislation for a separate department that year, the administration introduced similar legislation early in the next Congress. The bill, which provided essentially for "carving the E out of HEW and not treading on anyone else's turf,"[12] won easily in the Senate by a vote of 72 to 21 on April 20, 1979. Passage of the bill in the House was neither so swift nor so smooth.

During House floor debate on the bill, Representative Rosenthal (D, NY) charged that it was "the most intensely lobbied reorganization bill that has ever appeared in Congress."[13] Albert Shanker, president of NEA's rival organization, the American Federation of Teachers (an AFL-CIO affiliate with a half-million members), and many in the higher education field campaigned vigorously against a separate department. Shanker argued that it would be "a conspicuous target" for various interests wanting to cut government spending.[14] AFT's opposition probably stemmed as much, though, from fears that the much larger NEA would control the new department. At the same time, NEA forces were pressing members of Congress to vote for the new department. Commenting on NEA involvement, the Washington Post charged that "the bill is the inspiration of the NEA, an organization that has as much relationship to public schools as the plumbers union has to the plumbing business."[15]

The Carter administration, hungry for a legislative victory and well aware of such a victory's importance for Carter's renomination and reelection strategy, pressed equally hard for the bill's passage. The importance of continued NEA support became clear at the Democratic convention; of the 664 delegates or alternates who were union members, 464 were both NEA members and Carter delegates. The enthusiastic support of NEA members was apparent in the important Iowa caucuses also.[16]

Congressional resistance nonetheless continued to be strong. When the bill finally passed the House on July 11, 1979, it did so by only a four-vote margin (210-206), and with several highly controversial amendments. Most of the amendments dealt with such issues as prohibiting busing for desegregation, forbidding numerical quotas in affirmative action measures, denying abortions to department personnel, and the like. The Skelton amendment, however, was aimed at insuring that the department would not have the power to control local decisionmaking in education: there could be no cutoff of funds for the purpose of imposing department decisions relative to curricula, program of instruction, administration, personnel, and the selection of library resources, textbooks, and other instructional materials except where specifically authorized by law.[17]

Although the conference compromise, which passed both houses in late September 1979, eliminated all of the House amendments, it did contain a strong prohibition against any interference by the department in matters that are the responsibility of state and local authorities. Absent the fund-cutoff prohibition, though, the conference wording did little to assuage the fears of opponents of an education department. One congressman, noting that the creation of a department was only fulfilling a campaign promise, commented that the bill should have been awarded "the Special Interest Memorial Prize of 1979."[18] President Carter signed the act creating the Department of Education on October 17, 1979, and on December 6, Shirley M. Hufstedler was sworn in as the first secretary. Five months later, on May 4, 1980, the new department assumed official responsibility for education programs and policy.

Federal initiatives to encourage and aid education had been nearly as slow in coming as had creation of an education department. The principal impetus for national involvement came when President Lyndon Johnson signed the Elementary and Secondary School Act into law on April 11, 1965, as part of his "Great Society" program. Responsibility for administration of the act was lodged in the Department of Health, Education, and Welfare's Office of Education, which, to allay apprehensiveness about federal encroachment, was prohibited by the act from exercising "any direction, supervision, or control over curriculum, program of instruction, administration, or personnel of any educational institution, school, school system, or over the selection of library resources, textbooks, or other printed or published instructional materials by any educational institution or school system. . . ."

Over the next decade and a half Congress proceeded to lodge in OE more than 120 programs with increasingly detailed directions to state, local, and postsecondary school systems. The programs were contained in several hundred pages of legislation, and were reinforced by almost two thousand pages of agency-developed regulations.[19] The proliferation of narrowly defined categorical programs, each with its own legislative authority or separate funding, has run rampant in the education field. Programs funding metric education, consumer education, arts projects, career education, population education activities, homemaker courses, ethnic studies, environmental courses, women's educational equity projects, biomedical enrichment, bilingual education, and a host of others have been created by Congress and are administered and controlled from Washington by the Education Department (formerly by OE). From an initial budget of $538 million, the elementary and secondary education funds increased to nearly $5 billion by 1977 and jumped to $7 billion by 1980. In higher education, the funding of student-aid programs grew from $383 million in 1966 to $5.6 billion by 1980.[20]

Each year there is additional pressure from interest groups to create, or protect, narrowly conceived categorical grant programs to fund their special projects. In an effort to bring about some simplification in the administration of this hodgepodge of federal education programs, Congress consolidated certain categorical education programs in the 1974 Education Amendments Act. For example, categorical programs for library and instructional materials were combined with guidance counseling and testing programs and with programs for strengthening particular academic subjects. The consolidation, however, did not last long. In 1978 counselors and librarians claimed that when they were forced to compete for the same limited funds, local school districts tended to fund one group or the other, not both. In response to these complaints, Congress in the 1978 Education Amendments Act created separate spending authority for all types of activities involving guidance, counseling, and testing.[21]

Congress has clearly played a major part in expanding the federal role in the education field. Many members and their constituents nonetheless remain suspicious and even fearful of federal control over education policy. When funding is provided through narrowly defined categories there is an obvious federal influence on local curriculum decisions. In spite of all the carefully worded protestations to the contrary that are found in most education statutes, the federal government is today involved decisively, if indirectly, in many local elementary, secondary, and higher education policy decisions.

Where federal education programs are concerned, Congress is caught between powerful pressures to direct more money toward an ever-increasing list of specific areas, on the one hand, and equal pressures to keep "that meddlesome Uncle Sam" out of local education politics, on the other. In the fifteen years between 1965 and 1980, Congress has supported significant increases in federal funding for education, and targeted a sizable portion of those funds by creating categorical grant programs. Such programs entail many administrative decisions--among others, application forms need to be designed; selection criteria developed; systems for enforcement devised--any or all of which may have serious consequences for local education. As long as Congress continues to increase the federal involvement in education, there will be an enormous and powerful need for it to have some control over administrative actions if members are to be in a position to protect their constituencies. It is not surprising, then, that the education subcommittees have used the legislative veto provisions as a tool to force the executive to negotiate, and to negotiate seriously with them about the content of agency administrative decisions. There is ample documentation to indicate that negotiation, not the power to veto, is the ultimate goal of the education committees in placing legislative veto controls over education regulations.

Education and the Legislative Veto, 1972 to 1978: Negotiation

During the first year of the Basic Educational Opportunity Grants Program (BEOGP) passed by Congress in 1972, there were "extensive informal meetings" on the content of the family contribution schedules between OE and the staff of the House and Senate committees that have substantive responsibility for the program.[22] In subsequent years the meetings were less frequent, and there were, instead, annual hearings at which OE representatives, the interested public (consisting for the most part of college financial aid officials represented by the National Association of Student Financial Aid Administrators [NASFAA]), and the subcommittee members and staff hashed out the specific details of the agency's proposed schedule. The hearings for the academic year 1974-1975 family contribution schedule are illustrative.

On September 24, 1973, OE published its proposed family contribution schedule for academic year 1974-1975 in the Federal Register, giving the public sixty days in which to submit written comments. At the same time that the public comment period was taking place, OE submitted the proposed schedule to Congress--well in advance of the February 1, 1974, deadline imposed by the 1972 Education Amendments. Six hearings were held by the House Special Subcommittee on Education (November 6, 30; December 4, 5, 20; and April 11, 1974). A single hearing was held by the Senate Subcommittee on Education on October 11, 1973. The gist of the testimony at all the hearings was the encouragement of OE's relaxation of the eligibility standards for grants under the program.

In his opening statement at the Senate subcommittee hearings, Chairman Claiborne Pell (D, RI) laid out his concerns:

> Many on the Hill believe that the Office of Education is operating the program in a manner which is somewhat restrictive and skews the law to its own view. . . . Unfortunately, through administrative actions, many of the programs are being predicated on much too stringent needs criteria. . . . The agencies should be warned that unless administrative steps are taken to change the thrust of Office of Education activities, legislative action could well be in the offing.[23]

The "legislative action" to which Pell referred in this veiled threat is, of course, passage by the House of a resolution vetoing the proposed schedule.

Chairman James O'Hara (D, MI) was no less pointed in his comments about the "rigidity of the schedule" at the House subcommittee hearings. After three days of hearings in November and December during which suggestions to broaden eligibility for the BEOGP were proposed and discussed at length, O'Hara summed up the results:

> The Commissioner proposed making several changes in the existing schedule, including allowing a deduction from the expected family contribution where the discretionary income is less than zero, adding an inflation factor to the family size offset to reflect the increase in the consumer price index, and eliminating the "other assets" item from the calculation of net worth.

> The Commission also indicated that they would be willing to listen to suggestions from the Congress with respect to the treatment of social security income attributable to the student. We have negotiated further with the Commissioner and his staff and there has been some agreement to provide for some liberalization of the treatment of social security income in cases where discretionary income of the family has gone below zero.

> Commissioners Ottina's letter of December 18 explains in detail the most recent administration offer. His office and mine have been seeking a clarification of the measurement to be used in calculating the inflation factor to be applied to the Orshansky low-income thresholds, and I trust we can arrive at an understanding this morning with the Commissioner. [Emphases added.][24]

The picture painted in this excerpt and by much of the hearing transcript is more akin to the bargaining of a labor-management contract session than to either a congressional hearing or an administrative rulemaking procedure. One reason for the negotiation strategy was the ambiguity of the law itself. In testimony about BEOGP, one representative described the problem: "There wasn't agreement in this Congress when the law was passed. We were all tied up in some pretty tough controversy and the intent of Congress was not clear as you can find out by talking to some other Members of the Congress who were involved at the time."[25] The subcommittee, through negotiations with the agency, was able, then, to "make clear" its own interpretation of the not-so-clear intent of Congress. The problem created by relaxation of the eligibility criteria, in the absence of additional funding, was also brought out in the hearing testimony: "To the extent you provide money to the middle income students when there are limited amounts for BOG (basic opportunity grants) you are taking it away from the lower income kids."[26]

The time constraints created by the congressional review process have fostered compromise because everyone has known that if appropriate approval of the schedules were not to occur, the entire program would be in jeopardy. The limited number of participants in this undertaking made the negotiating process possible and the necessary compromises easier to come by. According to Bruff and Gelhorn's findings, each year OE has offered to meet the expressed concerns of the subcommittees part way. Such compromised issues have then been dealt with again in the next year's round of hearings on the family contribution schedule. Bruff and Gelhorn worry that in order to preserve this "negotiating stance with the agency," the subcommittee may have been encouraged to avoid reporting out veto resolutions and have thus avoided the full congressional review procedure required by the law.[27] Furthermore, if expansion of eligibility under the BEOGP had been subject to the full legislative veto process or to the normal legislative amendment process, it is doubtful that eligibility for the program would have expanded so rapidly.

Negotiation has also been the major strategy for OE and the subcommittees under the 1974 provision that applies the legislative veto across the board to education regulations. OE was largely a grant-making agency (this is true of its successor, the Department of Education, as well), and most regulations developed by it resulted from new or reauthorized legislation. More education programs are on approximately five-year reauthorization schedules. For example, the elementary and secondary education programs were reauthorized in 1974 and again in 1978; legislation for reauthorization and modification of higher education programs was passed in 1976 and again in 1981. After each reauthorization, OE must develop new sets of regulations and revise existing regulations to address new programs and substantial changes in ongoing programs. These new and revised regulations are intended to govern the programs involved until the next cycle of reauthorization.

Bruff and Gelhorn found that negotiating took place when such extensive sets of new regulations were necessary because of congressional dissatisfaction with past performance. Following adoption of the 1974 amendments to the General Education Provisions Act (GEPA), HEW, though reluctant, was nevertheless "brought into an 'exhaustive' series of about twenty meetings with congressional staff from both houses, in order to ensure that the staff's view would be considered in drafting regulations."[28]

Later Representative William D. Ford (D, MI) described how the legislative veto provision had worked prior to the four vetoes on education regulations in 1980:

What has happened here, until your most recent opinion
[Attorney General Benjamin R. Civiletti's opinion of
June 1980 directing the secretary of education to
ignore the veto of the department's regulations] was
that HEW and now the Department of Education, came up
here and discussed what the regulation was going to be
and presented to the committee what it was going to do.
If, at our staff level, it produced a reaction saying
wait a minute, that is not what the committee intended,
it got changed. . . . It wasn't intended as a way in
which we would have conflict. It was a way in which we
avoid conflict. . . .[29]

Consultation and negotiation over the content of
proposed rules, however, were not indicated as the purpose
of the legislative veto provision in either the law or its
accompanying report. In fact, both emphasize that the
review of a proposed rule is to be restricted to a
determination of its consistency with the act from which it
derives its authority. In addition, the report specifies:
"Disapproval is the only action the Congress can take under
this procedure. It cannot amend. . . ."[30] And yet, Bruff
and Gelhorn found that the review process under the 1974
amendments has "in a large part operated outside the formal
and open procedures that were presumably intended for
it."[31]

Consultation procedures between the Department of
Education and Congress have actually been institutionalized. (Bruff and Gelhorn point out that this was true at
OE as well.) The regulations process of the department
includes a procedure for "Clarification of Congressional
Concerns" that directs the assistant secretary for
legislation to arrange meetings with congressional staff
promptly after reauthorization or the adoption of major
legislation to help clear up points of congressional
concerns.[32] Such a system allows guidance on the political
acceptability of a rule to be sought in the absence of
definitive statutory guidelines. Negotiations over the
Title IX regulations are a case in point.

Title IX was adopted in conference without hearings or
a committee report to guide agency rulemaking. The
enabling legislation provided for no exceptions to or
exemptions from its ban on sex discrimination in
educational programs receiving federal financial
assistance. HEW's Office of Civil Rights spent over two
years developing a proposed rule; discussions with
congressional staff were a part of the effort. More than
9,700 comments on the rule were received during the 120-day
public comments period, a time when agency personnel were
meeting with members and staff of the committees of both
houses. Certain changes were made by the agency in
response to this public and congressional input; the Bruff
and Gelhorn study cites the addition of a self-evaluation
requirement for institutions receiving grants as one

example, and attributes it to congressional pressure on the agency brought about by the lobbying of some women's organizations.[33]

The final regulations that emerged from this protracted process were not issued until the fall of 1975. Soon after they were transmitted to Congress as required by Section 431 of the GEPA, several concurrent resolutions of disapproval were introduced in the House. After holding hearings on one of these, the Subcommittee on Postsecondary Education of the House Committee on Education and Labor reported it favorably to the full committee. Under pressure from the women's organizations, the full committee then referred the resolution of disapproval to the Equal Opportunities Subcommittee, where it died. The forty-five-day period for disapproval lapsed before any action was taken on any of the other resolutions of disapproval.

There is little doubt, though, that the issue that occasioned the most impassioned reactions to the Title IX regulations was women and interscholastic athletics. It was a controversy that was reduced in the media and in the halls of the Capitol to Big Ten football vs. women's rights. The language of Title IX offered no guidance on resolution of the controversy . The 1975 regulations had finessed the problem by the use of unclear and confusing regulatory language on the subject of women and college sports programs. Furthermore, during the period from 1975 to 1978, HEW did little to enforce the provisions affecting athletics, and Congress did not press it to more vigorous enforcement.[34] In 1978, however, the administration at HEW issued proposed guidelines clarifying the earlier regulations and providing for improved enforcement efforts. When it became clear to Congress that the department intended to issue its proposed guidelines as a final rule, the leadership moved quickly to forestall the process. In a private, off-the-record meeting with Secretary Joseph Califano, House Majority Whip John Brademas, Speaker "Tip" O'Neill, Majority Leader James Wright, and House Education Subcommittee Chairman William Ford pressed the secretary not to issue final regulations because it would then be required for them to be submitted to Congress for possible review. Califano later described the meeting:

> O'Neill set me down to his right, puffed on his cigar, and asked, "Joe, how can you do this to your alma mater, Holy Cross? The Jesuits will never speak to you again". . . . Wright spoke seriously about Texas and politics, Brademas mentioned Notre Dame, and both he and Bill Ford argued that sending the guidelines to the House for a vote posed an impossible political dilemma for Democratic congressmen: forcing them to vote to

reject the position of women's groups or to take an unpopular stand against college football.[35]

Advocates of applying the legislative veto to administrative rules and regulations have argued that the veto would force Congress to face up to the "difficult task" of dealing with the "difficult decisions" posed by broad legislative mandates delegated by Congress to the executive.[36] There was little stomach in Congress, though, for exercising its legislative veto power to review the controversial Title IX regulations in this case. The legislative veto was insufficient to force Congress to act in the absence of the will to act. Rather than the more visible process of amending the law or openly vetoing the regulation, Congress chose instead to avoid confronting the issue in public by negotiating with the department in private. In later testimony, Representative Ford defended such an approach. "That is the kind of confrontation we try to avoid--destroying a good law because an administrator gets out of sync with the people who wrote the law, or, if you will, in the case of Title IX, the popular prejudices of the moment."[37] Based on such logic, it follows that the agency should develop its regulations in concert with "the popular prejudices of the moment," not in accord with the law passed by Congress. Yet, in attaching legislative veto power over education regulations, it appeared that Congress had in mind preventing exactly this sort of agency action.[38]

Throughout the period from 1972 to 1978 negotiation with HEW's Office of Education was a major tactic used by the education subcommittees to resolve their dissatisfaction with regulations developed by the agency under notice-and-comment procedures of the Administrative Procedure Act. The changing of regulations substantially in response to congressional pressures averted actual vetoes. The informal influence meant that the subcommittees and their members were able to effect changes in policy without having to follow the full process of legislative amendment. This "cooperative" relationship appeared to deteriorate at about the same time that it became clear that legislation creating a Department of Education would pass. In light of President Carter's expressed concern about the new department, and his strong relationship with the powerful National Education Association, the committee feared that the new secretary would be less responsive to it. This situation posed the potential for the disruption of the committee's influence and control over education regulations, and may very well have been the motivation behind the four education vetoes of 1980. Analysis of the education vetoes underscores their use by the committee to make clear to the new department who its boss really was.

Education and the Legislative Veto,
1979 to 1980:   Conflict

The Education Amendments Act of 1978, signed into law by President Carter on October 1, 1978, reauthorized for five years with amendment a number of programs that constitute the major portion of federal aid to elementary and secondary schools. Funding authorizations for the programs included in Titles I through XIII of the act ranged from $10.305 billion in fiscal year 1979 to $12.178 billion in 1983. Hearings on the proposed changes were held in both houses during consideration of this legislation. In the House, the subcommittee on Elementary, Secondary, and Vocational Education held seventy-five days of hearings from May 10, 1977, to March 6, 1978, on the programs contained in the reauthorization legislation—the most extensive ever conducted by Congress on federal aid to elementary and secondary education. Testimony in the record makes clear the incredible level of detail addressed by both committee members and witnesses. The report developed by the Committee on Education and Labor to accompany the House bill (H.R. 15) includes extraordinarily specific instructions as to the committee's intent in the bill's many changes of existing law.[39]

Pursuant to his authority to promulgate regulations to administer Office of Education programs, the commissioner of education published approximately twenty-three sets of revised regulations in proposed form at various intervals throughout 1979 for all programs affected by the 1978 amendments; publication was followed in each case by a public comment period of at least thirty days. This was no small undertaking; the changes involved cover 237 pages of the law.[40]

It was a process that was made even more complicated by the diversion of a considerable amount of the OE staff's energies to the battle over a separate department of education, as well as by the confusion and uncertainty among the staff generated by an unknown future.[41]   Leadership at OE had been unsettled for some time. For example, in the twelve years prior to the creation of the Department of Education (ED), there had been fourteen commissioners of education at the agency. But this was even more the case during the period of congressional action on legislation concerning a new department. In June 1979, Commissioner Ernie Boyer resigned to take a position in the private sector, and no qualified outsider would consider accepting the vacant post. From June 1979 until May 1980, the acting commissionership was held first by Assistant Secretary for Education Mary Berry and then by Assistant Commissioner for Policy Studies Mike Smith. It was during this period of uncertainty and upheaval at OE that the congressional review and vetoes of the elementary and secondary education regulations took place.

After each set of proposed rules was published, the House Education and Labor Committee staff, under the direction of Chairman Carl Perkins (D, KY), undertook an exhaustive line-by-line review. Committee files, nearly a foot thick, covered with notations in several handwritings and colors of ink, reveal the extent of the review.[42] Comments in the margins of nearly every page of "Check this," "May be a problem," "Obvious inconsistency," and the like pinpoint staff concerns. As the staff completed each review, a letter from Perkins to Acting Commissioner Mary Berry called attention to the provisions that, in his view, were excessive or inconsistent with the law. Approximately twenty-three such letters--one for each set of proposed regulations--were sent.[43] In some cases Perkins relayed his guidance on the law before the agency even published a proposed regulation. In one letter, for example, he states:

> As you know the law is silent on how a State is to distribute its Title IV-D money among local school districts. I presume that regulations will be developed to clarify this issue. In developing these new regulations, I urge that States not be required to fund each school district within the State.[44]

Neither the Senate majority or minority staffs, nor the House minority staff made any effort to undertake such a review of proposed or even final regulations. A Senate majority staff member commented on the failure to do a thorough review: "We do not have the time, the staff or the inclination to do so."[45] Any review done by these staffs is "reactive to constituent complaints."[46]

Publication of final regulations for the elementary and secondary education programs began in March and April of 1980. Approximately two weeks prior to publication of each set of final regulations, Acting Commissioner Smith sent a written response to Perkins's earlier letters that provided a detailed explanation regarding each point raised: where the regulations would be altered to take into account the chairman's concerns, and where the regulations would be issued as proposed despite the chairman's disagreement with them.[47] Soon after the final regulations were published in the Federal Register, Perkins introduced resolutions of disapproval for three sets. Senator Claiborne Pell (D, RI) and Representative William Goodling (R, PA) each introduced a resolution of disapproval to overturn other sets of regulations. Four of these legislative vetoes were ultimately passed by both houses.

The Arts in Education Regulations

One program reauthorized by the 1978 amendments provided funds to encourage and assist state and local educational agencies to establish and conduct programs in which the arts are an integral part of elementary and secondary school curricula.[48] Only a few substantive changes were made in the program that had been established by the 1974 Education Amendments. Although a $20 million authorization was provided for, only about $1 million was finally appropriated. Proposed revised regulations were published in the Federal Register on June 18, 1979.[49] On August 8 Perkins wrote to Acting Commissioner Berry complaining that the proposed regulations added several requirements to the program that were not in the law. The final regulations, published on April 3, 1980, contained at least three of the requirements that had offended Perkins: formation of a local advisory council for each project; a project must address at least four art forms, including dance, music, theater, and the visual arts; and matching federal funds with local or state funds.[50]

By law, OE was required to respond to comments made during the public comment period and to publish its response along with the final regulations.[51] In response to Perkins's comments, and in defense of its actions, OE noted that the formation of an advisory committee, and the addressing of four art forms were both almost identical to provisions in regulations that had been in effect since 1974. Congress had not indicated, by amendment or in legislative oversight hearings, any problem with either of these concepts. A lengthy explanation of the importance of the requirements and the rationale for them was included in the agency's March 20, 1980, letter to Perkins and in the documentation accompanying the published final regulations.[52]

To justify the imposition of the new matching-funds requirement, the agency argued that in light of the small size of the appropriations it could use only a "seed-money" grant strategy. The matching requirement was designed to insure that the federal government did not simply "rent" projects that would have no chance of surviving once federal funding ended.[53] The House report to accompany the 1978 amendments had specifically addressed insuring continued local commitment to federally funded innovative programs in its discussion of problems under Title IV--Consolidated Programs:

> As noted before, a major problem in Federal innovative programs is getting the local districts to continue the projects from their own funds once Federal funding terminates. . . . Also, according to the Rand study, the reason many Federally-funded innovation projects are not continued after the grant period is over is because "few districts adequately prepared themselves for sustaining . . . even successfully implemented projects."[54]

Although similar concerns are not specified in the title documentation under which the arts program falls (Title VI--Miscellaneous Programs),[55] the similarity in types of programs and funding levels of both these titles might lead a prudent observer to conclude that the problems of insuring local commitment would be the same.

The OE explanations were clearly unsatisfactory to Perkins, and on April 24, 1980, he introduced House Concurrent Resolution 319 for the purpose of "disapproving the final regulations for the arts in education program" because of "their inconsistency with the authorizing legislation." The reasoning is set out in detail in the resolution, and the final paragraph of the explanation states:

> The Committee recognizes that the Commissioner must have some authority to make decisions regarding Federal competitive or discretionary grant programs. However, there is strong evidence that the addition of requirements of such magnitude as cost-sharing and advisory councils exceeds the Commissioner's discretionary authority. The fact is, several other education statutes do explicitly mandate matching of Federal funds or advisory councils. The existence of these mandates in other education laws is the result of conscious decisions by Congress that such mandates are necessary for those programs. Similarly, the lack of any such mandates in the arts in education law indicates a conscious decision on the part of Congress not to impose those requirements.[56]

The House vote on House Concurrent Resolution 319, disapproving the final regulations for the Arts in Education Program, and in House Concurrent Resolution 318, disapproving the final regulations for an education appeals board, occurred on May 12, 1980. Debate on the resolutions took place under Clause 3 of Rule XXVII of the <u>Rules of the House</u>, which allows for suspension of the rules for a limited debate (forty minutes divided between majority and minority). Following a brief explanation of the provisions of Concurrent Resolution 318 by Perkins, Representative John Buchanan (R, AL), a member of Perkins's Education and Labor Committee, spoke even more briefly in support of the resolution. No other representatives spoke on the issue. When the speaker <u>pro tempore</u> called the question on the motion to suspend the rules and agree to the concurrent resolution, the "yeas and nays" were demanded by Representative Steven Symms (R, ID). Turned down by the chair, Symms objected to the vote on the grounds that a quorum was not present and made a point of order to that effect. The chair then postponed action on Symms's point of order, allowing Perkins to move and debate the second concurrent resolution (House Concurrent Resolution 319).

Once again, Perkins and Buchanan each spoke in favor of disapproving offending regulations by passage of the second resolution. At the chair's call of the motion, a "division" was demanded by Representative John Rousselot (R, CA). The vote tally in the Congressional Record: "Yeas, 8, nays, 0. So (two-thirds having voted in favor thereof) the rules were suspended and the concurrent resolution was agreed to."[57]

Rule XXVII of the Rules of the House has three clauses: Clause 1 provides that "2/3rds voting, a quorum being present" (emphasis added) may suspend the rules; Clause 2 provides for a tallied vote on the motion if requested; and Clause 3 provides for limited and equally divided debate on the matter at hand. It seems clear from the record described above that both resolutions of disapproval were passed with only eight members present and voting--far fewer than the 218 members required for a "quorum being present." This, then, appears to be a clear violation of Rule XXVII. Such exercise of the legislative veto power raises serious questions. For example, can the House be held effectively or legally responsible and accountable for an action of only eight of its members, especially action not in accordance with its own rules?

Three days later, on May 15, 1980, the Senate voted by an unrecorded voice vote to pass the House Concurrent Resolutions 318 and 319, thus effectively vetoing the regulations involved.[58]

The Education Appeal Board

The 1978 Education Amendments mandated the formation of an education appeal board within HEW for the purpose of conducting audit appeal hearings, cease-and-desist hearings, and withholding hearings.[59] On May 25, 1979, OE published proposed rules for public comment in the Federal Register concerning the rules for the conduct of proceedings to be followed by the appeal board.[60] Chairman Perkins wrote to Acting Commissioner Berry on August 7 commenting upon the board. Prior to publication of the final regulations, Acting Commissioner Mike Smith responded to Perkins's letter, noting that several provisions of the regulations had been changed as a result of Perkins's comments and those of others. Among several provisions that were not changed and that had been objected to by Perkins was one giving the chairperson of the appeal board authority to grant an extension of the statute's thirty-day limit for submission of an application for board review of an audit determination. Smith explained:

> Although the legislation does not provide for an extension of the 30-day time period for filing an application for review, the Title I Audit Hearing

Board--the predecessor to the Education Appeal
Board--found that some cases involved such complicated issues or so many different localities that 30 days
did not allow an appellant sufficient time in which to
prepare an application for review. The Title I Board
Chairman, having received a fair number of requests
from appellants for extensions of the 30-day time
period, attempted to accommodate the appellants if the
request appeared reasonable. We believe that the
Education Appeal Board should have the same
flexibility.[61]

At issue are appeals by state and local agencies from
final audit determinations made by HEW personnel. Those
agencies that do not file a timely appeal lose all of their
administrative and judicial remedies; thus, the filing of
an appeal is a crucial step, often with millions of dollars
at stake. Sometimes, because of the complexity of the
matter involved, or because of unexpected local emer-
gencies--or even because of mistakes belatedly discovered
in an appeal filed on time--a state or local agency may be
unable to meet the thirty-day deadline. According to
departmental files, there were twenty-two cases from 1973
to 1980 in which an extension was necessary, and in none of
the cases was a board hearing delayed because of the
extension. In later testimony, Education Secretary
Shirley M. Hufstedler commented on the legal authority and
reasoning for the agency's actions:

When the Administration decided that the Hearing Board
should be expanded and given specific legislative
authority, it drafted a bill to do so. The bill was
adopted without substantial change by Congress as part
of the Education Amendments of 1978. Neither the
Administration's proposal nor the enacted law
contained a specific authority to extend the filing
deadline; but both contained a provision allowing the
Board to prescribe rules to govern its proceedings,
including rules about such matters as the "notice of
the issues to be considered." Neither the
Administration nor the Congress expressed any
intention to abandon the Title I Audit Hearing Board's
consistent practice of extensions for good cause.
Certainly the legislative history shows no desire to
require States and local governments to forfeit
enormous claims if they cannot meet the thirty-
day deadline despite good-faith efforts to do so.[62]

The reasonableness of this approach was underscored by
Education and Labor Committee member George Miller (D, CA):

I dare say that if that 30 days had been strictly
adhered to, there is probably not a member on this
committee who would not be running and trying to make a

case that there were unforseen circumstances, that
there was good cause that the appeal should not be lost
by a locality within our district, that the deadline
was arbitrary and this was not what the Congress meant
because we obviously wanted to follow the rule of the
reasonable man. All of those cases would have been
brought because our district would have lost some
funding if they had not complied after the audit.[63]

Chairman Perkins was apparently not swayed by this
logic, however, and on April 24, 1980, he introduced House
Concurrent Resolution 318 for the purpose of disapproving
the regulations covering an education appeals board. As
noted in the above section, the resolution was passed by a
vote of 8 to 0 by the House on May 12, and by an unrecorded
voice vote in the Senate on May 15.

Law-Related Education Regulations

The Senate version of the 1978 Education Amendments
included an amendment authorizing the commissioner of
education to make grants and contracts for the provision of
law-related education designed to equip nonlawyers with
knowledge and skills pertaining to the legal system.
Although the House bill had no such provisions, $15 million
was authorized for a law-related education program by the
conference committee compromise. Approximately $1
million was eventually appropriated.

Statutory guidance on this new program was decidedly
skimpy. The initial section of the act, which set forth the
rationale for congressional action, stated:

Because of a widespread lack of understanding of how
our system of law and legal institutions works, and
because such an understanding is an essential
component in developing faith and appreciation in our
democratic system, Congress finds that there is an
urgent need for Federal involvement designed to
encourage and support the development of law related
programs.[64]

The statement of purpose was augmented by a list of seven
potentially legitimate activities that might be funded
under the act. Financial assistance under the act was to be
made only upon application to the commissioner, and "shall
be submitted at such time, in such form, and containing such
information as the Commissioner shall prescribe by
regulation." There is no further guidance as to program
design or content within the one-page statute.

On June 29, 1979, the commissioner published proposed
regulations—based on findings of the OE Study Group on Law-
Related Education and on recommendations of interested

members of the public--for public comment in the <u>Federal Register</u>.[65] Chairman Perkins wrote to Acting Commissioner Berry on September 4, calling attention to several regulations that he thought added requirements beyond those in the legislation. On April 17, 1980, Acting Commissioner Smith responded to Perkins, indicating a number of specific changes that had been made to bring the language of the regulations closer to that of the statute. Smith explained OE's legal authority and reasons for keeping three of the regulations to which Perkins had objected: (1) a complete schedule of matching requirements for different categories of grants; (2) limits on the time an individual grantee can continue to receive funds under the act; and (3) creation of four categories of grants, each with its own requirements, its own competition for funds, and its own reservation of funds.[66] The final regulations, including these three, were published in the <u>Federal Register</u> on April 24, 1980. In attached documentation, the acting commissioner defended OE's strategy in implementing these requirements for the program:

> The statute provides a broad framework for the program and enables various categories of funding to be established to meet the evolving needs of the field. The Commissioner believes that it is important to focus the program in this way.

> To leave the program open and let applicants apply against the statute, as suggested by the commentor, could result in no discernible national impact.

> It is well-established in law and in practice that executive agencies may regulate to interpret a statute and to fill in its gaps. Section 408 of the General Education Provision Act expressly confers broad authority upon the Commissioner of Education to promulgate legislative rules that are necessary to administer Office of Education programs.

> The Commissioner believes that the cost-sharing requirements are reasonably necessary to carry out the purpose of the statute to encourage law-related education programs. This statutory purpose necessarily includes the objectives of spreading law-related education and institutionalizing it as an ongoing part of educational programs.

> The Commissioner believes that without graduated cost sharing few programs will be sustained after the expiration of Federal funding. . . .[67]

Perkins did not agree, and on May 7, 1980, he introduced a concurrent resolution of disapproval for the purpose of vetoing the law-related education regulations as a clear example of overregulation, restrictive regulation, and regulation in excess of the law. Debate and voting on the resolution took place on May 19 under a motion to suspend the rules and agree to House Concurrent Resolution 332. After Perkins and Buchanan spoke in favor of vetoing the regulations, the question was called and passed. In this case, no tally of the vote was asked for, and thus the number of members voting remains a mystery.[68] The resolution was similarly debated and passed in the Senate on the following day.

Title IV-B Regulations: The Gym Equipment Issue

Title IV, Part B, funds are intended to support the purchase of library resources, textbooks, equipment, and materials suitable for use in providing education in academic subjects, and which are to be used for instructional purposes only. During the 1978 hearings held by the House Committee on Education and Labor, witnesses testified that Part B funds were being used to buy equipment that made no contribution to instructional programs, such as general office equipment, including typewriters and filing cabinets; ice machines; uniforms; gym equipment, such as bleacher seats and basketballs; and even, in one instance, a background music system.[69] Reacting to the information, the committee amended the statute to make it "crystal clear that Title IV-B funds are to be spent only for the purchase of library resources and equipment that will be used for instructional purposes."[70] To clarify further its intentions, the committee explained in its report on the 1978 Education Amendments Bill (H.R. 15):

> Use of Title IV-B funds for acquisition of instructional materials relating to nutrition education, for example, does not violate the intent of this Committee. The Committee does not intend, however, that IV-B funds be used to purchase food or stoves on which to cook nutritional meals. Although acquisition of materials designed to impart knowledge relating to music education or physical education could be viewed as acceptable uses of IV-B funds, the Committee does not view band instruments or gym mats and parallel bars as acceptable uses of these funds. . . . Accordingly, the Committee directs the U.S. Office of Education to take these comments into consideration when promulgating regulations pursuant to the Title IV-B legislation. [Emphasis added.][71]

When OE published proposed regulations for Title IV-B, physical education equipment and musical instruments were explicitly excluded from the definition of "instructional equipment." But when the final regulations were published in the <u>Federal Register</u> on April 7, 1980, the meaning of "instructional equipment" had been expanded to include both:

> "Instructional equipment" means equipment that is appropriate for use in providing education in academic subjects in elementary and secondary schools and that is used to teach or learn an academic subject. The eligibility of instructional equipment is determined by its intended use and its direct relationship to instruction in an academic subject. . . . The term does not include general purpose classroom or library furniture, shelving, stoves, refrigerators, bleacher seats, equipment for staff offices or other equipment not directly related to instruction in academic subjects. The term, however, <u>does include musical instruments and physical education equipment if used for instructional purposes</u> in music or physical education classes in the school's regular instructional program. [Emphasis added.][72]

On April 30, 1980, Senator Pell introduced Senate Concurrent Resolution 91 to veto OE's final regulations covering Title IV programs. He explained in the resolution the reasons for the action:

> The proposed regulation allows <u>for the purchase of band instruments which are used in an instructional program. The Committee has no quarrel with this interpretation</u>, since the definition of "academic subjects" specifically includes the arts. However, the Committee believes that inclusion of physical education equipment is a clear violation of the law and of Congressional intent. [Emphasis added.][73]

Although the House and Senate committees agreed that purchases of gym equipment should be prohibited, they differed on purchases of band instruments. Policy disagreements between the House and Senate, such as this, underscore the difficulty an agency may face if it uses the language of the report emanating from either house as definitive guidance on the legislative intent of Congress as a whole. In this case, a potential deadlock was averted by narrowing the issue to the matter of gym equipment only.

In defending its addition of gym equipment as a permissible expenditure category for Title IV-B funds, OE stated that more than a hundred objections to the exclusion of gym equipment had been made during the public comment period. In the House floor debate on Senate Concurrent Resolution 91, Representative William Goodling (R, PA) responded to such a line of reasoning:

It should be noted that since gym equipment was not included in the draft regulations or in earlier regulations, there was no incentive for persons agreeing with this exclusion to write, and inclusion or deletion of an item in the regulations should not be dependent upon the number of letters received but rather by the law and the intent of Congress. . . . If an agency or department is going to respond to how many letters they get in opposition to something I will guarantee they are going to get an awful lot of mail and then they will be up here asking for money to open their mail because everyone will know that they are moved not by what the Congress had legislated but by what somebody wrote in some letter.[74]

Senate Concurrent Resolution 91 was passed by the Senate on May 20 and by the House on May 21.

Summary

Although there were several other efforts, especially by minority members of the House Education and Labor Committee, to veto regulations promulgated by OE to implement the 1978 Education Amendments, none was successful. Ranking minority member Goodling, for example, introduced a concurrent resolution on May 14, 1980, to disapprove the final regulations pertaining to the Adult Education Program. The forty-five-day review period lapsed, however, before the committee took any action on it. A similar effort was made by John Ashbrook (R, OH) to veto regulations dealing with an OE requirement that affirmative action efforts be used as one of many bases for determining grant recipients, and it met the same fate.[75]

The perception at OE was that the success of a veto effort was dependent entirely upon the support of Committee Chairman Perkins. It appears from the committee files on its review of the regulations implementing the various programs authorized by the 1978 Education Amendments that there were numerous other examples of questionable agency action equal to or exceeding those of the vetoed regulations. Many of these, according to OE staff, involved issues that were far more controversial than the issues raised by the four vetoed rules, and for this reason such regulations had been avoided. Only regulations that were the least likely to be divisive seem to have been selected by the chairman for actual exercise of the veto power. Perkins's control over the veto process is evident from start to finish--from the initial review of the proposed rules, through the introduction of the resolutions and action of the committee, right up to final action on the floor. The motivation for this sudden shift from the established practice of negotiating with OE over the

content of regulations to what appears to be a carefully
orchestrated effort to set up a conflict situation between
OE and its congressional oversight committees is, however,
far less evident on the surface.

The Department of Education versus
Congress: The Face-off

Within two and a half weeks from the date that
Secretary Shirley M. Hufstedler and the new Education
Department assumed responsibility for the education
programs, May 4, 1980, the four vetoes of education
regulations discussed above occurred. As noted, two of the
concurrent resolutions passed on May 15, two on May 21. By
statute the department was required to respond to this
congressional action by modifying the vetoed regulations.
Faced with this necessity, the new secretary, a former
lawyer and judge on the U.S. Court of Appeals for the Ninth
Circuit, requested of the attorney general a formal opinion
with respect to the vetoed regulations. About her reasons
for doing so, Hufstedler commented:

> I was fully aware that the administration had
> consistently taken a position that denied the
> constitutional authority to Congress to veto
> regulations. . . . I was also aware that if I
> respected the congressional veto, thereby denying
> what I knew was the policy of the administration, I
> would also be provoking lawsuits. . . .[76]

On June 5, 1980, Attorney General Civiletti replied
with a thirteen-page response to the secretary's request.
Following twelve pages of detailed explanation of the
constitutional issues raised by the legislative veto
procedure found in Section 431 of the General Education
Provisions Act, Civiletti concluded that the procedure was
invalid because it "intrudes upon the constitutional
prerogatives of the Executive." The letter ended:

> More important, I believe that your recognition of
> these concurrent resolutions as legally binding would
> constitute an abdication of the responsibility of the
> Executive Branch, as an equal and coordinate branch of
> Government with the Legislative branch, to preserve
> the integrity of its functions against encroachment.
> I therefore conclude that you are authorized to
> implement these regulations.[77]

Relying upon the Civiletti opinion, which was viewed
by ED General Counsel Betsy Levin to be "binding as an
expression of the administration's position," Hufstedler
issued a decree to department personnel to disregard the
congressional veto action entirely.[78] One week later, on

108

June 12, 1980, Perkins and thirty-two of the thirty-six
committee members wrote to Hufstedler urging her to comply
with the vetoes, warning that failure to do so would be an
"arrogant course . . . irresponsible action and a sad way for
you as a new Secretary to begin your operations."[79]
The lines were drawn setting the new department on a
collision course with its House oversight committee.
Unless one side or the other backed off, the only possible
resolution would have to come from the courts.
At a White House news briefing on June 21, 1978--the
same day that Carter's message opposing the legislative
veto was transmitted to Congress--Attorney General Griffin
B. Bell and Assistant to the President for Domestic Affairs
and Policy Stuart E. Eizenstat had made it clear that in a
spirit of comity the administration would avoid a
confrontation with Congress on major policy matters. In
response to a reporter's question of whether a situation
could be envisioned in which the administration would
disregard a congressional veto and do what it wanted to do,
Bell replied:

> I think it could come to it. I don't think it would on a
> major question. For example, if the Congress said to
> some small agency, "Don't spend any money."--suppose
> they are supposed to give out money.--"Don't spend any
> money unless we approve it." They would be taking
> over that agency. That is the sort of thing. "Or
> don't issue any regulation unless we approve it."
>
> So six months would go by and we would say to the agency,
> the President would, "Why haven't you done something
> about these regulations?" "Well, we can't get
> Congress to approve them." They are intruding into
> something they shouldn't be in. That sort of thing
> could come up--I don't believe, pending court
> resolution, we are going to have major confrontation.

The briefing continued, with the same reporter
pressing for clarification of Bell's position:

> Q. In other words, you wouldn't ever do this on
> something like war plane sales or some major foreign
> policy question?
>
> Attorney General Bell: That is where . . . we would
> have to exercise comity. . . . I think we are trying to
> make the point, and we have been trying to make it about
> a year by negotiation. We have not been successful
> and the flood continues, and so we are staking out
> another position to be firmer. I can't imagine us . . .
> creating a major confrontation. But we could have
> some minor confrontation.

Q. If you are making a Constitutional issue on this, why are you only doing it on the minor things, not the major things? What is the point?

Attorney General Bell: We want to keep the government in balance as much as we can. That is what comity is, be civil and have due regard for other people's views. . . .[80]

It may, of course, be mere happenstance that Carter's message to Congress and the press briefing came just before passage of the 1978 Education Amendments and subsequent action by Perkins's committee to subject the regulations implementing that act to exhaustive review. But there is little doubt that the legislative vetoes of the regulations offered the administration just the sort of minor issue that might result in only a "minor confrontation"; the administration may have felt compelled to respond consistently with the firmer position it had staked out. According to White House and Justice Department spokesmen interviewed in June 1980, just after Hufstedler's edict to ignore the vetoes, there was little probability of a challenge to the vetoes in the courts. "It would be unlikely," according to one White House spokesman, "that any member of the public would have sufficient grounds for a case."[81] In the absence of a court-imposed resolution, however, the "minor confrontation" had the potential to balloon into a major problem for the new department, which was already on shaky ground with many members of Congress as well as with many of its clientele groups. If ever there was a time when a department was in need of the protection and nurturance that a supportive congressional oversight committee could offer, this was it.

Secretary Hufstedler appeared to be well aware of the need to resolve the situation. Throughout the summer, ED undertook an extended review of the regulations at issue; Justice Department and White House attorneys were involved, at least to some extent. Upon completion of the review, Hufstedler wrote to Perkins that while she still regarded the disputed regulations as legally valid, she was changing some of them and was instituting a new procedure for drafting regulations.[82] It was a masterful "peace offering." The department agreed to change one regulation immediately in response to the committee's concern; to change two others but to postpone the changes until the next fiscal year; and, after presentation of a lengthy defense of the need for one regulation and the department's authority to act, to leave that regulation unchanged.

The department backed down on the vetoed regulations dealing with Title IV funds, prohibiting the purchase of gym equipment in order to "meet concerns expressed by Congress"; musical equipment, including band instruments, was left permissible. Although the secretary stopped somewhat short of acknowledging departmental error, she did admit that based on a "meticulous review of the entire legislative history and the statute . . . it was more probable than not that Congress did not intend to fund the purchase of gym equipment."[83]

Immediate change in the regulations of the Arts in Education and the Law-Related Education Programs was deemed impractical because of timing, and illegal under provisions of the Administrative Procedure Act, which, because of the magnitude of the changes required to address congressional concerns, meant amending the regulations under notice-and-comment procedures. At the time of the veto, the Arts in Education Program had pending more than 280 applications; the Law-Related Education Program, 160 applications. Hufstedler explained the predicament:

> The applicants needed our final decisions quickly so they could make hiring decisions and take the other steps necessary to start up their projects for the coming school year. If we had amended the regulations and reopened the competition, no orderly planning process would have been possible. In fact, it is very unlikely that we could have made awards before the end of the fiscal year, when the funds would have expired.

As proof of ED's good intentions, the secretary sent proposed regulations to the Federal Register for both programs that eliminated all the regulations that the committee had criticized.

> Instead the goals they sought to achieve--such as community support and ability to survive when Federal funding ends--have been stated in general terms as selection criteria. Thus, instead of being required to match Federal funds, applicants will simply be judged in part on whether their project is likely to continue without Federal funds.

The department's conciliatory approach did not extend to the vetoed regulations involving an education appeals board. Hufstedler defended ED's legal authority in spite of the literal language of the statute that limited the time for an application for review to thirty days:

> Now this question, of course, I must view from the perspective of many, many years on the bench. When the end product of giving total, literal interpretation to one segment of the statute reaches results that are extraordinarily harsh or absolutely unconscionable, one has to ask the question, "Did Congress intend that?"

> You answer that in connection with the totality of the statute, of which that segment was a part.

In this particular instance, the literal language says 30 days. That means if literally applied it would require a forfeiture of all sorts of rights involving millions of dollars to obtain relief, either through administrative proceedings or through the courts.

Now we do not attribute forfeiture intentions to Congress unless the language is very, very clear. We look at the history of this legislation and we note that it came about after the original audit procedure, the audit hearing board, had been established with a set of regulations that advised 30 days, but permitted very much like many, many other statutes for extension of such time upon good cause shown in the interest of justice.

Congress said nothing in the statute about intending to overturn that prior administrative construction . . . we would not attribute to Congress an intention to impose a forfeiture unless Congress had said, expressed the intent, that the 30 days was jurisdictional.

In response to these overtures from the secretary, Perkins said at the oversight hearing he scheduled to address the matter that he was "willing to develop procedures to insure that the Department is given full and fair notice of any intent on our part to disapprove regulations," and that he "would certainly be agreeable to open communication with the Department at all stages in the development of regulations." He then introduced the secretary, who, "in order to promote an orderly presentation of the testimony" requested the privilege of having Mr. John Harmon of the Attorney General's Office testify first. Then for fully half of the four-hour hearing the chairman and the committee members vented their anger at the administration upon Mr. Harmon. Perkins charged that the administration had "usurped the rights of the Congress"; that the Civiletti opinion was "not worth the paper it was written on"; and that in writing regulations the administration acted "like a blind dog in a meat house wandering around." The comments of other members were in a like vein.

When Hufstedler took the chair to testify, a more friendly mood prevailed. Representative Goodling said of the secretary's strategy: "I think it was an ideal way to move, because all the wrath that my colleagues may have been bestowing upon you—poor Mr. Harmon had to take it. I think it was a good maneuver." The secretary was assured of the committee's good will by Representative William Ford: "I don't detect on this committee, in any quarter, any antagonism toward you or your Department because of the circumstances that bring us together here today." The only member who pressed the secretary on the constitutionality

of her action was Representative Ken Kramer (R, CO). (Soon
after, Kramer, seventeen other representatives, and three
senators--all but one of the group were Republicans--
entered a civil suit for declaratory and injunctive relief
against Hufstedler's actions in regard to the
congressionally vetoed regulations: _Kramer_ v. _Hufsted-_
ler, Civil No. 80-7111, U.S. District Court for Colorado
[withdrawn].)

In her testimony, Hufstedler summed up the result of
the department's actions in modifying the vetoed
regulations, and pointed out: "In responding to the
modifications suggested by Congress, I have done so not
because I thought there was a violation of that statute in
the prior regulations, but because I wanted to show in a very
concrete way responsiveness to the concerns expressed by
Members of Congress." This controversial topic laid to
rest, she then explained the new departmental regulations
process. It was designed "to insure careful attention to
legislative intent and congressional concerns" and "to
increase the dialogue between the regulation drafters and
the Congress."

The extent of Hufstedler's commitment to a more
cooperative role with Congress in developing regulations
was made explicit by much of her testimony. She expounded
on the wisdom of this approach:

> I can tell you that after many, many, many years of
> divining congressional intent, I have discovered that
> it is often easier to define congressional intent by
> talking to the people who wrote the statute rather than
> depending entirely upon the literal words of the
> statute.

With the pipe of peace thus passed between the committee and
the secretary, and with the constitutional crisis "washed
away by the efforts, the very good efforts of the Secretary
of Education to revise these rules," the hearing closed.

The Department of Education and Congress:
Back to Negotiations

If the congressional vetoes were meant to send a
message to the new Department of Education about the
committee power, the message was received and apparently
heeded. The department modified its regulations process
to expedite consultation with its oversight committees in
the development of regulations. The internal memorandum
institutionalizing the new approach described the role of
the Office of the Assistant Secretary for Legislation:

> This office is in a key position to know congressional
> concerns with a familiarity that goes beyond a careful
> reading of committee reports and floor debates. This

information must be fully integrated into the
regulations process at the earliest stages and used as
a check to ensure that the provisions of the proposed
and final regulations meet the concerns of Congress.[84]

The memorandum also directed the assistant secretary for
legislation to arrange meetings with congressional staff to
discuss congressional concerns.

"Congress's vetoing of the four education
regulations," according to one committee staffer, "has
resulted in a much closer relationship between the agency
and the committee. Now ED is consulting with committee
staff over proposed regulations much more closely."[85] The
committee influence was not seen by this staffer as
violative of the rulemaking procedure of the Administrative
Procedure Act nor as intrusive into the executive domain:
"It is O.K. as long as questions are within the scope of the
'intent' of the law." And about issues that are ambiguous
in, or absent from, the statute: "The committee and
committee staff are best able to say what the law means."[86]

Former Assistant Attorney General Robert Dixon, Jr.,
expresses his reservations about this kind of relationship,
an "extraconstitutional negotiating power." He argues:

A practical result of the veto power, whether or not
any vetoes actually occur, is to force on the agencies
a negotiation process "with teeth" as a condition for
avoiding a threatened veto. In effect, the personnel
of the agency is involuntarily enlarged to include a
new set of powerful advisors not appointed by or
controlled by the Executive, in derogation of the
Executive's appointment and removal power in Article
II. . . . The functional result of such a review
process is not to create significant ongoing
administrative authority in the Congress or even one
house thereof, but in the key members of the relevant
subcommittees--a membership by definition nonrepre-
sentative and subject to all the vagaries of periodic
realignment of subcommittee assignments. In this
context the "congressional veto" can become more a
fiefdom concept than a grand democratic device for
controlling the bureaucracy.[87]

A similar point was made by Attorney General Civiletti
in his opinion to Hufstedler:

No doubt congressional review provides a check on
agency action, just as committee review or committee
chairman review would provide a check. But such
review involves the imposition on the Executive of a
particular interpretation of the law--the interpretation of the Congress, or one House or one committee,
or one chairman--without the check of the legislative
process which includes the President's veto.[88]

The issues involved in the four vetoed education regulations were relatively minor and thus engendered little controversy. As one staffer pointed out, "If they had not been for the most part 'cut and dried' it would probably not have been possible to get concurrent resolutions acted upon by both houses within the forty-five-day time limit. There are simply too many opportunities for a member who disagrees with a veto to thwart the process."[89] In spite of this reality, the department was willing not only to alter all but one of the vetoed regulations but to formalize a negotiating relationship with the committees for future regulation development. This capitulation to congressional committee pressures and demands is not too surprising. As Harold Seidman has pointed out, "Collusion between the legislative and executive bureaucracies to alter administrative policies is not an unknown phenomenon."[90] Moreover, for a new department with a divided clientele, such a strong liaison with its congressional oversight committees could be advantageous if not essential.

                            Summary

     Although it might at first appear that Congress has exercised its power to veto education regulations in a manner consistent with its statutory authority--a review by the full Congress based on the regulations' consistency with the authorizing statute--on closer look it becomes apparent that the full Congress was by no means involved, and that although the immediate vetoes were carefully restricted to agency actions that were arguably in excess of or contrary to legislative intent, the ultimate congressional goal was to ensure the committees' ability to review substantively future education regulations.
     The possible disruption by the formation of a separate department of the close and cooperative relationship the congressional committees had developed with the Office of Education is the most likely explanation for Perkins's action to exercise the veto review power established by the 1974 Education Amendments Act. His willingness to devote a considerable amount of his own and the committee staff's time to building the documentation necessary to substantiate the veto effort was essential to its success. By avoiding controversial issues that might arouse opposition in the Congress, Perkins made possible action in both houses within the forty-five-day limit. Moreover, unlike environmental or energy regulation issues, little in the way of specialized technical knowledge was required to understand the education regulations. The ability to comprehend and decipher regulatory legalese was sufficient to the reviewing task, and the committee staff had a plentiful supply of lawyers. Perhaps most important of all, there was a substantial advantage accruing to the

chairman and the committee from the successful accomplishment of its purpose. By ensuring continuation of the negotiation strategy between the new department and the committees, committee members would be in a position still to protect their constituents.

What this means for the substance of education policy is difficult to determine, although the negotiation power of the veto appears to have been used in most instances to broaden eligibility--in other words, as a mechanism of distributive politics. The ultimate effect of the education vetoes' "negotiation powers with teeth" may be, however, an increase of the federal government's role in education. "Far more power is delegated in the company of legislative vetoes," according to Congressional Research Service's Louis Fisher, "than would have been tolerated without it."[91] The enormous growth in the number and the size of the federal government's education programs lends credence to this observation.

The next chapter deals with two very different applications of the legislative veto. Rather than applying the veto power to all rules of an agency, as in the Department of Housing and Urban Development, and the Department of Education examples, Congress chose instead to target the veto power to a specific delegation of rulemaking authority. In the first case study presented in chapter 5, Congress attached a legislative veto to the Federal Energy Regulatory Commission's mandate to develop an incremental gas pricing rule. In the second case study, the veto was applied to authority delegated to the National Traffic and Highway Safety Administration to develop a passive restraint rule. Motivation for congressional enactment and use of these targeted legislative vetoes was significantly different as well. Rather than being used as a mechanism for Congress to gain control over an agency's rulemaking process, as was true in the HUD and ED cases, the legislative vetoes in chapter 5 were added by Congress to avoid or postpone its need to make politically or technologically difficult decisions.

116

Notes

1. Harold H. Bruff and Ernest Gelhorn, "Congressional Control of Administrative Regulation: A Study of Legislative Vetoes," 90 Harvard Law Review 1369 (1976), p. 1383.
2. Ibid., p. 1385.
3. F. Forbis Jordan and Wayne Riddle, "Congressional Disapproval of Education Regulations" (Washington, DC: Library of Congress, Congressional Research Service, 1980), p. 147.
4. U.S. Congress, House, Subcommittee on Elementary, Secondary, and Vocational Education of the Committee on Education and Labor, Oversight Hearing on Congressional Disapproval of Education Regulations, 96th Cong., 2d sess., September 18, 1980, p. 24. Hereafter cited as Oversight Hearing on ED Vetoes.
5. 20 U.S.C. 1232(d).
6. U.S. Congress, House, Report to Accompany the Elementary and Secondary Amendments of 1974, Report 93-805, 93d Cong., 2d sess., 1974, pp. 72-73. Hereafter cited as 1974 House Report.
7. Ibid.
8. Bruff and Gelhorn, "Congressional Control of Administrative Regulation," p. 1387.
9. Skee Smith, "The U.S. Department of Education," American Education (Washington, DC: Government Printing Office, November 1979), pp. 6-7.
10. 125 Cong. Rec. H8595 (daily ed.), November 27, 1979.
11. Smith, "U.S. Department of Education," p. 6.
12. Joseph A. Califano, Jr., Governing America: An Insider's Report from the White House and the Cabinet (New York: Simon and Schuster, 1981), p. 285. For a more complete account of the politics behind ED's formation, see pp. 174-93.
13. 125 Cong. Rec. H8597 (daily ed.), September 27, 1979.
14. U.S. News and World Report, May 12, 1980, p. 49.
15. Quoted in Califano, Governing America, p. 184.
16. Ibid., p. 292.
17. 125 Cong. Rec. H8595 (daily ed.), September 27, 1979.
18. Ibid., p. H8598.
19. Califano, Governing America, p. 278.
20. Ibid., pp. 272-73.
21. U.S. Congress, House, Committee on Education and Labor, Excerpt of a Report on the Education Amendments of 1978, H.R. 15, 95th Cong., 2d sess., 1978, p. 62. Hereafter cited as 1978 Education Amendments Report-- House.

22. Bruff and Gelhorn, "Congressional Control of Administrative Regulation," p. 1382. (The authors cite interviews with congressional committee staff as their authority.)

23. U.S. Congress, Senate, Subcommittee on Education of the Committee on Labor and Public Welfare, Hearings on Family Contribution Schedules for the BEOGP, 93d Cong., 1st sess., 1973, p. 1.

24. U.S. Congress, House, Special Subcommittee on Education of the Committee on Education and Labor, Hearings on Basic Education Opportunity Grant Program, 93d Cong., 1st sess., 1973, pp. 165-66.

25. Ibid., p. 171.

26. Ibid.

27. Bruff and Gelhorn, "Congressional Control of Administrative Regulation," p. 1385.

28. Ibid., p. 1386.

29. Oversight Hearings on ED Vetoes, p. 41.

30. 1974 House Report, p. 73.

31. Bruff and Gelhorn, "Congressional Control of Administrative Regulation," p. 1387.

32. U.S. Department of Education, "Department of Education Regulation Process Memorandum" (internal memorandum from Deputy General Counsel for Regulation and Legislation Stewart A. Baker), September 25, 1980, p. 13 (Section II(B)(4)).

33. For more complete details, see Bruff and Gelhorn, "Congressional Control of Administrative Regulation," pp. 1388-90.

34. Califano, Governing America, p. 263.

35. Ibid., p. 267.

36. U.S. Congress, House, Rules Committee, Hearings before the Subcommittee on the Rules of the House on Regulatory Reform and Congressional Review of Agency Rules, 96th Cong., 1st sess., 1979, Part I, p. 11 (testimony of Representative Levitas).

37. Oversight Hearing on ED Vetoes, pp. 41-42.

38. In support of the need for the legislative veto power, 1974 House Report states: "For at least four decades now, the agencies of the Executive Branch have increasingly used their rule-making authority to 'correct' what they feel are the errors and ambiguities of the law."

39. 1978 Education Amendments Report--House, pp. 1-455.

40. 92 Stat. 2143-2380.

41. Interview with staff members, Office of Education, November 13, 1980.

42. Files of the House Education and Labor Committee, inspected in committee offices by author, June 11, 1980.

43. Interview with staff member, House Committee on Education and Labor, June 11, 1980.

44. Letter from Perkins to Berry, April 2, 1979, files of the House Committee on Education and Labor.

118

45.   Interview with staff member, Senate Committee on Labor and Human Resources, November 10, 1980.

46.   Interview with staff member, Senate Committee on Labor and Human Resources, November 9, 1980.

47.   Files of the House Committee on Education and Labor.

48.   10 U.S.C. 2961.

49.   44 Federal Register 35186.

50.   H. Con. Res. 319, 96th Cong., 2d. sess., 1980, p. 2.

51.   Administrative Procedure Act, 5 U.S.C. 553.

52.   Letter from Smith to Perkins, March 20, 1980, files of the House Committee on Education and Labor. See also 45 Federal Register 22743 (1980).

53.   Oversight Hearing on ED Vetoes, p. 69 (printed testimony of Secretary Hufstedler).

54.   1978 Education Amendments Report--House, pp. 64-65.

55.   Ibid., pp. 71-75.

56.   H. Con. Res. 319, 96th Cong., 2d sess., 1980, p. 3.

57.   126 Cong. Rec. H3487 (daily ed.), May 12, 1980.

58.   126 Cong. Rec. S5517 (daily ed.), May 15, 1980).

59.   20 U.S.C. 1234 a(b).

60.   44 Federal Register 30528.

61.   H. Con. Res. 318, 96th Cong., 2d sess., 1980, p. 3.

62.   Oversight Hearing on ED Vetoes, p. 68.

63.   Ibid., p. 56.

64.   20 U.S.C. 3002(d).

65.   44 Federal Register 38142.

66.   H. Con. Res. 332, 96th Cong., 2d. sess., 1980, p. 3.

67.   45 Federal Register 17882.

68.   126 Cong. Rec. H3408 (daily ed.), May 19, 1980.

69.   1978 Education Amendments Report--House, p. 63.

70.   Ibid. See also 20 U.S.C. 3101.

71.   1978 Education Amendments Report--House, p. 63.

72.   145 Federal Register 230604.

73.   S. Con. Res. 91, 96th Cong., 2d sess., 1980, p. 2.

74.   126 Cong. Rec. H3908 (daily ed.), May 21, 1980.

75.   Interview with staff members, Office of Education, November 13, 1980.

76.   Oversight Hearing on ED Vetoes, p. 77 (printed testimony of Secretary Hufstedler).

77.   Letter from Benjamin R. Civiletti to Shirley M. Hufstedler, June 5, 1980, in Oversight Hearing on ED Vetoes, p. 18.

78.   Washington Post, June 7, 1980, p. A1.

79.   Richard E. Cohen, "Legislative Veto Battle Escalates--Should Congress Have the Last Word?" National Journal, September 6, 1980, p. 1476.

80. White House, News Briefing, 2:40 p.m., June 21, 1978, pp. 7-8.

81. Interview with members, White House staff, October 1, 1980.

82. Cohen, "Legislative Veto Battle Escalates," p. 1476.

83. The remaining quotations in this section are all from testimony of witnesses at the Oversight Hearings on ED Vetoes.

84. "Department of Education Regulation Process Memorandum," p. 4.

85. Interview with staff, Senate Committee on Labor and Human Resources, November 10, 1980.

86. Ibid.

87. Robert G. Dixon, Jr., "The Congressional Veto and Separation of Powers: The Executive on a Leash?" 56 North Carolina Law Review, 427 (1978), p. 445.

88. Civiletti to Hufstedler, Oversight Hearing on ED Vetoes, p. 11.

89. Interview with staff, Senate Commitee on Labor and Human Resources, November 10, 1980.

90. Harold Seidman, "Legislative Veto: Two Views--One 'Yea,' One 'Nay,'" Staff: Congressional Staff Journal (Washington, DC: Committee on House Administration, Office of Management Services, September/October, 1980), p. 22.

91. U.S. Congress, House, Subcommittee on the Rules of the House Rules Committee, A Study of Legislative Vetoes (committee print), 96th Cong., 1st sess., 1979, p. 14.

5
The Legislative Veto as a Means for Decision Avoidance: Two Targeted Vetoes

Introduction

In the case studies presented in chapters 3 and 4, the ostensible purpose of the legislative veto provisions was to give Congress a mechanism to insure that the regulations developed by "unelected bureaucrats" to implement statutorily mandated programs would reflect the intent of the law. As the analysis in each case has shown, however, congressional exercise of the legislative veto power was aimed more at modifying existing law through committee- and committee staff-level negotiations.

Many members of Congress who have been vigorously opposed to such broad uses of the legislative veto because of the potential for such off-the-record negotiations have, nevertheless, supported legislative vetoes when they were targeted to a specific delegation of rulemaking authority. The case studies in this chapter involve restricted applications of the legislative veto to the authority of the secretary of the Department of Transportation to develop occupant-restraint regulations, and the mandate of the Federal Energy Regulatory Commission to develop an incremental gas-pricing rule. In both cases the legislative veto power was targeted at a specific agency regulatory authority, and in both cases the regulation involved was aimed at protecting the consumer at the expense of powerful industry groups. The controversial nature of these two regulatory areas is evident from their legislative histories. Both the occupant-restraint and the incremental gas-pricing regulation were subject to legislative veto provisions as a result of conference committee efforts to reach an accommodation between conflicting House and Senate bills.

Proponents of such limited applications argue that the legislative veto provides Congress with an acceptable and useful method for resolving difficult policy issues. Congressional use of the targeted veto is aimed, then, not so much at controlling the bureaucracy as at resolving internal disputes within Congress. As the analysis of the case studies in this chapter will show, however, the result is not the resolution of difficult policy problems but rather the postponement or avoidance of decision.

On May 20, 1980, the House of Representatives used its one-house veto power to overturn the Federal Energy Regulatory Commission's final incremental gas-pricing rule. Analysis of this successful veto effort will be presented first. Although congressional efforts to veto the passive-restraint rule in October 1977 were unsuccessful, the data from this case study will be presented to illustrate the limited power of the legislative veto review process when exercised within the constraints of Congress's own rules and procedures.

Incremental Gas-Pricing Rule

Federal regulation of natural gas pricing stems from a 1954 Supreme Court Decision. In <u>Phillips Petroleum Co. v. Wisconsin</u> (347 U.S. 672), the court ordered the Federal Power Commission to regulate the wellhead price of natural gas destined for the interstate market. Natural gas sold in intrastate markets was exempt from federal regulatory control, thus creating a dual-market situation: one price controlled, one free to vary prices with conditions.

Throughout the fifties and sixties the price of natural gas remained low, while production steadily increased. By the seventies, however, conditions had changed dramatically. First, production growth slowed considerably until, in 1976, production actually declined.[1] Meanwhile, demand continued to increase at an annual rate of about 5 percent. The imbalance brought on by the dual-market system further complicated the problem by setting up a supplier bias in favor of the higher-priced intrastate market. At the same time, the 1973 Arab oil embargo and subsequent events exacerbated the production shortage and dual-market problems by creating a substantially increased demand for the cheaper, price-controlled gas alternative. Gas producers argued that decontrol, which would allow prices to rise to offset the higher cost of drilling and exploration for deeper and more difficult to exploit gas reserves, was the only answer to the need for increasing supplies.

Natural Gas Policy Act of 1978

Pressed by the desirability of encouraging domestic alternatives to the Arab oil stranglehold on American domestic and foreign policies, and in the belief that there were enormous domestic gas reserves available to tap if the incentive were offered (a claim variously disputed and endorsed by experts at the time), President Carter elected to move at least somewhat toward decontrol. As part of his

National Energy Plan, he proposed solving the natural gas supply shortage by increasing the regulated price from $1.42/thousand cubic feet (Mcf) to $1.75/Mcf, with future price increases tied to the consumer price index, and to subject the intrastate market to the same price controls. Opponents of the president's plan fell into two camps: those who feared the inflationary impact and heavy cost to consumers, especially the poor, who depended upon natural gas for essential domestic uses; and those who argued that the plan provided too little relief for producers, and that complete decontrol was the only answer.

In Congress the controversial nature of the natural gas problem was soon evident. To pass the Natural Gas Policy Act of 1978 took eighteen months and "more floor hours, more committee hours, more conference hours and more task force hours . . . than any other issue before the 95th Congress."[2] Although the House and Senate produced substantially different bills on the issue, debate in both houses revolved around the same basic points: the need to deregulate in order to obtain new supplies versus the limited ability of consumers to pay significantly more to heat their homes.

Speaker Thomas P. O'Neill designated an ad hoc energy committee to consider the president's energy plan in the House. After rejecting the alternative concept of deregulation by a vote of 23-20, the committee reported out a bill similar in many respects to the Carter plan. Part D of the bill, which dealt with natural gas, provided for retaining controls, increasing the price, and extending controls to intrastate markets.[3] The committee added, however, a new provision calling for incremental pricing to insulate homeowners temporarily from further substantial price increases.

The incremental pricing mechanism is designed to require industrial users of natural gas to bear the cost of the more expensive new gas supplies until that cost reaches the equivalent price of alternative fuels, such as coal or oil.[4] The rationale of the incremental price concept is that it encourages those most able to switch to alternative fuels, the larger industrial users, to do so, and that it discourages waste of gas supplies resulting from the practice of rolled-in pricing--pricing that disguises the varying prices of alternative gas sources by averaging high- and low-cost gas sources. A more complete assessment of the incremental pricing device is presented later in the chapter. It is sufficient, at this point, to note that its intended purpose in the House bill was to provide a cushion for consumers against higher gas prices. It is important also to note that there was no provision in the House bill for legislative veto review over the incremental pricing plan to be developed by the Federal Energy Regulatory Commission (FERC). After five days of often heated debate among the proponents of immediate decontrol--those favoring continuation of the status quo, that is, regulated markets, and those anxious for compromise to prove congressional concern about the energy problem--the House passed the committee version by a vote of 230 to 180 on August 5, 1977.[5]

Senate consideration of the president's energy plan had different results. Decontrol proponents in the Senate enjoyed greater strength and had far greater success. Unable to agree on an alternative plan for natural gas pricing, the Senate energy committees simply reported out, with no recommendation, the president's version. After lengthy debate and numerous amendments culminating in a cloture vote, the Senate adopted a bill incorporating the so-called Pearson-Bentsen substitute by a vote of 50-46 on October 4, 1977. The Senate bill provided for immediate deregulation of new gas supplies subject to a limited authority in the commission to impose price ceilings. Limited incremental pricing was also included but was restricted to the pipeline level. Distribution utilities were not required by the Senate version to allocate the higher costs to low-priority industrial users, as in the House bill. In addition, there was no provision for legislative veto review of an incremental pricing rule.

These two bills encompassing fundamentally different concepts were then sent to the conference committee for resolution. There followed a marathon, ten-month conference struggle. In later reference to the problems faced by the conferees, one staff participant commented, "Dealing with energy legislation is like swimming in a kettle of spaghetti. You get tangled up in a controversy no matter which way you turn!"[6] Representative John D. Dingell (D, MI), chairman of the House Interstate and Foreign Commerce Subcommittee on Energy and Power, voiced a more poignant memory of the conference process: "We were almost like battered children out of the process. Neither side loved us."[7]

The conference committee product was an artfully crafted document born of intricate political deals and tradeoffs about which Dingell was later to say, "Even though I voted for the bill there were plenty of things at the time some of us knew were irrational, no matter which side you were on, but it was the only way to get the decision."[8] Also, at the time, an energy bill--any energy bill--was a top priority for the embattled Carter presidency.[9]

There were two major compromises involved in the conference committee's natural gas pricing scheme. Title I provided for a phased decontrol gradually lifting price controls over new gas supplies until they were completely removed in 1985. This represented something between the restrictive House version, which raised the controlled price but continued and extended controls, and the more liberal Senate version, which provided for immediate decontrol. Title II provided for implementation of an incremental pricing plan in two stages: the first to cover industrial boiler fuel facilities and to be effective one year after passage of the act; the second to cover other low-priority industrial uses and to be effective eighteen months after passage of the act. The conference committee also added a one-house thirty-day legislative veto over FERC's rule to implement only the second stage of incremental pricing.[10]

Implementation of the incremental pricing process in two stages was an apparent compromise between the restrictive Senate provision, which applied incremental pricing only at the pipeline level, and the more liberal House view that provided that all low-priority end users would be incrementally charged. The reasons for the addition of the legislative veto provision by the conferees, which appeared in neither the House nor the Senate bill, is far less clear. The section-by-section analysis that accompanied the conference bill simply describes the congressional review mechanism without offering any explanation for its addition. In fact, exactly what took place during the conference committee deliberations remains, for the most part, a mystery. All the "wheeling and dealing" was carried on behind the closed doors of the conference committee, which at that time was the only formal congressional forum that was still permitted to conduct its business in secret. As a result, there is little in the way of reviewable history from which to deduce congressional intent or reasoning. The absence of certainty as to intent or reasoning became an important factor when the House chose to exercise the conference-added legislative veto power eighteen months later.

Debate on the conference compromise in the Senate continued for nine days, during which time the bill was repeatedly "sold" as a compromise. Testimony, from opponents and proponents alike, makes clear that the purpose of the incremental pricing provision was to protect consumers.[11] Only once during the long debate was the legislative veto provision mentioned; this occurred in a brief exchange between Senators Henry Jackson (D, WA) and Charles Percy (R, IL). In answer to Percy's expressed concern over the possibility of industrial relocation as a response to incremental pricing, Jackson asserted: "This bill does not compel incremental pricing with respect to any industrial use other than in large boilers. Extension of incremental pricing beyond boiler use could be prevented by a majority vote of either House of Congress two years from now."[12] To the dismay of its opponents, who had variously labeled it "The Greatest Consumer Ripoff of This Century" and "An Abomination--But the Only Abomination in Town," the compromise passed the Senate on September 27, 1978, by a vote of 57-42.

Support for the natural gas pricing compromise was even less enthusiastic in the House. To avert certain defeat, its sponsors maneuvered to have it considered together with the four remaining parts of the original Carter energy package. By a single-vote margin, the resolution to accomplish this passed on October 13, 1978.[13]

The next day the total energy package passed, 231-168. Throughout the two-day debate, the only mention of the legislative veto was made by Representative Dingell, who explained that "the mandatory requirements of incremental pricing apply only to boiler fuel users. Any broadening of incremental pricing to a broader universe of industrial users is subject to congressional review and single House veto."[14]

The importance of incremental pricing to many who voted for the conference compromise as a means of insuring at least some measure of protection for consumers is far more clear from the record. For example, conferee Dingell flatly stated that "meaningful incremental pricing was an essential prerequisite, a sine qua non, to my acceding to deregulation."[15] In addition, an administrative fact sheet passed out to members during congressional consideration of the conference compromise stated: "This natural gas bill affords special protection to residential consumers in the interstate market through the 'incremental pricing' provision that first passes through to industry the costs of natural gas that exceed the current FERC new gas price. . . ."[16]

With a decided lack of enthusiasm, but pleased to be done with it, Congress sent the Natural Gas Policy Act, along with the other parts of the energy package it had approved, to the president, who signed them into law on November 9, 1978. From there the incremental gas-pricing "ball" moved into the FERC court, bringing with it all the unresolved controversy avoided by Congress in its effort to get a bill passed. The legislative veto device, however, was the very instrument by which FERC would return the ball to congressional territory, where under significantly different circumstances the less powerful and less organized consumer interest would be at a special disadvantage.

The Federal Energy Regulatory Commission and the Incremental Pricing Rule

Title II, Section 201, of the Natural Gas Policy Act (NGPA) directed FERC to prescribe and make effective, within twelve months of enactment of the act, a rule designed to provide for the pass-through of the costs of natural gas to boiler-fuel use of natural gas by any industrial boiler-fuel facility. This the commission did under the notice-and-comment provisions of the Administrative Procedure Act. FERC approved its final rule covering Section 201 on September 28, 1979, with an effective date of January 1, 1980.[17] Congress had not extended the legislative veto power over the Phase I rule, and thus FERC's publication of the rule as final was sufficient to make it operative.[18]

Section 202 of Title II directed FERC to develop, within eighteen months after enactment of the act, an amendment to the Phase I rule to expand application of incremental pricing to other industrial uses. This so-called Phase II rule would not become effective until after a thirty-day period of continuous session of Congress, during which time either house could adopt a resolution disapproving the rule. If FERC's Phase II rule were disapproved, the commission was authorized but not required to submit a revised rule not earlier than six months, not later than two years after adoption of the original disapproval resolution. The revised rule would again be subject to the one-house legislative veto review procedure.

The act furnished guidance on the types and sources of gas that were to be subjected to the rule's pass-through requirements and exempted certain facilities, such as schools and hospitals, as well as agricultural users from paying the incremental costs, but otherwise allowed the commission considerable discretion in determining the exact nature and types of facilities to be included under the rule. In addition, the commission was given substantial latitude for deciding the dollar amount and design of the pass-through requirement.

After completing work on the Phase I rule, FERC announced a proposed notice of rulemaking for the Phase II rule on November 15, 1979.[19] Public hearings were held throughout January 1980 in San Francisco, Salt Lake City, Chicago, Louisville, and Washington, DC. The comments of 522 individuals and organizations were directed primarily at the timing of the rule, its scope, alternative price ceilings, and the protections afforded by the rule for residential and other high-priority users. Four hundred fifty-one comments were made by, or on behalf of, industrial end users who were to be subject to the higher incremental prices, and by, or on behalf of, natural gas production or distribution companies; forty-five by members of Congress; three by spokespersons of other federal agencies; and sixteen by representatives of state regulatory commissions. Only seven comments were made by consumer groups or individual consumers.[20]

The proposed rule that elicited this interest provided for an approximately sixty-cent surcharge per thousand cubic feet of gas to be applied to all industrial users except those specifically excluded by statute. FERC claimed that in developing the rule it was attempting to meet the dual objectives it believed Congress had expressed in enacting the incremental pricing provision: (1) to prepare the natural gas market for deregulation in 1985, when, it was feared, prices would skyrocket--the so-called market-ordering objective; and (2) to give a measure of shelter from rising gas prices to residential and other high-priority customers.[21] The projected annual saving

128

for the protected classes was estimated to be between eighteen and twenty-three dollars per household. From the beginning, the commission voiced its doubts about the ability of incremental pricing to achieve the market-ordering objective.[22]

To understand the reasoning behind the incremental pricing debate, it is necessary to say a bit about gas pricing in general. Residential rates for natural gas have always been higher than industrial rates because gas is priced according to volume of usage, that is, the unit cost decreases as volume of use increases. In 1978 gas prices for industrial users averaged $1.91/Mcf; residential rates averaged $2.53/Mcf. In other words, residential costs per unit were 21 percent higher than industrial costs per unit. By the third quarter of 1979, prices for both categories had risen as a result of the phased decontrol provision of Title I of the Natural Gas Policy Act (NGPA). At the end of the third quarter of 1979, industrial users paid an average $2.32/Mcf; residential rates had risen to an average of $3.59/Mcf. Without the protection of any incremental pricing (remember that Phase I did not go into effect until January 1, 1980), residential users were paying 42 percent

Table 5.1

Industrial and Residential Per-Unit Costs for Gas,
1978 to Third Quarter, 1979

	1978 (per Mcf)	Third Quarter 1979 (per Mcf)	Amount Increase (per Mcf)	Percentage Increase
Residential	$2.53*	$3.59	$1.27	42
Industrial	$1.91	$2.32	$ .41	21
Residential surcharge	$ .62	$1.27	$ .65	105

Source: Compiled from data in U.S. Congress, House Committee on Interstate and Foreign Commerce, Subcommittee on Energy and Power, Hearings on Phase II Incremental Pricing of Natural Gas, 96th Cong., 2d sess., April 3 and May 6, 1980, pp. 3, 113. (Figures provided by the American Gas Association.)

*Mcf = thousand cubic feet of gas.

more than industrial users for each unit of consumption (see Table 5.1). Not surprisingly, there was a 15 percent increase in gas consumption by industrial users, while residential consumption remained constant.

The incremental pricing provision exacerbated precisely what it was designed to alleviate; in Representative Dingell's words, "The Natural Gas Policy Act reflects a policy decision to close the gap between industrial and residential rates."[23] The perception was that large industrial customers would be the first to benefit from new, usually more expensive, supplies of decontrolled gas, and that they should therefore begin to pay the true cost of the extra supplies that the rolled-in price-averaging practice disguised.

There is, however, more to the gas pricing problem. The cost of natural gas itself is actually only a small portion of the end cost to the consumer. In fact, only about 20 percent of a gas bill goes to buy the actual gas; most of the rest buys the pipelines. There is over $40 billion of principal and interest debt for pipeline construction in the United States that under Federal Power Commission rules pipeline companies are permitted to charge (along with operating costs and a small profit) to customers. Furthermore, the lion's share of pipeline construction costs is incurred for the pipelines to bring gas to individual homes. Construction of pipelines to deliver to many small-volume users, that is, households, is clearly more expensive than a direct line to a single large-volume industrial user. Natural gas providers argue that this economy of scale should be passed on to industry.[24]

Because the pipelines represent fixed costs, if they are not full--which they are not, nor have they ever been-- each cubic foot of gas bears a higher transmission burden. Put more simply, if a pipeline principal and debt payment were equal to $1,000/year and if 1,000 Mcf of gas passed through the pipeline per year, the cost for using the pipeline would be $1/Mcf of gas; if 2,000 Mcf passed through, the cost would be $0.50/Mcf; if 50 Mcf passed through, the cost would be $25/Mcf. Such being the case, it makes sense to encourage increased usage of gas; and it certainly would be counterproductive to push high-volume users off gas. This is one of the arguments of decontrol proponents against the incremental pricing scheme-- especially in light of the growing acceptance that domestic supplies of gas are nearly limitless.

An important question remains: At what point will greater gas production, brought about by the higher prices allowed under the NGPA, result in sufficiently more usage to lower the per-unit pipeline transmission costs enough to protect the small-volume user? Clearly, the 15 percent volume increase evident by the third quarter of 1979 under the NGPA phased decontrol was insufficient. At any rate, the sixty-cent surcharge for industrial users proposed by FERC in its Phase II rule would have still left a sixty-

seven-cent gap between the higher residential cost
($3.59/Mcf) and the lower industrial cost of $2.92/Mcf
($2.32 plus surcharge).

When FERC published its final Phase II rule on May 6,
1980, there were several changes from the proposed rule that
resulted in an even lesser cushion for the high-priority and
residential user. For example, the final rule exempted the
first 300 Mcf of gas used each day by each facility that
would be subject to the Phase II rule. To put this
exception into perspective, it took 55.1 Mcf to heat a four-
story, fourteen-room house and to run a gas stove, water
heater, and dryer in Connecticut in the thirty-one days
between January 14 and February 13, 1981; this translates
into 1.78 Mcf/day. Indeed, of 2,517 industrial facilities
studied by FERC, 59 percent, or 1,483, used less than the
average of 300 Mcf/day.[25]

Another change by FERC in the final rule was to
institute a single-tier price ceiling gauged to the cost of
No. 6 high-sulphur fuel oil, which had an average price in
May 1980 of $3 to $3.25/million BTU. The proposed rule had
called for a three-tier price ceiling based on the price of
No. 2 fuel oil (average price, $5.50/million BTU), No. 6
low-sulphur fuel oil (average price, $4 to $4.50/million
BTU), and No. 6 high-sulphur fuel oil. This change meant
that the surcharge would be significantly lower.

Together the changes resulted, FERC estimated, in a
saving of approximately $10/year/household, and a
surcharge cost of about $0.50/Mcf for a significantly lower
number of industrial users. The changes were made,
according to the commissioners, "to prevent industrial load
loss," which, they argued, would result in higher costs for
consumers.[26] The final rule, accompanied by the
commissioners' less than enthusiastic assessment of its
efficacy, was next subjected to the congressional veto
review procedure provided for under Section 202(c) of the
NGPA.

House Veto of the Incremental
Pricing Rule

Even before FERC issued its final Phase II rule,
Chairman Dingell's Subcommittee on Energy and Power held
hearings on the incremental pricing rule. The hearings
were reactive to an announcement by FERC of its "preliminary
decision" on the Phase II rule on March 20, 1980. Those
testifying on April 3, 1980, with one exception, were
representatives of gas suppliers or industries faced with
paying the incremental prices. The ten spokespersons
voiced unanimous opposition to the rule and urged its
veto.[27] Most also urged passage of the Preyer-Stockman
bill (H.R. 5862) and the Lugar-Stevenson bill (S. 2392),
which would repeal all of Title II's incremental pricing
provisions, including the already operative Phase I rule.

The only witness to testify in defense of the consumer interest was Edward Petrini of the National Consumer Law Center. His support was at best lukewarm: "While we believe that FERC's proposed phase II rule correctly extends incremental pricing to all industrial users, it is seriously weakened insofar as it fails to protect high priority consumers to the full extent contemplated by Congress."[28]

In attacking the rule, the powerful industry groups were able to raise the spectre of higher inflation, reduced domestic production of gas, the danger of industries' switching to oil, foreign competition, and even the possibility of industrial failures. To defend the rule, consumer groups needed to justify the value of the projected saving for housholds. Congressman Richardson Preyer's (D, NC) comments during the hearing went to the heart of the problem:

> I think the point we were concerned with is that $23 a year is a relatively modest saving. The question is whether it is worth the risk of higher prices of consumer goods which they would be paying, or whether it is worth the risk of switching so many gas users into other fuels and therefore loading a heavier price on them. We are running a <u>pretty big risk for a relatively minor benefit.</u> [Emphasis added.][29]

When FERC later revised its estimate down to a $10/year/household saving, the problem of rallying consumer support for the rule was further exacerbated.

On the same day that the final Phase II rule was issued and transmitted by FERC, a resolution of disapproval (H. Res. 655) was immediately introduced by Congressman Philip R. Sharp (D, IN). In contrast to the Education and HUD resolutions of disapproval, this resolution offered no reasoning for disapproving the rule. (The congressional review procedure of the NGPA provided no standards for its exercise; therefore, no explanation in the resolution of disapproval was required by the act.) The entire resolution merely read:

> Resolved, That the House of Representatives does not approve the proposed rule under section 202 of the Natural Gas Policy Act of 1978 [relating to incremental pricing of natural gas] a copy of which was transmitted to the Congress on May 6, 1980.

At 2 p.m. that day, Dingell's subcommittee convened a second hearing on the Phase II rule, at which FERC Chairman Charles B. Curtis and Commissioners George Hall, Georgiana Sheldon, and Matthew Holden, Jr., were the sole witnesses present. Over the next hour and a half the commissioners and members of the subcommittee discussed the problems with the rule.

The tone of the hearing was immediately established by Dingell, who thanked his "old friend" and former counsel to the Energy and Power Subcommittee, Curtis, for "a job well done" and for his "assistance" to the committee. Representative Clarence J. Brown (R, OH) next extended his thanks "to the Commissioners for their honesty in pointing out the problems with the entire concept of incremental pricing." Even Sharp, author of the veto resolution, commended the commissioners for taking their mandate "very seriously."

Testimony from the commissioners made clear their belief that an extension of incremental pricing would not accomplish the congressional purpose to order the marketplace in preparation for decontrol. In commenting on the congressional purpose of providing a cushion for the consumer against higher prices, Curtis held out the hope that "given due consideration to the burdens on industry," the rule would "achieve some measure of price shelter for residential users, schools, hospitals, and agricultural users." Questioned about the level of shelter, Curtis revised the commission's earlier prediction of $20 to $23/year/household downward to $10/year/household. He also admitted that there would be "significant problems with implementing this rule," and that therefore the commissioners had a "certain lack of enthusiasm for it." "The Commission," according to Curtis, was "fully prepared for Congress to exercise its judgment on this matter."[30]

Somewhat incredulous, Representative Tom Corcoran (R, IL) expressed surprise at the nature of the hearing, "having expected that the Commissioners would be here to tell us why we ought to go ahead and permit the phase II rule to go into effect." Rather, he drily noted, they appeared to be making "a request that we vote in favor of the resolution of disapproval."[31]

Perhaps the comments of Congressman Albert Gore, Jr. (D, TN) best reflect the irony in the hearing:

> This is an interesting procedure we are going through here today. I found it fascinating. . . . Those who worked so long on the Natural Gas Act came to think of it as kind of a member of the family. It was here for months and years, and if you go back and look at the arguments that took place at the time it is quite interesting because quite a few people said, "Consumers, after all, will be protected by the incremental pricing sections in this bill. So we should not be overly concerned about the impact of deregulation." But as I say, it looks like brain death may have already occurred, and the merciful course of action may be to avoid prolonging the suffering. . . . I intend to put the patient out of his misery in support of Mr. Sharp's resolution.[32]

Following the hearing, the subcommittee by voice vote reported the resolution of disapproval favorably to the full committe, which on May 7, the next day, passed the resolution, also by voice vote. The committee report to accompany H. Res. 655 left no doubt that the commission had been required to issue a Phase II rule. The argument in the report against the rule refocused on the debate on the changed nature of energy markets since the passage of the 1978 law, and recommended that "the motivation for expansion of incremental pricing at this time needs to be reassessed in light of these changed circumstances."[33]

Debate and vote on the resolution occurred on May 20, 1980. Congressman Sharp and many other members raised the problem posed by incremental pricing in light of the drastically changed economic and market conditions in the two years just past. Oil prices had doubled, causing energy prices to increase substantially. Demand had fallen off sharply. Inflation, accompanied by high interest rates, appeared to be pressing the nation into severe recession. Added to all this was the fact that by 1980 the natural gas market was in a period of temporary supply surplus, in contrast to the supply shortages of 1978, thus making the demand-restraint incremental pricing mechanism unnecessary and counterproductive. Some members also lamented the inadequate knowledge, data, and experience available to the commission on the workings of the incremental pricing mechanism, because less than a year had gone by under the Phase I experience. Others voiced concern that the benefits would be very small for the protected class of users, while the burdens on the industrial sector would put some industries at risk during a time of great economic difficulty.

Only Representative Toby Moffett (D, CT) defended the rule. Admitting that the rule was so weak that in fact it might be hard to justify, Moffett argued that "the principle of incremental pricing is at stake here and a weak rule for some use is better than no rule, and a weak rule that can be improved is better than no rule." This was especially true because FERC had made it clear that unless it were pressed to do so by Congress, it would not reissue a new rule under its authority of Section 202. Moffett pointed out that the message from Congress in the debate and vote on the veto would be loud and clear: "Do not come back with another rule, FERC!" By vetoing the rule, he charged, Congress would be backing away from the principle of consumer protection articulated so strongly in the NGPA and its legislative history.[34]

With little other evidence of dissent, the House of Representatives voted 369 to 34 to veto the incremental pricing rule. There is small doubt that the effective result of this action was to change the policy of existing statutory law.[35] It was, in Congressman David Stockman's

(R, MI) words, a way to have "a second look at the policy that
we could not be certain of . . . to correct an error in policy
that would otherwise go into effect regarding the natural
gas market."[36] With such near unanimity on the wisdom of
this action, one might suppose that the normal legislative
response to policy alteration--amending the law--would
have been sufficient to the task of addressing incremental
pricing. The problem was not one of bicameralism, as one
Senate staffer pointed out: "If it had been a two-house
veto, it was highly probable that the Senate would have
followed its sister's actions. The one-house veto allowed
the Senate committee and staff to sigh a collective breath
of relief at not having to pursue the hearing and floor vote
process."[37] Because the incremental pricing idea
originated in Congress, it is equally unlikely that an
amendment overturning the Phase II provision would have
been vetoed by the president. The veto's utility had other
origins.

"It was clear," according to one staff participant in
the lengthy 1978 conference committee deliberations, "that
phased deregulation could not have passed without
incremental pricing to protect consumers. There was
simply no question about that."[38] Incremental pricing was
at the time, however, merely an untested, theoretical idea.
No one knew quite how it would work, or even exactly how it
should be designed. "The legislative veto provision was
used as a way around the incredible technological complexities of the incremental pricing concept."[39] It was a
way of holding out the prospect of consumer protection to
members who insisted on that as a prerequisite for their
support of the phased decontrol while allowing them to
postpone a decision about exactly what incremental pricing
was and how it would work. It did not appear to be
contemplated as a mechanism for dumping the incremental
pricing idea altogether. But a year and a half later
Congress was no more willing and no more able to deal with the
complexities of the incremental pricing concept or with the
problem raised by decontrol, that of balancing industrial
costs versus consumer protection. Indeed, the controversy over gas decontrol was much the same in 1980 as it had
been in 1977-1978. The battle lines between those favoring
and those opposed to deregulation of pricing were similarly
drawn, but it was not at all clear which side might emerge the
winner if the question were reopened in Congress again.
There was a good chance that the carefully crafted, phased
decontrol compromise might fall.

At the April 6 hearing on incremental pricing,
Chairman Dingell warned of what might occur if Congress were
to deal with the incremental gas pricing problem by amending
the NGPA, as H.R. 5862 and S. 2392 proposed to do.

I know that if we go to a bill which would eliminate
incremental pricing . . . we are going to also be going
into the question of natural gas pricing generally.

> We are going to open up the entire Natural Gas Policy
> Act. You are going to find the entire question . . .
> lying before the Congress and lying before the
> subcommittee. . . . If we open the issue up it is not
> going to be just whether we are going to have a repeal of
> the provisions of that statute referring to
> incremental pricing but it is going to relate to the
> entire question of total deregulation of natural
> gas. . . . You might find that you are going to have
> before one body or the other, or maybe both, the
> question of whether or not we are going to reimpose
> regulation because there are some who would like that
> too . . . or we will just embroil ourselves in such
> intolerable controversy the subcommittee not only
> will not be able to deal with the question about which
> you complain . . . but we are not going to be able to deal
> with any of the other energy questions which are very
> difficult and which are bothersome.[40]

The legislative veto provision in the Natural Gas
Policy Act offered members of Congress a conflict-avoidance
route out of the continuing natural gas controversy. The
provision not only narrowed and limited the issue to be
addressed but also provided for expedited procedures for
its consideration by Congress, including a debate confined
to ten hours and a prohibition against amendments to the
resolution itself.[41] There were clear advantages to
Chairman Dingell and others interested in protecting the
hard-fought NGPA compromises in using the legislative veto
as a way to deal with the incremental pricing problem.
Congress was thereby able to respond to industry pressure,
changed circumstances, and even a possible policy error in
the law. But there are real problems for democracy in using
the procedural shortcut to lawmaking offered by the
legislative veto.

The Federal Regulatory Commission Veto
and Democratic Principles

First among the problems for democracy posed by the
legislative veto is the diminished role of the consumer.
Even though the high visibility of the incremental pricing
issue insured broad congressional participation--unlike
the low-visibility issues in the ED and HUD cases--the speed
of the process, combined with limiting the issue, militated
against the effective participation of the less-organized,
less-powerful consumer interests. In the normal slow-
moving legislative process, more time would have been
available for consumer interests to mobilize behind the
rule. Lacking the power and resources of the big industry
lobbies, consumer groups were simply unable to respond
quickly.

The use of the legislative veto in the manner described raises another problem for democratic and constitutional values. It appears clear that the NGPA could not have been enacted without the incremental pricing provision. If the provision could not have been included without also including the legislative veto procedure, as Congress later argued in its amicus curiae brief before the court in the FERC case (Consumers Energy Council of America et al. v. FERC; chapter 2 contains an analysis of the decision), then it seems obvious that the legislative veto has made exercise of the legislative power possible in this case. Exercise of the legislative power, however, was made difficult under the Constitution for a purpose: the requirement of presentation to the president and for concurrence by two legislative bodies representing two different constituencies for lawmaking was meant by the Framers to act as a constraint on the growth of the federal power. If the legislative veto is used as a means to pass a law that would otherwise fail under this constitutional test, it may be that its use is responsible for excessively extending the federal government's powers. The NGPA is by no means the only example of the energy committee's resort to the legislative veto device as a way to postpone difficult and controversial decisions. The Energy Security Act of 1980, which among other things set up the Synfuel Corporation, for example, has more than twenty legislative veto-type provisions.[42] Would the federal government be in the synfuel business today without the legislative veto? For citizens concerned about the intrusiveness of government into their lives, this is a question worth consideration.

To be sure, the legislative veto in the FERC case offered Congress an avenue of escape from a controversial issue. It was able to get rid of an unpopular provision in the law without opening up the whole controversial subject of natural gas policy. But if there indeed was sufficient support in Congress for changing national policy on natural gas pricing, either back to total regulation or to immediate or accelerated decontrol, then the legislative veto may have allowed and encouraged Congress to avoid its responsibility. In this case the legislative veto may have been used to perpetuate a status quo that no longer enjoyed majority support. No doubt life on the Hill was made more pleasant by avoiding the embroilment of members of Congress in a conflict over natural gas pricing policy, but whether democratic and representative values were served as well is certainly debatable.

Yet another problem is raised by the legislative veto as used in the incremental pricing case. The existence of the veto may have stimulated or enabled FERC to develop a weak or flawed rule, thus ensuring its ultimate veto. This was the charge leveled at FERC by consumer groups and by consumer advocates in Congress. It is manifest that the FERC rule with its projected ten-dollar annual saving for a household altered the focus of the debate on incremental pricing; debate no longer centered on balancing the need to encourage new gas supplies against the residential consumer's ability to pay but instead focused on the small saving for the residential consumer against the increased costs to industrial consumers. Would FERC have developed a rule better to protect consumers had it been faced with the certainty of having to live with the rule? Later comments made by the commission indicate that this would have been a quite probable result. The comments are discussed below.

Finally, whatever the merits of the concerns raised by the legislative veto that have been addressed thus far, at the very least one must be concerned about the wasted two years of FERC time and the cost of this manner of lawmaking. The fact that the commission was less than enthusiastic about the possibilities of designing a reasonable Phase II rule was evident almost from the beginning of the rulemaking process. Relations between Congress and FERC were clearly cooperative, and it appears clear that members of the energy subcommittees and their staffs were aware of the commission's problems at the start. As a National Journal article queried at the time, "Was It Really Necessary?"[43] One consumer group charged the whole process "demonstrated the absolute disutility of such procedural shortcuts to effective lawmaking."[44]

The Incremental Pricing Issue
Moves to the Court

About two weeks after the House veto of the Phase II rule, a number of consumer groups petitioned for a rehearing with FERC, asking the commission to make the rule effective in spite of the House veto because the one-house procedure was unconstitutional. In its August 1, 1980, denial of the petition, FERC stated that "sound administrative practice requires the presumption of constitutional validity of the statutes entrusted to this Commission for implementation."[45] Although this action ran contrary to President Carter's order that agencies ignore legislative vetoes, FERC's status as an independent agency exempted it from the president's direct control.

On the same day, fearing that if the veto provision were declared unconstitutional the Phase II rule would take effect, the commission withdrew the rule completely. FERC argued that the commissioners "might well have very serious reservations as to the wisdom of making the Phase II rule effective" because it "had not yet independently evaluated whether the Phase II rule meets the social and economic goals of the Title II incremental pricing program."[46] They could hardly have made more clear their original motives in developing a rule for sacrificial offering to the congressional veto.

Following this action, the consumer groups filed a second petition on September 2, 1980, for a rehearing,

challenging the commission's authority summarily to revoke
the rule; they argued that to revoke FERC should have
followed notice-and-comment provisions of the Administrative Procedure Act (APA). FERC also denied this petition,
and on September 26, 1980, the consumer groups moved to
challenge both the constitutionality of the veto and the
revocation order in court.

On January 29, 1982, the District of Columbia Circuit
Court of Appeals found the revocation order to be invalid
and Section 202(c), the one-house congressional review
provision, to be unconstitutional, and ordered that the
Phase II rule become effective absent further commission
action under provisions of the APA to amend or postpone the
rule. (The basis of these findings is discussed in chapter
2, and thus is not dealt with here in any detail.) The case
is now on appeal to the Supreme Court, and as yet there has
been no implementation of the incremental pricing rule.
Counsel for the consumer groups, Alan B. Morrison, predicts
that FERC will move to postpone the effective date through
notice-and-comment proceedings. Because of the provision
in the rule for a ninety-day delay of its effective date
after the thirty-day congressional review process--which
the agency will read to begin after the court ruling--there
will be ample time to stop the rule before its effective
date.[47]

To the costs incurred, and the time wasted by FERC and
Congress in their charade to develop a rule for sacrifice to
the veto, now must be added the cost and time of the courts as
well as the cost of the lawyers' fees to FERC, Congress, the
Justice Department, gas producers, industry groups, and the
consumer groups, who were all involved in the lawsuit. The
"shortcut" provided by the legislative veto procedure ended
up as a cumbersome and lengthy process. Furthermore, under
provisions of the NGPA, it appears that some sort of Phase II
incremental pricing rule will need to be developed. If
Congress desires to prevent its going into effect--or to
prevent time being wasted on the rulemaking process again--
it will have to amend the law anyway. The only way use of the
legislative veto procedure would become a viable
alternative again would be for the Supreme Court to reverse
the lower-court ruling.

Passive Restraint Rule

In the second case study involving a targeted veto, the
passive restraint rule, the veto effort, as noted before,
failed. In the long run, however, the outcomes have
actually been more successful in stopping the rule from
becoming effective. This is not attributable to the
legislative veto power but rather to the numerous other
avenues short of amendment available to members of Congress
who are bent on delaying or thwarting agency actions
pursuant to statutory rulemaking authority. The tactical

problems members face in using the legislative veto power on a highly visible issue in the absence of an overriding consensus to do so are illustrated by the developments in the passive restraint case., To understand the issue involved, we must go back to the National Traffic and Motor Vehicle Safety Act of 1966.

National Traffic and Motor Vehicle Safety Act of 1966

In the same tradition as the Occupational Safety and Health Act of 1970, which directed the secretary of labor to make the nation's workplaces safe, and the Consumer Product Safety Act of 1972, which directed the Consumer Product Safety Commission to make the nation's consumer products safe, the National Traffic and Motor Vehicle Safety Act of 1966 directed the secretary of transportation to make the nation's motor vehicles safe. Unlike the Natural Gas Policy Act, the National Traffic and Motor Vehicle Safety Act, which was unanimously passed by Congress, has a legislative history apparently free of controversy. Controversy arose later, however, when the secretary of transportation moved to implement the act's broad and vague mandate.

The section of the act bearing on the case study presented here directed the secretary of transportation to establish federal motor vehicle safety standards. In constraining the secretary's discretion to act, Section 103 mandated that "each such Federal motor vehicle safety standard shall be practicable, shall meet the need for motor vehicle safety and shall be stated in objective terms."[48] Guidelines for prescribing standards under this section were couched in broad terms that allow the secretary enormous discretion and latitude. For example, in prescribing standards under Section 103, the secretary was (1) to consider relevant available motor vehicle safety data, (2) to consult with the Vehicle Equipment Safety Commission, (3) to consider whether any such proposed standards are reasonable, practicable, and appropriate for the particular type of motor vehicle, and (4) to consider the extent to which such standards will contribute to the carrying out of the purposes of the act. There was little else in the form of guidance on congressional intent either in the act or its legislative history.

Until 1974 the secretary's authority to issue safety standards under the act was subject to no further constraints—except, of course, review by the courts. In the early 1970s the Ford Motor Company developed a system that required seatbelts to be fastened before a car could be started or that continuously buzzed if seatbelts were not fastened after a car was started. This so-called seatbelt interlock system was then pressed upon the Department of Transportation (DOT) by the company as a "better idea" than the then-existing departmentally proposed passive

passive restraint systems.[49] Responding to this pressure, the Republican administration at DOT issued a standard requiring the interlock system in all 1974 and 1975 model cars. Public reaction was swift, negative, and intense. Congress was deluged with complaints blaming the "hare-brained" scheme on bureaucratic zeal. Somehow in the uproar the auto industry's role was ignored or forgotten.

The congressional reaction to the citizen outcries was to overturn the interlock standard. A provision contained in the House bill but not in the Senate bill appeared in the conference compromise of the Motor Vehicle and School Bus Safety Amendments of 1974; it directed DOT to eliminate the standard requiring the seatbelt interlock system and the continuous buzzer system. The conference committee added a further restriction on the secretary's authority to issue safety standards dealing with occupant restraint systems in the form of a legislative veto provision, which had not appeared in either the House or Senate versions of the bill. Like that in the natural gas case, this legislative veto provision was a conference committee invention. It provided that no occupant restraint system other than a belt system could become effective until after Congress had been given an opportunity to consider such a standard for sixty days of continuous session. During the sixty days Congress could, by concurrent resolution, vote to overturn the standard.[50]

The only time Congress has attempted to use its veto power under this provision occurred in 1977 and involved the passive restraint standard. A bit of history behind this standard is essential to an understanding of the controversy over its implementation.

Passive Restraints

Quite simply, a passive restraint system is one that requires no active participation by a car occupant to make it effective. There are essentially two technologically available ways for instituting such a system. One, the passive belt, was developed by Volkswagen and made available on Volkswagen Rabbits in the mid-1970s; it works by automatically engaging a belt when the door of the car is closed. The second is the so-called air bag or air cushion that is housed under the dashboard of a car and automatically inflates when the car undergoes the sudden jolt of an impact. Prodded by DOT and Congress to begin to develop passive restraint options, American automobile manufacturers reluctantly chose the air-bag alternative. Thus, most of the later furor over the passive restraint rule centered on the air bag.

Air bags were first patented in the early 1950s, and by 1968 Eaton Yale and Towne, Inc., the major air-bag developer, demonstrated to the National Highway Safety Bureau a model that it claimed could be ready for mass production and installation within four years.[51] In June of 1969, DOT issued its first notice of proposed rulemaking for an "Inflatable Occupant Restraint System," with a proposed effective date for the rule of January 1, 1972. The date was later postponed by DOT until 1973, while a court case was heard testing the validity of the department's authority to issue such a rule. The court in this case, Chrysler v. Department of Transportation (472 F.2d 659) concluded that the passive restraint standard was valid and that the air bag was a practical and legal device to meet the performance requirement of the standard, but ordered DOT to revise test specifications and to amend the rule so as not to eliminate convertibles and sports cars.

While the agency responsible within DOT, the National Highway Traffic and Safety Administration (NHTSA), proceeded to modify its test specifications, General Motors (GM) moved to forestall the mandatory-standard approach by offering to include the air bag as an option in the luxury line of its 1974 model cars. Departing from its original projection of one million air-bag-equipped cars--stated during a congressional hearing--GM scaled its estimate down to 150,000. Far fewer than even the second figure were ever produced: about 10,000. In 1976 GM ceased the air-bag option altogether.

Meanwhile, NHTSA's testing continued, congressional hearings pressing for action became an annual event, and car insurance companies actively promoted the passive restraint concept in the hope of lowering the astronomical hospitalization and injury costs of car accidents. Finally, after promising to issue a final rule that year, Secretary of Transportation William Coleman announced a voluntary "demonstration project" to manufacture 500,000 air-bag-equipped cars beginning with the 1978 model year. Within a month, the number became 60,000, and the model year became 1979, based on an agreement Coleman had forged with GM and Ford.

Soon after the Carter administration took over in Washington, newly appointed Secretary of Transportation Brock Adams announced at a press conference that he was voiding the agreement with GM and Ford, and that he would immediately hold a public hearing on the passive restraint systems. In June 1977, following the April hearing, Adams announced his decision to require passive restraints for all new large-size cars by September 1981; for all new medium-size cars by September 1982; and for all new cars by September 1983. At this point the passive restraint issue moved to the congressional arena for consideration under its legislative veto procedure.

The Air-Bag Veto Attempt

Opposition to the air-bag rule was led in the Senate by Robert P. Griffin (R, MI) and in the House by Bud Schuster (R, PA); both introduced resolutions of disapproval to overturn the secretary's action.[52] By the end of August, Schuster's resolution had over 160 cosponsors. In September, hearings were held by the House Subcommittee on Consumer Protection and Finance of the Interstate and Foreign Commerce Committee, and the Senate Subcommittee on Consumers of the Commerce, Science, and Transportation Committee.[53] Both subcommittee chairmen, Representative Bob Eckhardt (D, TX) and Senator Wendell Ford (D, KY), were avid supporters of air bags and of the secretary's passive restraint standard. Spokespersons at the hearings favoring the air bags included public health officials, doctors, and individual insurance companies, as well as the Insurance Institute for Highway Safety, the Epilepsy Foundation, the United Auto Workers, the American Automobile Association, and air-bag manufacturers. Speaking in opposition to the rule were representatives of GM, Ford, American Motors, and manufacturers of seatbelts. Controversy swirled around the scientific and technological validity of various tests made on air-bag effectiveness that had been run by NHTSA, the auto companies, and the insurance industry. Opponents decried the lack of "real-world" data. Supporters pointed out the problem of amassing such data in the absence of air-bag-equipped cars for purchase. Chairman Ford queried, "Do you see any irony in the fact that industry claims more data is needed yet it is impossible to buy a domestically produced automobile in this country at this point in time equipped with an air-cushion restraint system?"[54]

Although the hearing records are replete with reprints and analyses of the scientific findings of the various studies, the actual issues in the controversy were not technological in nature. Rather, they involved economics (protecting the automobile industry) and political philosophy (the government role in regulating car safety). The opposition's philosophical misgivings were expressed by Representative Schuster with his charge that the rule "chips away needlessly at our individual freedom."[55] But opponent Senator Griffin's support instead for a mandatory seatbelt law with misdemeanor charges for failure to abide by it makes the governmental intrusiveness of the air-bag standard pale by comparison. It seems plausible from reading the hearing record that the major impetus for the battle against the air bags came from the powerful and economically pressed automobile industry, which was able to win the support of numerous individual members.

After the hearings were completed, each subcommittee recommended to its full committee that the resolution of disapproval be rejected. In the House, action never went beyond the full committee due to a series of parliamentary maneuvers, including points of order and ignored quorum calls, that delayed and eventually blocked action. With time running out on the sixty-day review time limit, the full committee by a vote of 16-14 finally tabled the resolution on October 12, 1977.

Action in the Senate committee was subjected to similar parliamentary maneuvers, but in this case the opposition wielded this tactical power to force a vote on the resolution. By a vote of 9-7 the full committee agreed to report the resolution to the floor with a negative recommendation. By the time the resolution reached the floor of the Senate on October 12, the House committee had already voted to table the resolution. Because a veto required the resolution to be passed in both houses, the Senate debate and vote was, as Senator Ford pointed out, merely "pro forma."[56] After a lengthy debate rehashing the issues raised in the many days of hearings, the Senate voted 65-31 to table the resolution of disapproval.

Thus, it appears that the air-bag proponents won the war. It was, however, only one battle in the long air-bag war.

After the Veto Failed--The Death of the Air Bags

Following their failed attempt to use the legislative veto to kill the air-bag rule, opponents shifted the battle site to the appropriations committees. There they were successful in attaching riders on the House's Department of Transportation appropriations bills for fiscal years 1979 and 1980, prohibiting the use of any funds to enforce the air-bag rule. Although the Senate bills did not contain a similar provision in either year, the prohibitions survived in the conference compromises both years. At worst, the prohibitions were considered "symbolic slaps" because enforcement funds would not be needed until the fall of 1981.[57] Yet, the action surely sent a message to the auto companies, assuring them that the fight was not yet lost, and probably made likely erosion in their commitment of time, research, and funds in gearing up for implementation of the rule.

Then in 1981 the battle moved back to the authorization committees with attempts to defer the effective dates of the standard, rolling back the implementation date until the model 1983 cars, and making small-model cars first in line for the requirement rather than the large-model cars provided in the rule. Requirements for air bags in all models remained scheduled for the 1984 model year.[58] This provision was contained in the conference compromise. After winning easy approval in the Senate before the 1980 election recess, the conference compromise became bogged down in the House. When the lame-duck 96th Congress returned after elections, the House was unable to break its deadlock over the transportation authorization bill containing the new passive restraint schedule. The 96th Congress adjourned <u>sine die</u> without completing action on the bill, thus effectively killing the compromise version.

Anti-air-baggers were finally successful with the arrival of regulatory reform, Reagan style, at NHTSA. In November of 1981, new NHTSA Administrator Raymond A. Peck, Jr., overriding staff recommendations and a sheaf of analyses, decided to withdraw the air-bag standard altogether.[59] The availability of passive restraints is now a matter of the car manufacturers' voluntary efforts to make them available as an option. If experience over the last decade and a half is any indication, air bags are unlikely to appear in car models in the foreseeable future.

Targeted Use of the Veto: An Assessment

Many members of Congress who oppose extending the legislative veto to cover all rulemaking nevertheless argue that if it is targeted to highly visible controversial issues, it enables Congress to reconcile differences that would prevent the enactment of legislation. In the two case studies presented in this chapter, some problems with this approach have been exposed.

In the FERC case, it became clear that postponement of difficult technological choices did not necessarily mean that they were any easier to deal with later. The technology remained uncertain, and Congress remained bitterly divided over the question of gas regulation versus gas deregulation. Incorporation of the legislative veto device had made possible amassing sufficient support for the bill's enactment but the compromise was later nullified by the focusing on a single aspect of a broad and complex program that had emerged from much give and take by many affected interests. Use of the legislative veto to aid lawmaking in this manner raises serious questions in light of our democratic principles.

If members of Congress lend their support to bills arrived at by compromise in the belief that their position can later be protected by using the legislative veto power, the air-bag case might serve as a warning. If there is sufficient resistance to use of the veto, and especially if the committee chairmen involved are opposed, there are ample parliamentary devices available to them to stall or thwart action on the veto--especially since action must be completed within definite and short, in congressional terms, time limits. Moreover, with only one issue to address, a minority is less likely to have the maneuverability to force action in its favor. In other words, powerful and organized interests are not always the winners in a legislative veto battle.

Notes

1. In 1960 natural gas production equaled 13 trillion cubic feet; by 1970 it had soared to 22 trillion cubic feet; but by 1976 production had declined to 19.6 trillion cubic feet. For further elaboration on the history of natural gas regulation, see Michael J. Malbin, Unelected Representatives: Congressional Staff and the Future of Representative Government (New York: Basic Books, 1980), pp. 208-36; Paul W. MacAvoy and Robert S. Pendyck, Price Controls and the Natural Gas Shortage (Washington, DC: American Enterprise Institute, 1975), pp. 11-16.

2. 124 Cong. Rec. H13413 (daily ed.), October 14, 1978.

3. H.R. 6831, 95th Cong., 1st sess., 1977.

4. The incremental pricing concept was developed in 1974 by Leslie J. Goldman, aide to Senator Adlai E. Stevenson (D, IL).

5. For examples of the heated nature of this debate, see 123 Cong. Rec. 25897-26170 (August 1, 1977), and 123 Cong. Rec. 26448-82 (August 3, 1977).

6. Interview, staff member, Senate Energy and Natural Resources Committee, May 21, 1981.

7. U.S. Congress, House, Subcommittee on Energy and Power of the Committee on Interstate and Foreign Commerce, Hearings on the Phase II Incremental Pricing of Natural Gas, 96th Cong, 2d sess., April 3 and May 6, 1980, p. 118. Hereafter cited as 1980 Phase II Hearings.

8. Ibid., p. 117.

9. Carter's April 1977 pronouncement of his intention to attack the nation's energy problems with the fervor of the "moral equivalent of war" had by summer of 1978 become bogged down in Congress. About the only piece of legislation still standing any chance of passage that had not been completely gutted by congressional amendments was the natural gas pricing proposal now dubbed "the Energy Bill."

10. 92 Stat. 3371, Title II--Incremental Pricing, Section 201(a), (b), and (c).

11. See, for example, the debate on the final day of passage in the Senate, at 124 Cong. Rec. 31817-47 (September 27, 1978).

12. 124 Cong. Rec. S15220 (daily ed.), September 15, 1978.

13. The vote was 207 to 206; 124 Cong. Rec. H12810.

14. Ibid., pp. H13114-15.

15. Statement released to the press by Dingell on May 2, 1978, quoted by Toby Moffett, at 126 Cong. Rec. H3846 (daily ed.), May 20, 1980.

16. Ibid.

17. 44 Federal Register 57726 (October 5, 1979).

146

18. At the same time that FERC adopted the Phase I rule, it adopted an exemption to the rule delaying the three-tier pricing system provided within the rule and provided instead for a single-tier system tied to the lowest No. 6 high-sulphur fuel oil price. The exemption was subsequently extended through 1981. Both amendments to the Phase I rule, though not the rule itself, were subject to congressional review and possible veto—neither was vetoed by Congress.

19. 44 Federal Register 67170.

20. 1980 Phase II Hearings, p. 319.

21. Ibid., p. 207.

22. Ibid., pp. 261-74. (The commission devoted thirteen pages in the final rule documentation to explaining "The Inability of Title II to Achieve Marketing Ordering.")

23. Ibid., p. 2

24. Editorial, "Cheap Gas for Brooklyn," Wall Street Journal, reprinted in 124 Cong. Rec. 31829 (September 27, 1978).

25. 1980 Phase II Hearings, p. 359.

26. Ibid., p. 202.

27. Ibid., see especially pp. 5, 27, 45, 105, 124.

28. Ibid., p. 151.

29. Ibid., p. 162.

30. Quotations in the last two paragraphs are found in 1980 Phase II Hearings, pp. 200, 363, 367, 375, 381.

31. Ibid., p. 382.

32. Ibid., pp. 380-81.

33. U.S. Congress, House, Committee on Interstate and Foreign Commerce, Report to Accompany H. Res. 655, 96th Cong., 2d sess., May 12, 1980, pp. 3-5, 8.

34. 126 Cong. Rec. H3839-55 (daily ed.), May 20, 1980.

35. The District of Columbia Circuit Court certainly agreed that the veto had this effect. The decision held "that the veto of the Phase II rule effectively changed the law by altering the scope of FERC's discretion and preventing an otherwise valid regulation from taking effect." Consumers Energy Council of America v. FERC, 673 F.2d 425, January 29, 1982.

36. 126 Cong. Rec. H3841 (daily ed.), May 20, 1980.

37. Interview, staff member, Senate Energy and Natural Resources Commitee, May 21, 1981.

38. Ibid.

39. Ibid.

40. 1980 Phase II Hearings, p. 116.

41. The NGPA's congressional review procedure contained several other provisions for expediting consideration of the resolution, including directions to the speaker of the House and the president of the Senate to "immediately refer" a resolution to a committee; provisions for discharge from committees after twenty days; highly privileged motions to consider the resolutions on the

floor; and prohibitions against tabling and reconsidering votes.

42.   Energy Security Act of 1980, 94 Stat. 611.

43.   Christopher Madison, "Was It Really Necessary?" National Journal, May 24, 1980, p. 866.

44.   126 Cong. Rec. H3850 (daily ed.), May 20, 1980, reprint of a letter from Public Citizen.

45.   FERC Order Denying Rehearing on Revocation of Amendments, Order No. 80 (October 2, 1980), reprinted in 45 Federal Register 71780 (October 30, 1980).

46.   Ibid.

47.   Telephone interview, Alan B. Morrison, February 16, 1982.

48.   80 Stat. 718, Section 103(a).

49.   U.S. Congress, Senate, Subcommittee on Consumers of the Committee on Commerce, Science, and Transportation, Hearings on the Passive Restraint Rule, 95th Cong., 1st sess., September 8, 9, 14, 21, 1977, p. 180. Hereafter cited as Senate Passive Restraint Hearings.

50.   U.S. Congress, House, Committee on Conference, Report to Accompany S. 335, Report No. 93-1452, 93d Cong., 2d sess., October 8, 1974, p. 6108.

51.   The history of the air bags that follows is adapted from an Insurance Institute for Highway Safety Report reprinted in Senate Passive Restraint Hearings, pp. 152-55.

52.   H. Con. Res. 273 and S. Con. Res. 31, 95th Cong., 1st sess., 1977.

53.   See Senate Passive Restraint Hearings and U.S. Congress, House, Subcommittee on Consumer Protection and Finance of the Interstate and Foreign Commerce Committee, Hearings on Passive Restraint Hearings, p. 43.

54.   See Senate Passive Restraint Hearings, p. 43.

55.   Ibid., p. 129.

56.   U.S. Congress, House, Subcommittee on Rules of the House Rules Committee, Studies on the Legislative Veto, committee print, prepared by the Congressional Research Service, 96th Cong., 2d sess., February 1980, pp. 574-78.

57.   Judy Sarosohn, "Opponents of Air Bags Threaten House Battle Over Compromise Rule," Congressional Quarterly, August 9, 1980, p. 2294.

58.   Ibid.

59.   Michael Wines, "Reagan's Reforms Are Full of Sound and Fury, But What Do They Signify?" National Journal, January 16, 1982, p. 98. Convinced that Peck's actions were illegal, State Farm Mutual Automobile Insurance Company and a group of other auto insurance interests petitioned for review of the recision order. On June 1, 1982, the U.S. Court of Appeals for the District of Columbia ruled that NHTSA's actions had been "arbitrary and illogical" (State Farm Mutual Automobile Insurance Co. v. DOT, 680 F.2d 206). The case is now on appeal to the U.S. Supreme Court.

6

The Legislative Veto of Regulations: Consequences for Democratic Policymaking

Among advocates of the legislative veto, the prevailing diagnosis of the American regulatory malaise is that regulatory agencies fail to follow the law. The prime sponsor of the legislative veto, Representative Elliott Levitas, argues that broad-scale adoption of the veto offers "the people, through their elected representatives, an input into and a control over the rules that govern their lives."[1] The legislative veto, he claims, makes the rulemaking process more democratic, more open, more accountable, and more responsible. It also gives Congress a powerful lever to insure agency adherence to statutory mandates. Furthermore, the attention of Congress itself is refocused on the making of regulations, encouraging the review and excision of offensive rules before their adoption. Thus, the legislative veto, its proponents maintain, enables Congress to prevent the promulgation of bad regulations by overzealous bureaucrats.

If absence of statutory guidance instead of—or in addition to—bureaucratic excess is seen as the regulatory problem, the legislative veto is offered by its sponsors as an equally efficacious solution. In support of this, they reason that because the legislative veto gives Congress "the ultimate responsibility for regulations which flow from the laws," it encourages, even forces, Congress to draft laws more carefully.[2] This more precise guidance would do away with the problem-causing vague delegations to agencies.

Not all supporters of the legislative veto over rulemaking forecast such promising results. Some defend it on more pragmatic grounds. In the opinion of Government Specialist Louis Fisher of the Congressional Research Service, selective use of the veto offers Congress an expeditious means of resolving divergent points of view.[3] When Congress is not ready to establish exact policy, either because of controversy over policy choices within the body itself, or because of unknown or unpredictable results of a particular policy choice, the veto allows for a flexible delegation of rulemaking to the executive. Without the veto, according to James Sundquist, Congress would probably withhold delegation, instructing the administrative agency to return with proposed legislation rather than proposed rules.⁴ This, both Fisher and Sundquist argue, would mean less power for the executive, greater delays, and a more convoluted legislative process.

The supposed purpose of the legislative veto is, then, really twofold. On the one hand, it is promoted as a democratic device of control to enable Congress to make sure that unelected bureaucrats follow the intent of the law in their rulemaking activities. On the other hand, it is promoted as a useful mechanism for conflict resolution within Congress to enable Congress to give the executive agencies the necessary leeway to deal with complex regulatory problems. As the case studies presented in this analysis show, however, congressional use of the legislative veto power has thus far accomplished neither of these objectives. The Department of Housing and Urban Development (HUD) and the Department of Education (ED) veto provisions, which appear to have been enacted as a means to bind the agencies closely to statutory intent, were actually exercised to impose a negotiation process between the agency and subcommittee members and their staffs. The process was not used to insure adherence to the law but rather as a means to amend the law or to achieve the staff or subcommittee's interpretation of the law by dictating the content of agency rules. The legislative veto in the Federal Energy Regulatory Commission (FERC) case may, indeed, have enabled Congress to delegate a responsibility to the executive branch that it would have been unable to do without the veto. The veto did not, however, aid in resolution of conflict within Congress; it merely allowed Congress to postpone resolution to another day.

The Legislative Veto and Democratic Control

Addition of legislative veto power over housing and education rulemaking procedures has, to be sure, caused a change in the nature of regulatory decision making in these policy arenas. The change, however, has not been in the direction of a more open and democratic process predicted by legislative veto proponents. Instead, regulatory decision making in the housing and education cases has been moved toward a more closed process best characterized by the distributive arenas of subgovernment politics.

Move to Distributive Arenas

In subgovernment policymaking Congress is able to deal with difficult redistributive governmental policies by converting them into discrete distributive issues. By disaggregating policy into small segments and limiting the number of participants, Congress can give relief from the costs of redistributive policy to disadvantaged interests without appearing to withdraw congressional support from the broader social goals legislatively embraced. The HUD case studies illustrate congressional use of the legislative veto to accomplish such an end in relation to the goals of fair housing and energy efficiency.

In the spatial deconcentration regulation case, public-housing construction firms and suburban officials were "protected" from the costs of pursuing the congressionally mandated goal of providing fair housing opportunities for minorities in publicly funded housing. This was accomplished by confining the issue to a single agency rule and by a sub rosa review process that involved only a few members of one congressional committee. Protection of special-interest groups from the costs of statutorily mandated social goals is equally evident in the thermal standards case. In a review process completely lacking in quality and thoroughness, the committee simply accepted the word of the powerful masonry industry and, in consequence, exempted it from the HUD-developed insulation requirements.

Use of the legislative veto in such a manner raises questions of both procedural and substantive fairness. Recent efforts by Congress and the courts to open up the rulemaking process have been aimed at protecting all interests involved--at preventing "deals" that exclude certain parties. For example, Congress has directed some agencies to solicit views from specific groups, to provide opportunities for oral testimony, to allow rebuttals to testimony by groups with a stake in the matter at issue, and so forth. Congress has even gone so far in many cases as to provide funding to enable groups and individuals who might be affected by an agency's rulemaking to participate in notice-and-comment rulemaking procedures if they cannot otherwise afford to do so. All these "sunshine" efforts have aimed at assuring procedural equitability, that is, at assuring a reasoned decision-making procedure that is based on a fairly compiled and representative record. In the HUD rulemaking procedures, all affected parties had the opportunity to be heard. In the congressional committee's thermal standards and spatial deconcentration review procedures, some interests were excluded. If protecting the interests of the "people" means protecting suburban and construction people at the expense of blacks and other minorities, or protecting the masonry industry people at the expense of the other building-materials industries people and the consumer, then the legislative veto has accomplished its purpose. But affording special advantages to certain private interests because of their superior financial resources or influence is not typically understood to be a goal of democratic government. It is, however, a typical tendency of the distributive nature of subgovernment policymaking.

It is true that access to members of Congress may be simpler in that one's representative or senator is relatively easy to reach, while it may take more effort to track down the responsible "nameless" bureaucrat. Access, however, is not equivalent to political "clout," and clout is the essential ingredient in motivating a busy member of Congress to spend time on a legislative veto proceeding involving low-visibility regulations--as were the HUD regulations in these case studies. The most likely result of expansion of the legislative veto to such low-visibility regulatory policy areas is an enormous increase in special-interest pleading from powerful lobbyists who have lost their case or fear losing their case at the agency, and who have the necessary power and financial resources to pressure members or their staffs into action. It is unlikely that those who would speak for the general interest--it is the public that is the intended beneficiary of much of the current governmental regulatory effort, i.e., to provide a cleaner environment, a safer workplace, consumer protection from harmful products or fraudulence, and a more open political process--would have enough notice of, or be sufficiently organized to participate effectively in, the "quicky" proceedings of legislative veto reviews. This raises the problem of actual, as well as procedural, fairness, especially in cases where disproportionate influence with the committee and staff is exercised by the interest to be regulated, as was true in the HUD and FERC cases. The outcome of the legislative review process over the spatial deconcentration proposal, the thermal regulations, and the incremental gas-pricing rule was to undermine the directives to regulate enacted into law by the full Congress. Modifications to previously agreed-upon policy decisions were made to protect powerful interests at the expense of the general interest.

Off-the-record, closed-door negotiations over the substance of policy is another characteristic of subgovernment politics. The case studies presented here show this to be the result of the negotiation power that accompanies the legislative veto. HUD rulemaking under its legislative review process, for example, has demonstrated this tendency. Most major regulations developed by HUD since adoption of the legislative veto review process in 1978 have been revised as a result of objections raised by individual members of Congress or committee staffs. Most staff comments have been informal, in other words, unrecorded. Furthermore, the waiver system included in the HUD veto procedure has been used for off-the-record, quid pro quo trades in a new form of logrolling, not among the fellow members of Congress but between committee leadership and the department. The power to hold off the signing of a waiver request has enabled committee leadership to bring about changes in the rule in question or other pending regulations in return for congressional signatures.

Unrecorded negotiations between agency personnel and committee staff patently played a major role in the development of regulations to implement Title IX's ban on sex discrimination as well. Comments on other education issues from the education oversight committees, especially from House Committee Chairman Perkins, were clearly expected to be taken by the Department of Education as directives from Congress. Institutionalization of a process to expedite communications between the department and its oversight committees following the 1980 legislative veto confrontations gives evidence of the department's intention to consult much more with the committees over the content of regulations in the future. Closer ties between agency staff and congressional staff occasioned by the legislative veto review power may, in fact, insure that regulations will be altered, changed, or eliminated in response to pressure from "elected" members of Congress or their staffs. There is no assurance, however, that this review and interpretation of the law by individual legislators or their staffs will have the same outcome as an equivalent review by the full Congress. The unrepresentative nature of subcommittee membership is reflective of the congressional selection process, which tends to match committee assignment to constituent service needs—a tendency that is especially true of the substantive committees most involved in regulatory oversight—further compounds the problem. Indeed, the result of the negotiation power exercised by subcommittee members and the staff may be to undermine the intent of the Congress as a whole. The expansion of eligibility for basic education grants far beyond that anticipated by the original enabling legislation—as a result of committee pressure—is indicative of the subversion.

Further, when the legislative veto power is used to eliminate a rule—either overtly, as in the FERC case, or covertly, as in the spatial deconcentration case—the result is a policy void. When members are unsure or cannot agree about what should be done about pressing social and economic problems, the legislative veto enables them to "paper over sticky issues by assuring themselves another shot after the regulations are drafted."[5] Just as Fisher, Sundquist, and others argue, the legislative veto may enable Congress to delegate authority to the executive to do something about the problem at hand, but, if the veto is later used completely or selectively to negate executive branch efforts to do something, it not only blurs accountability and responsibility for government action but quite possibly negates policy and program objectives entirely.

Use of the legislative veto as a means for committees, individual members of Congress, or congressional staff to impose their own interpretations of policy or desires for policy changes raises various problems for democratic values. The regional and special interests represented by

individual senators and representatives are expected to
pass through a "constitutional averaging process based on a
specific, preestablished weighting system designed to cut
across potential factional interests."[6] By requiring
majority support from both houses as well as the signature
of the president to enact each piece of legislation, the
goals of a government in which national concerns
predominate are protected. These constitutional requirements for legislative action were meant by the Framers to
prevent the legislature from precipitating into dominating
factions.[7] Extension or alteration of constitutionally
enacted programs and policies by legislative veto power
exercised by narrowly interested subcommittees and their
staffs work to promote, not to rise above, factional
interests. This can have, and has had in the case studies
presented here, the effect of undermining national
governmental goals and priorities expressed in the programs
and policies of duly enacted law.

Committee and Staff Power Aggrandizement

Another result of applying the legislative veto to
rulemaking is that it transfers power from agencies and the
administrative hierarchy to congressional committee
members and professional staff. In their earlier study,
Bruff and Gelhorn found that the chief effect of the
legislative veto was an increase in the power of
congressional subcommittees and their staffs and an
increase in the practice of negotiating over the substance
of rules.[8] Evidence from the HUD and ED case studies
further substantiates this. In both cases, the
legislative veto was used to enable subcommittee members
and subcommittee staff to participate prospectively in
executive rulemaking processes. It is especially
apparent from evidence in the ED case that subcommittee
staff became involved as effective administrative decision
makers in the department's rulemaking process--not on equal
footing with agency staff but, as a result of the potential
for a legislative veto, a powerful and often decisive final
arbiter of the substance of agency rules. To be sure, the
heavy workloads and time pressures of both congressional
staff and subcommittee members prevent such involvement
from being constant. Like much of congressional oversight
of executive action, the legislative veto negotiation
process is initiated <u>ad hoc</u> by constituent complaints.
The occasional nature of the intrusion does not make it less
objectionable, though, especially in light of the
procedural and substantive fairness problems raised by the
financial power and influence inequities inherent in the
reality of who can and will motivate members and their staff
to act.

Since most of the regulatory product does not command the front page, much of the congressional involvement will, in reality, be performed not by members of Congress but by congressional staff. This could hardly be more clear than it was in the ED case. Congressional staff, however, are just as "unelected" and "nameless" as their executive bureaucratic counterparts. In light of recent studies chronicling the rise in power of congressional staff and the loose, sometimes nonexistent, level of management and control exercised over staff by their elected congressional masters, it is reasonable to conclude that they are subject to even less control than are executive bureaucrats whose rulemaking activities are at least constrained by provisions of the Administrative Procedure Act and other requirements for procedural fairness. With allegiance usually specifically tied to an individual member and his or her reelection prospects, or, even more specifically, to staff future employment opportunities, the motivation behind staff pressures to alter the content of rules is necessarily suspect.

Even if Congress were to undertake a thorough, unbiased review confined to insuring agency adherence to statutory intent, as the House education subcommittee allegedly did in its review of the rules implementing the 1978 Education Amendments, the legislative veto would raise problems of accountability and responsibility. If Congress were to extend this concept to all agency rulemaking, a comprehensive review could be accomplished only by a vast expansion of congressional staff. To provide the necessary expertise to review much of the regulatory product, the staff would need to include scientific, economic, and technological experts-- essentially, small versions of the executive agencies themselves. The regularized and repetitive routine of such an undertaking would mean that this increased staff would quickly become institutionalized and bureauc- ratized. Such a counter-bureaucracy strategy would soon evolve into an equal problem of control for Congress.

The Legislative Veto and Conflict Resolution

Use of the legislative veto to facilitate the amassing of sufficient congressional support for legislation to propose or renew governmental programs and policymaking authority has been suggested, by many, as the primary value of the device. If Congress were to be prevented from using the legislative veto by court action that declared the veto unconstitutional, those who invest the veto with the conflict-resolution function raise the spectre of loss of power to the executive or the congressional imposition of even more objectionable constraints over delegations of power to the executive branch. In the past, subscribers to this view have cautioned congressional self-restraint in recourse to the legislative veto expedient, usually recommending that it be applied only to important presidential-level decisions and proposals. Legislative vetoes over presidential organization plans, arms sales proposals, exercise of the war power, and emergency gas rationing plans have typically been cited as necessary and proper veto uses. Until recently, defense of the legislative veto from this camp has not extended to the across-the-board, generic veto or to broad-scale expansion of the legislative veto to blanket agency rulemaking authority. Its proved utility as a lubricant to reduce the high levels of friction within the halls of the Capitol that are created as members of Congress try to develop and pass legislation addressing social and economic needs has caused its popularity to soar, however. This has been especially evident since the 95th Congress (1977-1978). Passage in the Senate on March 24, 1982, by an overwhelming majority (69-25) of a two-house, generic legislative veto provision to cover almost all regulations issued by government agencies is only the most recent example of the growing proclivity in Congress for the legislative veto solution.[9]

Perhaps the best illustration of the apparent use of a legislative veto provision as a means for Congress to deal with its internal conflicts may be the case of the Federal Trade Commission. Action regarding the commission's rulemaking under the legislative veto authority added by the Federal Trade Commission Improvements Act of 1980 has come too late to be included as a complete case study in this research. A brief analysis of events thus far is nonetheless useful in addressing the utility of using the veto as a means for Congress to resolve conflicts.

The Federal Trade Commission Example

The Federal Trade Commission (FTC) is not an agency that spews out hundreds of rules per year. In fact, of the more than twenty trade regulations rules (TRRs) that have been proposed by the commission since the 1974 Magnuson-Moss Act first conferred explicit rulemaking authority on the FTC, by the end of 1982 only three had been promulgated as final rules. This low rate of rule production is due, in part, to the time-consuming, formalized rulemaking procedure imposed on the FTC by the Magnuson-Moss Act, and in part, to the controversial nature of the areas over which the FTC has chosen to institute its rulemaking efforts. Rulemaking proceedings conducted by the commission to develop regulations for the funeral home industry, for the insurance industry, for used-cars sales, and for children's television advertising have been vehemently attacked by the public as well as by many members of Congress.

Controversy over the commission's regulatory role prevented Congress from agreeing upon reauthorization legislation for the FTC in 1977, 1978, and 1979. For those years the FTC existed on continuing authorization resolutions while members of Congress battled over what its powers should be. A majority in the House favored attaching a one-house legislative veto over all FTC rulemaking authority as a means for Congress to control the commission's rulemaking activities. Prevailing sentiment in the Senate remained opposed to the veto, favoring, instead, withdrawing from the FTC its authority to regulate in specific areas. In May 1980, after the latest continuing authorization lapsed, effectively putting the FTC "out of business" for a day, both houses finally agreed to accept a conference compromise that included a two-house, ninety-day legislative veto provision. There is little doubt that inclusion of the legislative veto played a decisive role in allowing Congress to reach agreement over the FTC reauthorization legislation. On February 28, 1980, the House, by close to a two-thirds majority, voted to direct its conferees to "hold fast" to the one-house legislative veto provision contained in the House bill.[10] In the words of one congressman, "A legislative veto will be included or else there will be no FTC bill."[11] The clear message to those supportive of the FTC and its rulemaking role was that the legislative veto was the price they would have to pay.

By accepting the legislative veto, FTC supporters were able to insure that the conference compromise allowed the commission to continue its rulemaking proceedings in several areas that had been expressly eliminated in either the House or Senate versions of the reauthorization legislation. For example, the House bill contained restrictions preventing the FTC from regulating the funeral home industry or investigating the insurance industry for the purpose of developing regulations. The Senate bill contained a similar restriction on FTC action aimed at the insurance industry; did not forbid regulation of the funeral home industry; but targeted children's television advertising, used-cars sales, and trade group industry standards as areas specifically off limits for FTC rulemaking activities.[12] The legislative veto offered Congress a means to avoid deciding what the FTC should regulate.

Soon after Congress voted itself veto power over FTC regulations, the commission announced its intention to promulgate a final rule for regulating the funeral industry--this decision was made because the commission believed that the funeral rule was the most "congressional veto proof" of all the FTC's controversial rule initiatives.[13]

Internal commission politics involving Reagan's newly appointed chairman, James C. Miller III, and Timothy

I. Muris, the new Bureau of Consumer Protection chief,
quickly altered the commission's plans, however. The
funeral rule was moved to the "back burner"--where it
remained until the spring of 1982--in favor of pressing
ahead on a used-cars-sales rule. Whether the decision was
tied to the new administration's deregulatory strategy
remains unknown. It is clearly evident, however, that the
used-car and automobile industry, which has a more
organized and powerful national lobby than the funeral
industry, was far more capable of mounting a veto fight in
Congress.

In the 1975 Magnuson-Moss Act, Congress directed the
FTC to develop a rule to regulate the sales and warranty
practices in the used-cars business if the commission
determined regulation to be "necessary."[14] After
rulemaking proceedings lasting more than five years, the
commission published a final rule on September 10, 1981,
requiring a dealer to attach a sticker to a used car stating
whether there was a warranty and listing any major known
defects. Protection from future liability was afforded
the dealer by a statement on the sticker noting that there
might be defects unknown to the dealer. It did not require
the dealer to inspect the car nor to have it inspected--a
claim later erroneously made by used-car dealers in their
campaign to force Congress to veto the regulation.
Commissioner Patricia P. Bailey's cost estimates were about
eighteen cents for printing the sticker plus the cost of
filling it out. The rule was a watered-down version of
earlier commission proposals that had offered substantially more protection to potential buyers.[15] Whether the
version offered any protection at all to the consumer is
certainly debatable.

In spite of the FTC's apparent efforts to come up with a
rule that could survive a congressional veto review,
several resolutions of disapproval were quickly introduced
in both houses. As a result of a series of parliamentary
maneuvers by Senator Robert Packwood (R, OR), an actual veto
in 1981 was avoided. Part of the maneuvering involved "an
agreement" to adjourn the first session of the 97th Congress
sine die on December 20, 1981--one day short of the required
ninety-day review period. The effective result of this
action was a "pocket veto" of the used-cars rule.

In January 1982, when the 97th Congress reconvened for
its second session, the used-cars rule was resubmitted
"automatically" and the ninety-day review period began
anew.[16] Despite a concerted effort by consumer groups to
defend the rule--an effort that resulted in literally
hundreds of supportive articles and editorials in
newspapers and by the broadcast media around the country--
it was overwhelmingly vetoed by both houses of Congress.[17]
As one observer noted, "The used car lobby is said to be so
strong that no manner of importuning can persuade Congress
not to veto the rule."[18] Exasperated staffers at the
commission have voiced their concern: "If the FTC can't

successfully write <u>this</u> rule, can it write <u>any</u> rule?"[19]
And if it cannot, then the authority granted by Congress to
the FTC seems at best a hollow delegation.

Inclusion of the legislative veto to enable Congress
to pass a piece of legislation--as evidenced in the case of
the Federal Trade Commission--leads to several tentative
conclusions. The legislative veto may well facilitate a
congressional decision to delegate to the executive branch,
but it does not resolve conflict within Congress itself.
Because agreement in Congress on the need for regulation and
the direction that regulation should take has not been
reached, delegation of authority accompanied by
legislative veto restraint tends to be defined in a broad,
open-ended, even vague manner. Thus, little in the way of
guidance on congressional intent is provided to the agency.
It is not flexibility that is delegated so much as
uncertainty. "Conflict resolution" by this method might
best be termed the "we'll-deal-with-it-later" mentality.
As to regulation of used-cars sales, the passage of time did
not work to lessen conflict. This was also true in the case
of FERC's incremental gas-pricing rule.

Focusing review on single issues rather than on an
agency's regulatory mandate in its entirety--as happened in
the case of the Federal Trade Commission--does allow,
however, for containment of conflict within Congress. The
forces in opposition need only to convince a sufficient
number of the members of Congress that a particular rule is
too burdensome. Responsibility is then left with the
agency to develop a better rule. No guidance need be
offered by Congress as to what might make a better rule.

In the belief that some legislative action--any
legislative action--is better than no legislative action,
the legislative veto is promoted as a necessary and useful
device for dealing with policy conflicts within Congress.
Little is gained by the executive, the citizenry, or
Congress when it is used to hide unresolved, often
unresolvable conflict. Covering up controversial and
unresolved issues with the symbols of agreement does not
make them vanish. In fact, the legislative veto appears to
keep both Congress and the executive from resolving such
issues.

It is insufficient to hold out the threat of other more
deleterious congressionally imposed restraints that would
be applied to executive regulatory actions if the veto
provisions were prohibited. In the same years that the
legislative veto has increased in popularity as a means for
Congress to control the executive, Congress has employed
its other available mechanisms of control with equal
enthusiasm. For example, in 1970 only twelve programs were
subject to an annual authorization process. By 1978 this
number had increased to thirty programs, and by 1980 fully a
quarter of the legislative output provided for expiring
authorizations.[20] Appropriations riders, another "worse

fate" for the executive that Fisher argues would be used in the absence of the legislative veto, have exhibited similar surges of growth during the past decade. In 1977, for example, Congress passed 172 general provision limitations couched in fiscal terms. In 1980 Congress passed 207 of these appropriations riders--a 20 percent increase in three years.[21] Many of these fiscal limitations and annual authorization provisions were aimed at the very agencies that were saddled with legislative veto review provisions. When the legislative veto failed to eliminate the air-bag rule, opponents quickly resorted to an appropriations rider prohibition. Annual authorizations were already a reality for the Department of Housing and Urban Development before Congress added its legislative veto review process over the department's rules. Congress has not used the legislative veto instead of other devices in its arsenal of weapons to restrain the executive branch; it has used the veto in addition to its other alternatives.

The Legislative Veto and the Rulemaking Process

The case studies presented here provide no evidence in support of the proposition that legislative vetoes will increase democratic control over government regulation. Neither do they substantiate the claim that vetoes can be used to resolve policy conflicts within Congress on regulatory issues. More to the point, evidence from the case studies indicates that the legislative veto causes additional problems for the rulemaking process. First, by delaying the development of rules, the veto has caused increased uncertainty for regulated groups and the public. Second, the legislative veto review process has meant increased workloads for both Congress and the administrative agencies, with few if any positive effects on the regulatory product. Finally, the constitutional check of agency discretion provided by the judiciary branch is undermined by the negotiation process that accompanies most legislative veto review procedures.

Delay, Uncertainty, and Confusion

Legislative veto review delays caused special problems for the grant programs at HUD and ED. Both departments were faced with the need to develop regulations to inform grant applicants of the eligibility and selection criteria the agency would apply in deciding who would receive funds. Rules had to be proposed in accordance with public notice requirements of the Administrative Procedure Act or of statutory provisions applied to individual programs, which ranged from thirty to ninety days. Final rules needed to be issued in time for applicants to follow them in developing grant proposals. Enough time also needed to be provided for the department's selection process. All of these had to be accomplished before the end of the fiscal year (September 30) or funding authorizations would lapse. In addition, Congress made major changes in HUD's grant programs each year in its annual authorization bill, often not completing action on the bill until late in November of even December. This left the agency with ten months or less to complete its rulemaking before the September fiscal- year deadline. ED, too, was faced with this problem, although with a five-year reauthorization cycle the effect of the foreshortening was confined to programs under that year's reauthorization schedule. Proponents of the legislative veto argue that its thirty-, sixty-, or ninety-day delay is of little significance when compared to the lengthy time frame of most agency rulemaking procedures. They fail, however, to differentiate the effect of the legislative veto delay when applied to the tight time schedules of grant agencies facing annual award constraints and the rulemaking proceedings that last literally years, as, for example, in the FTC's used-cars rule proceedings.

The ninety-day congressional review of the used-cars rule actually covered 115 days before Congress "pocket vetoed" it by adjourning in 1981, and 272 days before the final veto of the rule on May 20, 1982. Bruff and Gelhorn cite a similar example in their study involving the 94th Congress, when it adjourned before the review period for the Federal Elections Commission's rules to govern the 1976 election had expired.[22]

Another example of the effect of the veto review delay is provided by FTC's amendment to its games-of-chance rule, which governs practices in the grocery and gasoline retailing industries. Even though the "rule" in this case was only an amendment to an existing rule, it had to undergo the legislative veto review process. The purpose of the change was to ease the compliance burden by modifying the public posting and record-keeping provision in the original rule. Nearly a year elapsed from the time the commission issued the final rule change in August 1980 until it was able to be made effective in July 1981. The delay was due to a veto review procedure made much longer by adjournment sine die of the 96th Congress in December 1980. In this case an agency effort to lessen the regulatory burden on businesses was held up for almost a year by the veto review power.[23]

Increased Workloads and Shift in Agendas

Administrators at both HUD and ED complained of the vexatiousness of scheduling rulemaking around congressional breaks and adjournments. Under constant pressure from constituents who need to know the rules in order to coordinate grant application strategies, as well as the constant pressure of the clock to beat the deadline of the end of the fiscal year, neither department can afford to have its rules bogged down by long congressional breaks, such as are typical at Easter, in the summer, and at election time. Most agencies dealing with legislative veto review procedures must also be concerned about a possible doubling of the delay period if they misjudge the congressional calendar and allow a "pocket veto" to occur. The monitoring of the scheduling process necessary to deal with these contingencies has "greatly complicated" HUD's regulatory process, according to a former assistant secretary.[24]

HUD officials have also complained about the paperwork attendant upon veto proceedings. Without doubt, the legislative veto process has also caused the education subcommittee staff members to labor more mightily, although they have not yet been heard to complain. If more committees were to undertake such thorough veto reviews, the total increased demands placed on the staff of Congress would probably cause a reaction.

Certainly the agenda of Congress has been affected by the veto procedures in these case studies. Extra hearings were held by the House Committee on Banking, Finance, and Urban Affairs, by the House Committee on Education and Labor, by the House Subcommittee on Energy and Power, by the House Subcommittee on Consumer Protection and Finance, and by the Senate Subcommittee for Consumers. Clearly, staff time was required to make ready for the hearings. Agency personnel had to appear on Capitol Hill, which means that agency staff had to prepare testimony and brief top administrators on the issues. Floor time for debate and votes was consumed by both houses in the education veto effort, by the House in the incremental gas-pricing rule veto, and by the Senate in the air-bag veto attempt. Although these instances may not seem to have added oppressively to the workload or to have caused a noticeable shift in the agendas of either Congress or the executive branch, if Congress were to expand the legislative veto to cover more agencies or all agency rulemaking, these effects would be greatly compounded.

One further effect of the legislative veto on agency agendas was cited by a former HUD official. As agency staff became familiar with the trauma of congressional review proceedings, avoidance behavior developed within the agency, creating a hesitancy to change existing rules in order to escape possible legislative vetoes.

Judicial Review

The function of court review of agency action is to interpret the statutory delegation and to determine whether the administrative decision is in compliance with that delegation.[25] When Congress assumes this reviewing role by vetoing regulations developed by an agency, courts are prevented from exercising review, "even though under prior decisions on the same statute, or on analogous statutes, they might have upheld the agency's exercise of discretion."[26]

"And if the rule is not vetoed," as Judge Wilkey points out in his opinion in Consumers Energy Council of America et al. v. Federal Energy Regulatory Commission, "the courts are presented with a difficult question of how much weight, if any, to give to the implicit congressional finding that the rule represents a proper exercise of statutory discretion."[27] Recent veto provisions have attempted to avoid this problem by including a statement providing that congressional inaction on or rejection of a resolution of disapproval shall not be deemed an expression of approval of such a rule. Despite such disclaimers, according to Robert S. Gilmour, "courts find it difficult to ignore the legal reality that, once a veto is in place, Congress then has a scheduled opportunity to review every regulation covered for consistency with legislative intent."[28]

An even greater problem for court review is caused by the off-the-record negotiations between agency staff and congressional committee members and their staffs that has been shown to occur under most legislative veto provisions. Over the past decade, courts have come to "insist that agencies create a careful record of their legislative activity" so that the court may have a reviewable record to consider in its judicial determination of whether an agency regulation is in compliance with the law.[29] Where unrecorded contacts from individual members of Congress or their staff have had an effect on the substantive content of agency regulations, the court is left with no means to ascertain the basis on which the agency has made its determination. That congressional review under the legislative veto negotiation power is "entirely standardless and may be conducted without equal participation of interested parties" further adds to the problem for court review.[30]

Conclusion

Congressional use of the legislative veto power over the rulemaking process has thus far had none of the functional consequences promised by its proponents. It has not been used as a device to make rulemaking more democratic nor has it proved useful as a means to resolve conflict within Congress. In fact, the dysfunctional consequences of the veto may compound, not solve, the regulatory problem in the United States.

A process that was designed to open up rulemaking to democratic control has instead forced regulatory policy decisions into subsystem politics, where pinpointing characterized by the pork-barrel politics of public works decisions that have been roundly criticized for their geographic and constituent-interest parochialism and for their inability to define national priorities or coordinate multiple policy initiatives.

The aim of resolving conflict within Congress has not been realized either. Rather, Congress has grasped the legislative veto device as a means to avoid or postpone decisions. As a result, it was able to pass legislation making action possible on controversial problems, but majority support for the direction of that action was by no means obtained or assured. When the executive then attempted to exercise its authority to regulate under the legislative delegation, congressional conflict resurfaced and the veto was used as a means to negate the regulation. Such resolution as did occur as a result of the legislative veto was done in negotiations between congressional staff and agency staff--not between the president and Congress. The results were rarely reviewable by anyone not directly involved, including other members of Congress.

Not only does the legislative veto fail to solve the many problems of regulation but, if Congress continues to rely on the veto over the regulatory area, its utility may be undermined in other areas where it has served as a useful device of comity between the president and Congress, such as arms sales, reorganization, and war powers. Regulatory issues and agency administrative actions offer far more "promise" for court involvement, as witness the current crop of cases involving gas-pricing rules, used-cars rules, and suspension of deportation rulings. Although the Supreme Court could refuse to hear veto cases, or rule narrowly on a case at hand, there is always the chance that the court could declare the veto to be unconstitutional in all situations. When Congress resorts to the veto with such frequency in this manner, it flirts with the possibility of total loss of the veto device--presidential overreliance on the impoundment power might serve as a useful parallel warning to Congress of the inherent dangers of this approach.

If the legislative veto is not the answer, what <u>can</u> Congress do to deal with very real and pressing regulatory problems? The much-touted deregulatory approach of the Reagan-style regulation revolution has arguably slowed the heretofore regulatory gallop to a canter, but it has by no means stopped the growth of regulation, and there is no indication that it has cut back the total regulatory product. It would be naive to assume that governmental regulation can be or will be stopped, or even significantly slowed. Unless Congress stops creating and changing laws, or spells out every detail of governmental action in statutory law--most unlikely, given the enormous difficulty in getting majority agreement on even the most general details of legislation--agencies will by necessity have to fill in the specifics through the regulation statutory law--most unlikely, given the enormous difficulty in getting majority agreement on even the most general details of legislation--agencies will by necessity have to fill in the specifics through the regulation process.

This does not mean that the legislative branch must let the administrative agencies take over governmental decision making. Solutions to the problems of democratic control over administrative action are, however, neither magic nor popular. What is required of Congress is more carefully thought out and more completely spelled out laws. It is not that Congress must legislate specific details, but that it must be more precise about what it wants to accomplish and at what cost when balanced against conflicting goals. There is a long road for Congress to travel between "glittering generalities"--of, for example, "go thou and make the workplace safe"--and specific requirements--of, for example, only 1,000 micrograms of cotton dust allowable per cubic meter of air in a factory.

Where technology is uncertain or too complex, Congress can require the agency to develop a proposal or alternative proposals for congressional consideration. Of course, this would make decision making in Congress more difficult and create more conflict, but it would result in accountable action, which, after all, is what members of Congress are paid to deliver. It would also prevent the decision-avoidance route offered by the legislative veto: "Do it, but not this way!"

What citizens and members of Congress alike must recognize is that there are no grand or simple solutions to our problems, whether the problems be procedural, like control over administrators, or substantive, like dioxin tolerance and how much should be paid to get rid of unsafe amounts. If we want decisions made democratically, Congress must be willing to endure the frustrations and internal stress of moving slowly and incrementally toward carefully articulated and agreed-upon goals. And, as citizens we must be willing to reward and honor members who do so.

Notes

1.   U.S.   Congress,   House,   Committee   on   Rules,
Regulatory   Reform and Congressional   Review of   Agency
Rules: Hearings   before   the Subcommittee on   Rules of
the House on HR 1776 and Related Measures,   96th   Cong.,
1st sess., p. 3.   Hereafter cited as Rules Report.
2.   Ibid., p. 13.
3.   Louis   Fisher,   "Congress   Can't Lose on Its Veto
Power," Washington Post, February 21, 1982, p. D1.
4.   James L. Sundquist, The Decline and Resurgence
of Congress   (Washington,   DC: Brookings   Institution,
1981), p. 357.
5.   Steven   V.   Roberts,   "Congressmen Seeking Turf
Executive Calls Its Own," New York Times, March 28, 1982,
p. E5.
6.   H. Lee Watson, "Congress Steps Out: A Look at
Congressional Control of the Executive," 63 California Law
Review 983 (1975), p. 1036.
7.   For a more complete analysis of the legislative
veto's effect on factions, see ibid., pp. 1032-43.
8.   Harold Bruff and Ernest Gelhorn, "Congressional
Control   of   Administrative   Regulation: A   Study   of
Legislative Vetoes," 90   Harvard Law Review 1369 (1977),
p. 1420.
9.   Diane   Granat,   "Two   House   Legislative   Veto
Included: Senate   Unanimously   Passes   Broad   Regulatory
Reform,"   Congressional   Quarterly,   March   26,   1982,
pp. 701-2.
10.   Judy   Sarasohn,   "FTC Funds Threatened by Veto
Dispute," Congressional Quarterly, March 8, 1980, p. 635.
11.   Ibid., p. 636.
12.   James   W.   Singer,   "Out   Like a Lamb," National
Journal, May 24, 1980, p. 867.
13.   Arthur   L. Amolsh and Mimi Madden, "Funerals,"
FTC: WATCH, December 12, 1980, p. 7.
14.   Judy   Sarasohn,   "FTC Rule on Used Cars Sales
Provides   First   Major   Test   of   Congress   Veto   Power,"
Congressional Quarterly, November 7, 1981, p. 2180.
15.   Ibid.
16.   The "automatic" nature of the resubmission was
the   subject   of   another   internal   battle   among   the
commissioners.   Commissioner Pertschuk pressed for this
interpretation of the statutory language and won.
17.   The vote to kill the rule in the Senate on May 18,
1982, was 69-27.   During debate no more than a half-dozen
senators were ever present on the floor.   The House vote was
286-133 on May 26, 1982.   During debate in the House, one
member charged that the eighteen-cent rule was "so costly
and burdensome that it would further aggravate the already
ailing automobile industry."   Another member charged that
the veto process in this case represented a "contamination

of the political arena by campaign contributions."

18. Arthur L. Amolsh and Mimi Madden, "Used Car Veto Seen," FTC: WATCH, November 6, 1981, p. 12.

19. Ibid. Commissioner Bailey also raised this concern just after the used-cars rule was vetoed. "I think it does raise the question of what kind of consumer measures . . . will be possible." See Congressional Quarterly, May 22, 1982, p. 1189.

20. Rules Report, p. 1345 (testimony of Congressional Research Specialist Allen Schick).

21. Ibid.

22. Bruff and Gelhorn, "Congressional Control of Administrative Regulation," p. 1416.

23. Arthur L. Amolsh and Mimi Madden, "Games-of-Chance Rule Change Clears Congressional Veto," FTC: WATCH, July 24, 1981, p. 13.

24. U.S. Congress, Senate, Committee on Government Affairs, Subcommittee on Oversight of Government Management, Hearings on Oversight of Agency Compliance with Executive Order 12044, "Improving Government Regulations," 96th Cong., 1st sess., October 10, 1979, p. 43.

25. Consumers Energy Council of America et al. v. Federal Energy Regulatory Commission, 673 F.2d 425, January 29, 1982, p. 423. Hereafter cited as FERC Opinion.

26. Ibid.

27. Ibid.

28. Robert S. Gilmour, "The Congressional Veto: Shifting the Balance of Administrative Control," Journal of Policy Analysis and Management 2 (1982):21.

29. Ibid., p. 17.

30. FERC Opinion, p. 102.

Epilogue

Reacting to the announcement of the Supreme Court's landmark decision in <u>Immigration and Naturalization Service</u> v. <u>Chadha</u>, Jagdish Rai Chadha commented, "It still baffles me that such a small case as mine could become so important."[1] The court's decision in this "minuscule" case, as Chadha himself called it, appears to signal the end of the line for nearly two hundred statutory provisions containing legislative vetoes passed by Congress over the last fifty years. "The encompassing nature of the ruling," Justice Powell observed in his concurrence, "gives one pause."[2] When just two weeks later the court ruled, based on the reasoning in <u>Chadha</u> and without further comment, that legislative vetoes in two other pending cases were also unconstitutional, any doubts about the breadth or reach of <u>Chadha</u> were quickly put to rest. What follows is a summary of the history behind the case and an analysis of the court's opinion.

The <u>Chadha</u> Case: Summary and Analysis

The Statute

Congressional delegation to the attorney general of authority to suspend deportations of aliens goes back to the 1930s. At that time Congress was besieged by private immigration bills, and faced with frequent suggestions from the press that some members were receiving payments for sponsoring bills to allow certain aliens to remain in the country. To deal with the situation, Congress passed the Alien Registration Act of 1940, which allowed the attorney general to suspend deportation of a qualified alien unless the House and Senate passed a concurrent resolution disapproving the suspension. The 1952 Immigration and Naturalization Act altered the procedure, providing for a single-house veto over deportation suspensions. (See Appendix, Justice White's dissent, at pp. 192-200, for a more complete discussion of the background of these acts.)

It is the legislative veto in the 1952 act that Chadha challenged after the House of Representatives voted to cancel the attorney general's suspension of his deportation order.

Chadha's Deportation Case

Jagdish Rai Chadha, an East Indian born in Kenya, was admitted to the United States in 1966 on a nonimmigration student visa that expired on June 30, 1972. Ordered by the district director of the Immigration and Naturalization Service (INS) to show cause why he should not be deported for having remained in the United States for a longer time than permitted, Chadha conceded that he was deportable for overstaying his visa. He then submitted an application for suspension of deportation due to his fear of persecution on account of his race if he were forced to return to Kenya. An INS administrative hearing on Chadha's application was held and on June 25, 1974, an INS immigration judge ordered the suspension of Chadha's deportation. The judge found that Chadha had met the statutory requirements for suspension: he had resided continuously in the United States for over seven years, was of good moral character and would suffer "extreme hardship" if deported. As required by the 1952 act, INS on the same day conveyed a report of its order to Congress.

For the next year and a half Congress made no attempt to deal with the report on Chadha's deportation suspension. Had Congress taken no action before it adjourned on December 19, 1975, the case would have been closed and Chadha's status adjusted to that of a permanent resident alien. But on December 12, 1975, Representative Eilberg, chairman of the Judiciary Subcommittee on Immigration, Citizenship, and International Law, introduced a resolution that stated simply that "the House of Representatives does not approve granting of permanent residence in the United States to the aliens hereinafter named" (H. Res. 926). Chadha and five other aliens were singled out from 345 persons whose deportations had been suspended by the attorney general and were then before Congress. The resolution was not printed, nor was it made available to other members of the House before or at the time of the vote. The resolution was passed on December 16, 1975, without debate or recorded vote.

When Chadha moved to terminate the INS hearing convened to implement the resolution as passed by the House on the grounds that the House veto of his suspension was unconstitutional, the immigration judge held that he himself had no authority to rule on a constitutional question. Chadha's appeal to the Board of Immigration Appeals was dismissed for the same reason. With the assistance of Alan B. Morrison, director of litigation for Public Citizen (a nonprofit organization loosely affiliated with Ralph Nader), Chadha appealed his case to the United States Court of Appeals for the Ninth Circuit. In 1980, a three-judge panel ruled unanimously that the House was without constitutional authority to order Chadha deported, grounding its decision in the separation-of-powers doctrine. (See ch. 2, pp. 46-47, for a more complete discussion of the Appeals Court's ruling.) INS then appealed the decision to the Supreme Court. By separate resolutions in the Senate (S. Res. 40) and in the House (H. Res. 49) Congress authorized its own intervention in the case. Congress's motion to intervene was granted by the court, which then proceeded to hear argument on the case on February 22, 1982, and again on December 7, 1982.

The Supreme Court Decision

On June 23, 1983, by a vote of 7 to 2, the Supreme Court ruled the congressional veto in the Immigration and Naturalization Act unconstitutional. In what a New York Times editorial called a "supremely simple" decision, Chief Justice Burger, "writing like a patient schoolmaster," explained the court's reasoning in "familiar and basic terms. Remember what we all learned in social studies about how laws are made? Well," the editorial continued, "that's just how it should still work."[3] As Burger pointed out in his decision, the Constitution provides "a single, finely wrought and exhaustively considered procedure" for exercise of the legislative power of the federal government. "Explicit and unambiguous provisions of the Constitution," he went on, "prescribe and define the respective functions of the Congress and of the Executive in the legislative process."

To underscore the importance of the constitutional requirements found in Article I--passage by a majority of both Houses and presentment to the president--the opinion sets them out verbatim. Any actions taken by either house if "they contain matter which is properly to be regarded as legislative in character and effect" must conform with this constitutionally designed legislative process. And, lest there be any confusion about what the court would consider to be legislative in nature, Burger carefully spelled that out too: Legislative action is any action that has the "purpose and effect of altering the legal rights, duties, and relations of persons outside the legislative branch." This broad definition of legislative action leaves little room for congressional maneuvering to avoid the constitutional process.

Applying its rationale to the case at hand, the court reasoned that absent the veto provision, neither the House nor the Senate, nor both together, could effectively require the attorney general to deport an alien once the attorney general, in the exercise of legislatively delegated authority had determined that the alien should remain in the United States. The one-house veto operates in this case to overrule the attorney general and to mandate Chadha's deportation. In the absence of the House action, Chadha would have remained in the United States; therefore, Congress has acted and its action has altered Chadha's status. Congress can accomplish such an end only by following the Constitution's prescription for legislative action.

While recognizing the convenient nature of the shortcut offered by the veto, which enabled Congress to share authority over aliens with the executive branch, Burger forcefully defended the "step-by-step, deliberate and deliberative process" for legislative action set out by the Constitution. "The Framers," he said, "ranked other values higher than efficiency." The process clearly imposes burdens on governmental procedures that often seem "clumsy, inefficient, and even unworkable." Burger concluded: "With all the obvious flaws of delay, untidiness, and potential for abuse, we have not yet found a better way to preserve freedom than by making the exercise of power subject to the carefully crafted restraints spelled out in the Constitution."

In a separate opinion, Justice Powell concurred in holding the legislative veto in the Chadha case unconstitutional but did not agree with the court's basis for arriving at its decision. Powell argued that when Congress finds that a particular person does not satisfy the statutory criteria for permanent residence in this country, it has assumed a judicial function in violation of the principle of separation of powers. When Congress decides the rights of specific persons, it operates like a court but without the procedural safeguards court action insures, such as right to counsel. Individual rights are thereby subject to "the tyranny of a shifting majority." The case, he argues, should be decided on this narrower ground. His rationale is far closer to that of the Ninth Circuit's decision. Had the Supreme Court ruled on such a basis, Chadha would have left open the question of the constitutionality of most of the other existing legislative veto provisions.

In a vehement dissent, Justice White defended the legislative veto as "an important if not indispensable political invention that allows the president and Congress to resolve major constitutional policy differences, assures the accountability of independent regulatory agencies, and preserves Congress' control over lawmaking." In his view neither the Presentment Clauses of the Constitution nor the doctrine of separation of powers is violated by this "mechanism by which our elected representatives preserve their voice in the governance of the nation."

Decrying the majority decision, White attacked it for lack of judicial restraint. "To strike an entire class of statutes based on consideration of a somewhat atypical and more readily indictable exemplar of the class is irresponsible." White reminded the court of what Justice Brandeis had to say about passing upon the validity of an act of Congress. "The Court," Brandeis said, "will not formulate a rule of constitutional law broader than is required by the precise facts to which it is to be applied."

The essence of White's defense of the veto in the Immigration and Naturalization Act is that there had in reality been no delegation of power to suspend deportations in the first place. The legislative veto provision does not "prevent the Executive from accomplishing its constitutionally assigned functions" as the majority claimed. It is clear that the executive branch has no constitutionally assigned function of suspending the deportation of aliens. Over no conceivable subject is the legislative power of Congress more complete than it is over the administration of aliens. White defended the veto against the majority's attack by claiming that what was granted to the executive in the act was "only a qualified suspension authority and it is only that authority which the president is constitutionally authorized to execute." The Burger opinion, according to White, "reflects a profoundly different conception of the Constitution than that held by the Courts which sanctioned the modern administrative state."

In a separate dissent, Justice Rehnquist argued that the judgment of the Court of Appeals should be reversed on the grounds that the legislative veto clause was not severable from the delegation of power to the attorney general to suspend deportations. The Immigration and Naturalization Act contains a broadly encompassing severability clause:

> If any particular provision of this Act, or the application thereof to any person or circumstance, is held invalid, the remainder of the act and the application of such provision to other persons or circumstances shall not be affected thereby.

Despite this rather unambiguous language, Rehnquist found sufficient historical evidence in the continued refusal of Congress to delegate suspension power to the executive without attaching legislative veto power to prove that Congress did not intend the one-house veto to be severable.

Based on reasoning similar to the Fourth Circuit's in McCorkle v. U.S. (see chapter 2, p. 46), Rehnquist concluded that the lower court erred. Because the veto was not severable, the power to suspend deportations could not stand in isolation from the veto power. Without a suspension, Chadha would be deportable; thus, a court ruling on the veto's constitutionality would not help his case. Since there was no judicial remedy for his situation, the case should have been dismissed on those grounds.

Initial assessment of the scope of the <u>Chadha</u> decision, especially after the court's ruling on July 6, 1983, to uphold without further comment the lower court decisions in the incremental-gas-pricing and used-cars-sales rules cases (see chapters 5 and 6 for background on these cases), is that it is, indeed, a very broad decision. "It may be presumed," says Congressional Research Specialist in Public Law Morton Rosenberg, "that all congressional veto provisions are now constitutionally suspect notwithstanding the manner in which they are exercised or the subject matter they cover."[4] One issue left open--the question of severability in the approximately sixty currently operative acts with legislative veto provisions--may take years to resolve. Each act will need to be addressed individually, and court action must await the bringing of a case by an aggrieved party. Some, like the War Powers Resolution and the Arms Sales Act, which have never had their veto provisions exercised, may never get to court at all. The courts cannot rule hypothetically: Congress must actually vote to veto a presidential or executive action, and someone must be able to establish standing to challenge the action in court. In some cases the president and Congress may agree to continue recognizing the veto provisions in a spirit of comity, thus avoiding court involvement in the issue.

There is no doubt, however, that in the months and years ahead Congress will be faced with adjusting to life without the legislative veto. The next section provides an overview of the many alternative approaches that Congress will be considering.

Picking up the Pieces: Life after the Veto

The first congressional response to loss of the veto came less than a week after the Supreme Court decision. In considering reauthorization legislation for the Consumer Product Safety Commission (CPSC) the House of Representatives voted 238 to 177 to attach two alternative restrictions as veto substitutes, leaving to the conference committee the problems of deciding which to choose. One, offered as an amendment by Representative Waxman, would provide for a ninety-day delay before commission rules could go into effect, during which time Congress could pass a joint resolution disapproving the rule. (This is similar to the HUD "constitutional veto" provision discussed in chapter 3.) The other, offered by Representative Levitas, would provide that no agency rule could take effect unless adopted by a joint resolution. Essentially, this would mean that the commission's regulations would merely be proposals requiring action by both houses and signature by the president to become effective.

Reacting to the haste with which the House seemed willing to adopt these "untried and curious" procedures,

175

Representative Dingell commented:

> I would observe to the House that drafting this kind of broad, sweeping legislative package dealing with all manner of procedural change at 6:30 by the clock, on an evening when the House has had no opportunity to consider this is perhaps the worst way in the world that we can legislate.[5]

Some sort of quick response was probably inevitable. Whether Levitas is right in claiming that this "first one out of the bag is important" because it will "show where we're headed" is certainly debatable, however. It may be that this action was nothing more than symbolic muscle-flexing to send a message to regulators that the court decision did not give them carte blanche to ignore Congress. It can be hoped, though, that future response will be preceded by more careful analysis and consideration than was evidenced here.

Congress has already scheduled several hearings to address the veto issue in more detail. "Our hearing," said Senator Grassley, chairman of the Senate Judiciary Subcommittee on Administrative Practice and Procedure, which was to hold a hearing on July 18, 1983, "will serve as an overview and a signal that Congress isn't going to roll over and play dead."[6] It will also provide the first congressional forum for addressing the many suggestions—some new, some old—now being offered as veto substitutes. The following list summarizes various alternatives that Congress may be considering:

> Joint Resolution Veto. The so-called constitutional veto first suggested by Senators Levin and Boren, and applied to HUD's rulemaking since 1978.
> Joint Resolution of Approval. Representative Levitas's proposal for the CPSC, which would require agency rules to be sent to Congress as proposals that could not go into effect unless passed by both houses and signed by the president.
> Establishment of a Select Committee. A proposal by Representative Moakley in the past two Congresses to establish a permanent select committee of the House (Select Committee on Regulatory Affairs) to monitor rulemaking activities and to report to the House any rules it considers arbitrary, or that duplicate, overlap, or conflict with other federal regulations, or that impose an excessive burden, or that are beyond statutory authority. Action to overturn or alter the rule would require passage of a joint resolution.
> Congressional Challenge of Rules in Court. This idea was offered by Representative Pashayan during a special evening session of the House devoted to the legislative veto on June 29, 1983. It is a

convoluted combination of a sixty-day "report and
wait," a nonbinding two-house resolution of
disapproval that would create a "legal rebuttable
presumption that the regulations are beyond the
congressional intent of the statute," and new
statutory authority for any member of Congress,
acting individually, to challenge the regulation
in court.

<u>Summit Conference on the Veto</u>. This proposal,
which is being pushed by Representative Levitas,
would bring together legislators, administrative
officials, legal scholars, and other legislative
veto experts to come up with the best veto
alternative.

<u>Modification of House Rules</u>. Rules changes pushed
by the House leadership at the start of this session
limited the number and kind of riders that could be
attached to appropriations bills. Some members
would now suggest modifying these restrictions to
make it easier to stop an agency from implementing a
rule by attaching "no-appropriations" riders to
prevent the agency from spending appropriated
funds to enforce the regulation. A variation of
this would call for amending the House rules to
provide that if an authorizing committee voted to
disapprove an agency regulation, prohibitions to
block the spending of money to implement the rule
would then be in order.

<u>Constitutional Amendment</u>. Representative Jacobs
has already begun to solicit sponsors for a
constitutional amendment to give Congress the
express right to overturn administrative rules and
regulations. This would effectively negate the
court decision in <u>Chadha</u>.

<u>Moratorium on Executive Exercise of Veto-
Connected Powers</u>. This has been suggested as a
way to give Congress more time to respond to the new
situation.

<u>More Detailed and Precise Delegations</u>. This
suggestion is offered by some as somewhat of a
threat of what will happen if satisfactory veto
substitutes are not found; by others it is
suggested as a necessary and positive result of the
loss of the veto.

<u>Traditional Congressional Controls</u>. Many members
of Congress believe that the regulatory problem can
be dealt with quite satisfactorily with the
oversight tools already available to Congress:
hearings, reports, periodic reauthorizations,
appropriations control, and specific and tighter
restrictions on delegated authority.

It is from this smorgasbord, augmented no doubt by even
more alternatives as inventive members and their staffs

scramble for input and media attention, that Congress will
choose. The temptation to find another procedural
substitute will be great. As the case studies in this book
have illustrated, a primary advantage to Congress of the
veto has been its utility as a means to avoid sticky
substantive decisions. It has also proved to be an
effective lever to force agencies to negotiate with
subcommittee members and staff over the content of rules.
On fewer than a handful of occasions over the last decade has
it actually been used to veto a regulation. It cannot be
shown that the veto has made the rulemaking process more
democratic nor that it has made bureaucrats follow the
intent of the law more carefully. Members of Congress must
cut through all the rhetoric and sloganeering about the veto
to see what it actually does if they are going to try to
fashion an appropriate substitute.

Furthermore, if they are to deal effectively with the
regulatory problem, members will also need to be far more
realistic about what the problem really is. The roots of
the regulatory problem have been nurtured in the
legislative turf. Congress has passed laws directing the
executive branch to implement regulatory goals that often
conflict with one another. Duplication and overlap among
regulatory policies abound. There is a need to redefine
priorities and to provide coordination and consistency in
the regulatory scheme. Clearly, it is more politically
expedient to cast the problem in terms of the "tyranny" of
the bureaucrats vs. the "virtue" of the democratically
elected representatives. And it would be easier to latch
onto a catchy-sounding procedural gimmick than to tackle
the broad regulatory problems. Neither approach,
however, will aid Congress in addressing the real
situation.

The most obvious and democratically appealing outcome
of the veto's demise would be for Congress to define its
intent more carefully in the law. In spite of the many
predictions from members of Congress that loss of the veto
will mean very narrow writing of legislation and severely
circumscribed delegations in the future, this result is
neither assured nor easy to obtain. Congress must first
overcome its long reluctance and resistance to making
difficult policy choices.

In the case of the passive-restraint rule (chapter 5),
for example, there is no reason that Congress cannot step in
to resolve the question of whether cars should be equipped
with air bags. After fourteen years of rulemaking
proceedings, the evidence is available for congressional
action. What remains is a political decision that calls
for balancing the additional cost of providing air bags to a
product that has suffered significant losses due to
inflation, the recession, and foreign competition against
the savings in health costs and lives: How many of the 126
Americans killed on the highways each day would need to be
saved to make air bags worthwhile? Air bags would not save

them all, but air bags could save many. Senator Danforth
has introduced a bill to require that "each manufacturer of
passenger automobiles shall install airbags in each
passenger automobile manufactured on or after September 1,
1985."[7] If Congress is serious about wanting control over
regulators, this would be a good place to start. No matter
which way it decided, at least citizens would be able to
figure out whom to hold responsible, and at least they would
have, through their vote, some means of doing so.

Many of the suggestions listed above will fall of their
own weight. Pashayan's convoluted challenge procedure
and the constitutional amendment proposal seem to be prime
candidates to do so. Some, like the summit conference,
have already encountered significant resistance from
congressional leaders, perhaps out of fear that they might
lose control over the outcome. Still others, like
Levitas's joint resolution of approval, though attractive
sounding, have serious practical problems.

If an agency rule had to be passed by Congress before
becoming effective, the goals of fixing accountability and
responsibility for government action in the hands of
elected officials would be furthered. Undoubtedly there
are circumstances for which this approach would be most
appropriate. The incremental gas-pricing rule (chapter
5) is perhaps a case in point. In this case, conflict would
still have been confined to the single rule, and it appears
that there was insufficient support for the rule to pass
Congress in 1980. Knowledge that such a hurdle would have
to be surmounted in order for consumers to be protected,
though, might have prevented passage of the original
compromise in 1978 allowing for phased deregulation in the
first place. It has, in other words, some of the advantages
Congress has gained from the veto but not others.
Nevertheless, confined to a few highly visible and
important regulations, affirmative action by Congress
might be a useful and manageable response. But if it is
applied to the more than 3,700 proposed rules covering more
than 12,000 pages in the Federal Register that were issued
by government agencies in 1982, it would cause "an unholy
mess" in Congress.[8] The enormous difficulty the 97th
Congress (1981-1982) had passing even essential
reauthorization legislation around the crunch of budget
matters should provide sufficient evidence about the
current state of congressional floor schedules and
workloads. How could Congress find the time to deal with
such an additional burden?

As the HUD study (chapter 3) has shown, the joint
resolution of disapproval, especially when applied over
grant agencies on tight rulemaking schedules, can have the
same practical results (committee-level negotiation power
over agency rules) as the one-house veto. Based on this
case study, though, the question of whether this result is
one that Congress should try to replicate is certainly
debatable.

Congressman Moakley's proposal to create a select committee to provide some institutional coordination among the standing committees as a way to determine regulatory and legislative priorities where conflict and duplication exist between regulatory goals is an appealing suggestion. If Congress is to gain control over agency regulations in the Office of Management and Budget, it will have to provide itself with the institutional capacity to deal with the broad picture.[9] Without this capacity, Congress may very well soon find itself every bit as much at the president's mercy in regulatory matters as it was in budgetary affairs just a decade ago. Undoubtedly any proposal to centralize regulatory oversight will be vigorously opposed by interests in and out of Congress that are tied to existing committee boundaries. Perhaps it will take some specific overt presidential excess in the regulatory area, like the Nixon and Ford use of impoundments did for the budget process, to force Congress to overcome its institutional problems.

Even if Congress were to reject all of the veto substitutes, by no means would it be stripped of power over the regulatory agencies. Its traditional tools for control would still be available. Annual or expiring authorizations, already a reality for over a quarter of the legislative output, could be expanded to cover other programs. Hearings, mandatory studies and reports, specified deadlines for action, and investigations are also means of exercising congressional control over delegated authority.

Congress may find replacement of the veto more difficult in other situations, especially those involving direct accommodation between the president (as an individual) and the Congress (as a voting body) on issues like impoundment, war powers, trade, or arms sales. But even there, Congress may find that comity bult on mutual respect and mutually arrived at agreements may be far more advantageous than the veto device, which was born in these situations from conflict and mistrust. In most of the cases (with the exception perhaps of deferrals) what Congress has sought by adding veto power over the president's actions was less the power to negate than the right to be consulted and to have input into a decision before it was made.[10]

Congress faces many crucial decisions in the months and years ahead as it attempts to deal with the aftermath of the Chadha decision. The real challenge was succinctly summed up by one representative during the House's special session on the veto:

> Mr. Speaker, the genius of our constitutional system is that the Presidency and Congress will always exist and have to work together. In the resolution of any confrontation, even one as sweeping as Chadha, the question is whether the two, in reaching

accommodations that replace the veto, have learned the
lessons of recent history and can apply them with
common sense.[11]

Notes

1. <u>New York Times</u>, June 25, 1983, p. 8.
2. Quotations from <u>Chadha</u> can all be found in the excerpts from the case in the Appendix.
3. <u>New York Times</u>, June 26, 1983, p. 20E.
4. Morton Rosenberg, "Summary and Preliminary Analysis of the Ramifications of <u>INS</u> v. <u>CHADHA</u>, the Legislative Veto Case," CRS brief, June 28, 1983, p. 13.
5. 129 <u>Cong. Rec.</u> H4779 (daily ed.), June 29, 1983.
6. <u>Congressional Quarterly</u>, July 2, 1983, p. 1328.
7. George Will, "Court Ruling Fails to End Long War over Auto Airbags," <u>New Haven Journal Courier</u>, July 4, 1983, p. 6.
8. 129 <u>Cong. Rec.</u> H4779 (daily ed.), June 29, 1983 (quoting Representative Dingell).
9. For a detailed account and assessment of these recent efforts, see Robert S. Gilmour, "Presidential Clearance of Regulation," paper presented at the National Conference of the American Society for Public Administration, April 17, 1983.
10. For an assessment of alternatives to the War Powers Resolution approach, see Barbara Hinkson Craig, "The Power to Make War: Congress' Search for an Effective Role," <u>Journal of Policy Analysis and Management</u> 1 (1982):317.
11. 129 <u>Cong. Rec.</u> H4827 (daily ed.), June 29, 1983 (quoting Representative Moakley).

Appendix: Excerpts from the Epic Chadha Decision

IMMIGRATION AND NATURALIZATION SERVICE
v. CHADHA ET AL.

Appeal from the United States Court of Appeals
for the Ninth Circuit

No. 80-1823. Argued February 22, 1982--Reargued December
7, 1982--Decided June 23, 1983.

Chief Justice Burger delivered the opinion of the court, in
which Justices Brennan, Marshall, Blackmun, Stevens, and
O'Connor joined. Justice Powell filed an opinion
concurring in the judgment. Justice White filed a
dissenting opinion. Justice Rehnquist filed a dissenting
opinion in which Justice White joined.

[From Chief Justice Burger's opinion:]

[The Facts]

. . . Chadha is an East Indian who was born in Kenya and
holds a British passport. He was lawfully admitted to the
United States in 1966 on a nonimmigrant student visa. His
visa expired on June 30, 1972. On October 11, 1973, the
District Director of the Immigration and Naturalization
Service ordered Chadha to show cause why he should not be
deported for having "remained in the United States for a
longer time than permitted". . . . Pursuant to S 242(b) of
the Immigration and Nationality Act (Act), 8 U.S.C. S
1254(b), a deportation hearing was held before an
immigration judge on January 11, 1974. Chadha conceded
that he was deportable for overstaying his visa and the
hearing was adjourned to enable him to file an application
for suspension of deportation. . . .
    After Chadha submitted his application for suspension
of deportation, the deportation hearing was resumed on

184

February 7, 1974. On the basis of evidence adduced at the hearing, affidavits submitted with the application, and the results of a character investigation conducted by INS, the immigration judge, on June 25, 1974, ordered that Chadha's deportation be suspended. The immigration judge found that Chadha met the requirements of S 244(a)(1): he had resided continuously in the United States for over seven years, was of good moral character, and would suffer "extreme hardship" if deported.

Pursuant to S 244(c)(1) of the Act, . . . the immigration judge suspended Chadha's deportation and a report of the suspension was transmitted to Congress. . . .

Once the Attorney General's recommendation for suspension of Chadha's deportation was conveyed to Congress, Congress had the power under S 244(c)(2) of the Act . . . to veto the Attorney General's determination that Chadha should not be deported. Section 244(c)(2) provides:

> "(2) In the case of an alien specified in paragraph (1) of subsection (a) of this subsection--
> if during the session of the Congress at which a case is reported, or prior to the close of the session of Congress next following the session at which a case is reported, either the Senate or the House of Representatives passes a resolution stating in substance that it does not favor the suspension of such deportation, the Attorney General shall thereupon deport such alien or authorize the alien's voluntary departure at his own expense under the order of deportation in the manner provided by law. If, within the time above specified, neither the Senate nor the House of Representatives shall pass such a resolution, the Attorney General shall cancel deportation proceedings."

The June 25, 1974, order of the immigration judge suspending Chadha's deportation remained outstanding as a valid order for a year and a half. For reasons not disclosed by the record, Congress did not exercise the veto authority reserved to it . . . until the first session of the 94th Congress. This was the final session in which Congress . . . could act to veto the Attorney General's determination that Chadha should not be deported. The session ended on December 19, 1975. . . . Absent Congressional action, Chadha's deportation proceedings would have been cancelled after this date and his status adjusted to that of a permanent resident alien.

On December 12, 1975, Representative Eilberg, Chairman of the Judiciary Subcommittee on Immigration, Citizenship and International Law, introduced a resolution opposing "the granting of permanent residence in the United States to [six] aliens," including Chadha. . . . The resolution was referred to the House Committee on the

Judiciary. On December 16, 1975, the resolution was discharged from further consideration by the House Committee on the Judiciary and submitted to the House of Representatives for a vote. . . . The resolution had not been printed and was not made available to other members of the House prior to or at the time it was voted on. . . . The resolution was passed without debate or recorded vote. Since the House action was pursuant to S 244(c)(2), the resolution was not treated as an Article I legislative act; it was not submitted to the Senate or presented to the President for his action.

After the House veto of the Attorney General's decision to allow Chadha to remain in the United States, the immigration judge reopened the deportation proceedings to implement the House order deporting Chadha. Chadha moved to terminate the proceedings on the ground that S 244(c)(2) is unconstitutional. The immigration judge held that he had no authority to rule on the constitutional validity of S 244(c)(2). On November 8, 1976, Chadha was ordered deported pursuant to the House action.

Chadha appealed the deportation order to the Board of Immigration Appeals again contending that S 244(c)(2) is unconstitutional. The Board held that it had "no power to declare unconstitutional an act of Congress" and Chadha's appeal was dismissed.

Pursuant to S 106(a) of the Act, Chadha filed a petition for review of the deportation order in the United States Court of Appeals for the Ninth Circuit. The Immigration and Naturalization Service agreed with Chadha's position before the Court of Appeals and joined him in arguing that S 244(c)(2) is unconstitutional. In light of the importance of the question, the Court of Appeals invited both the Senate and the House of Representatives to file briefs amici curiae.

After full briefing and oral argument, the Court of Appeals held that the House was without constitutional authority to order Chadha's deportation; accordingly it directed the Attorney General "to cease and desist from taking any steps to deport this alien based upon the resolution enacted by the House of Representatives." The essence of its holding was that S 244(c)(2) violates the constitutional doctrine of separation of powers.

We granted certiorari . . . , and we now affirm.

[Jurisdictional Challenges Dismissed]

[Note: The next paragraph summarizes the court's decision on jurisdictional questions.

Before addressing the important question of the constitutionality of the one-house veto provision, the court considered and dismissed several challenges to its authority to resolve the issue. The court held that it had jurisdiction to entertain the appeal; that the one-house

veto provision was severable from the delegation of power to
the attorney general to suspend deportations; that Chadha
had sufficient standing to challenge the constitutionality
of the veto provision; that Chadha's marriage to a United
States citizen on August 10, 1980, did not make his case
moot; that the case did present the necessary adversarial
relationship to constitute a case and controversy; and that
the question involved was not a nonjusticiable political
question. Thus satisfied that the parties were properly
before the court, Burger proceeded to tackle the
constitutional issue.]

[The Constitutional Questions]

We turn now to the question whether action of one House
of Congress under S 244(c)(2) violates strictures of the
Constitution. We begin, of course, with the presumption
that the challenged statute is valid. Its wisdom is not the
concern of the courts; if a challenged action does not
violate the Constitution, it must be sustained. . . .
By the same token, the fact that a given law or
procedure is efficient, convenient, and useful in
facilitating functions of government, standing alone, will
not save it if it is contrary to the Constitution.
Convenience and efficiency are not the primary objectives--
or the hallmarks--of democratic government and our inquiry
is sharpened rather than blunted by the fact that
Congressional veto provisions are appearing with
increasing frequency in statutes which delegate authority
to executive and independent agencies. . . . But policy
arguments supporting even useful "political inventions"
are subject to the demands of the Constitution which defines
power and, with respect to this subject, sets out just how
those powers are to be exercised.
Explicit and unambiguous provisions of the
Constitution prescribe and define the respective functions
of the Congress and the Executive in the legislative
process. Since the precise terms of those familiar
provisions are critical to the resolution in this case, we
set them out verbatim. Art. I provides:

"All legislative Powers herein granted shall be vested
in a Congress of the United States, which shall consist
of a Senate and House of Representatives." Art. I,
S 1. [Emphasis added.]

"Every Bill which shall have passed the House of
Representatives and the Senate, shall, before it
becomes a Law, be presented to the President of the
United States. . . ." Art. I, S 7, cl. 2. [Emphasis
added.]

"Every Order, Resolution, or Vote to which the
Concurrence of the Senate and House of Representatives

may be necessary (except on a question of Adjournment)
<u>shall be</u> presented to the President of the United
States; and before the Same shall take Effect, <u>shall be</u>
approved by him, or being disapproved by him, <u>shall be</u>
repassed by two-thirds of the Senate and House of
Representatives, according to the Rules and
Limitations prescribed in the Case of a Bill." Art.
I, S 7, cl. 4. [Emphasis added.]

These provision of Art. I are integral parts of the
constitutional design for the separation of powers. . . .

[The Presentment Clauses]

The records of the Constitutional Convention reveal
that the requirement that all legislation be presented to
the President before becoming law was uniformly accepted by
the Framers. Presentment to the President and the
Presidential veto were considered so imperative that the
draftsmen took special pains to assure that these
requirements could not be circumvented. . . .
The decision to provide the President with a limited
and qualified power to nullify proposed legislation by veto
was based on the profound conviction of the Framers that the
powers conferred on Congress were the powers to be most
carefully circumscribed. It is beyond doubt that
lawmaking was a power to be shared by both Houses and the
President. . . .
The President's role in the lawmaking process also
reflects the Framers' careful efforts to check whatever
propensity a particular Congress might have to enact
oppressive, improvident, or ill-considered measures. . . .
The Court also has observed that the Presentment Clauses
serve the important purpose of assuring that a "national"
perspective is grafted on the legislative process. . . .

[Bicameralism]

The bicameral requirement of Art. I, SS 1, 7 was of
scarcely less concern to the Framers than was the
Presidential veto and indeed the two concepts are
interdependent. By providing that no law could take effect
without the concurrence of the prescribed majority of the
Members of both Houses, the Framers reemphasized their
belief, already remarked upon in connection with the
Presentment Clauses, that legislation should not be enacted
unless it has been carefully and fully considered by the
nation's elected officials. . . .
We see therefore that the Framers were acutely
conscious that the bicameral requirement and the
Presentment Clauses would serve essential constitutional
functions. The President's participation in the

legislative process was to protect the Executive Branch
from Congress and to protect the whole people from
improvident laws. The division of the Congress into two
distinctive bodies assures that the legislative power would
be exercised only after opportunity for full study and
debate in separate settings. The President's unilateral
veto power, in turn, was limited by the power of two-thirds
of both Houses of Congress to overrule a veto thereby
precluding final arbitrary action of one person. It
emerges clearly that the prescription for legislative
action in Art. I, SS 1, 7 represents the Framers' decision
that the legislative power of the Federal government be
exercised in accord with a single, finely wrought and
exhaustively considered, procedure.

[Constitutionality of the Legislative Veto]

The Constitution sought to divide the delegated powers
of the new federal government into three defined
categories, legislative, executive and judicial, to
assure, as nearly as possible, that each Branch of
government would confine itself to its assigned
responsibility. The hydraulic pressure inherent within
each of the separate Branches to exceed the outer limits of
its power, even to accomplish desirable objectives must be
resisted. . . .
Not every action taken by either House is subject to
the bicameralism and presentment requirements of Art. I.
Whether actions taken by either House are, in law and fact,
an exercise of legislative power depends not on their form
but upon "whether they contain matter which is properly to
be regarded as legislative in its character and effect."
Examination of the action taken here by one House
pursuant to S 244(c)(2) reveals that it was essentially
legislative in purpose and effect. In purporting to
exercise power defined in Art. I, S 8, cl. 4 to "establish an
uniform Rule of Naturalization," the House took action that
had the purpose and effect of altering the legal rights,
duties and relations of persons, including the Attorney
General, Executive Branch officials and Chadha, all outside
the legislative branch. . . . The one-House veto operated
in this case to overrule the Attorney General and mandate
Chadha's deportation; absent the House action, Chadha would
remain in the United States. Congress has <u>acted</u> and its
action has altered Chadha's status.
The nature of the decision implemented by the one-
House veto in this case further manifests its legislative
character. After long experience with the clumsy, time
consuming private bill procedure, Congress made a
deliberate choice to delegate to the Executive Branch, and
specifically to the Attorney General, the authority to
allow deportable aliens to remain in this country in certain
specified circumstances. . . . Disagreement with the

Attorney General's decision on Chadha's deportation—that is, Congress' decision to deport Chadha—no less than Congress' original choice to delegate to the Attorney General the authority to make that decision, involves determinations of policy that Congress can implement in only one way: bicameral passage followed by presentment to the President. Congress must abide by its delegation of authority until that delegation is legislatively altered or revoked.

Finally, we see that when the Framers intended to authorize either House of Congress to act alone and outside of its prescribed bicameral legislative role, they narrowly and precisely defined the procedure for such action. There are but four provisions in the Constitution, explicit and unambiguous, by which one House may act alone with the unreviewable force of law, not subject to the president's veto:

(a) The House of Representatives alone was given the power to initiate impeachments. Art. I, S 2, cl. 6;

(b) the Senate alone was given the power to conduct trials following impeachment on charges initiated by the House and to convict following trial. Art. I, S 3, cl. 5;

(c) The Senate alone was given final unreviewable power to approve or to disapprove presidential appointments. Art. II, S 2, cl. 2;

(d) The Senate alone was given unreviewable power to ratify treaties negotiated by the President. Art. II, S 2, cl. 2.

Clearly, when the Draftsmen sought to confer special powers on one House, independent of the other House, or of the President, they did so in explicit, unambiguous terms. These carefully defined exceptions from presentment and bicameralism underscore the difference between the legislative functions of Congress and other unilateral but important and binding one-House acts provided for in the Constitution. These exceptions are narrow, explicit, and separately justified; none of them authorize the action challenged here. . . .

The bicameral requirement, the Presentment Clauses, the President's veto, and Congress' power to override a veto were intended to erect enduring checks on each Branch and to protect the people from the improvident exercise of power by mandating certain prescribed steps. To preserve those checks, and maintain the separation of powers, the carefully defined limits on the power of each Branch must not be eroded. To accomplish what has been attempted by one House of Congress in this case requires action in conformity with the express procedures of the Constitution's prescription for legislative action: passage by a majority of both Houses and presentment to the president.

The veto authorized by S 244(c)(2) doubtless has been in many respects a convenient shortcut; the "sharing" with the Executive by Congress of its authority over aliens in this manner is, on its face, an appealing compromise. In purely practical terms, it is obviously easier for action to be taken by one House without submission to the President; but it is crystal clear from the records of the Convention, contemporaneous writings and debates that the Framers ranked other values higher than efficiency. The records of the Convention and debates in the States preceding ratification underscore the common desire to define and limit the exercise of the newly created federal powers affecting the states and the people. There is unmistakable expression of a determination that legislation by the national Congress be a step-by-step, deliberate and deliberative process.

The choices we discern as having been made in the Constitutional Convention impose burdens on governmental processes that often seem clumsy, inefficient, even unworkable, but those hard choices were consciously made by men who had lived under a form of government that permitted arbitrary governmental acts to go unchecked. There is no support in the Constitution or decisions of this Court for the proposition that the cumbersomeness and delays often encountered in complying with explicit Constitutional standards may be avoided, either by Congress or by the President. . . . With all the obvious flaws of delay, untidiness, and potential for abuse, we have not yet found a better way to preserve freedom than by making the exercise of power subject to the carefully crafted restraints spelled out in the Constitution.

We hold that the Congressional veto provision in S 244(c)(2) is severable from the Act and that it is unconstitutional. Accordingly, the judgment of the Court of appeals is <u>Affirmed</u>.

[From Justice Powell's concurring in the judgment opinion:]

The Court's decision, based on the Presentment Clauses, . . . apparently will invalidate every use of the legislative veto. The breadth of this holding gives one pause. Congress has included the veto in literally hundreds of statutes, dating back to the 1930s. Congress clearly views this procedure as essential to controlling the delegation of power to administrative agencies. One reasonably may disagree with Congress' assessment of the veto's utility, but the respect due its judgment as a coordinate branch of Government cautions that our holding should be no more extensive than necessary to decide this case. In my view, the case may be decided on a narrower ground. When Congress finds that a particular person does not satisfy the statutory criteria for permanent residence in this country it has assumed a judicial function in violation of the principle of separation of powers. Accordingly, I concur in the judgment. . . .

One abuse that was prevalent during the Confederation was the exercise of judicial power by the state legislatures. The Framers were well acquainted with the danger of subjecting the determination of the rights of one person to the "tyranny of shifting majorities". . . .

It was to prevent . . . abuses that the Framers vested the executive, legislative, and judicial powers in separate branches. Their concern that a legislature should not be able unilaterally to impose a substantial deprivation on one person was expressed not only in this general allocation of power, but also in more specific provisions, such as the Bill of Attainder Clause.

The Constitution does not establish three branches with precisely defined boundaries. . . . The Court thus has been mindful that the boundaries between each branch should be fixed "according to common sense and the inherent necessities of the governmental co-ordination" . . . . But where one branch has impaired or sought to assume a power central to another branch, the Court has not hesitated to enforce the doctrine. . . .

Functionally, the doctrine may be violated in two ways. One branch may interfere impermissibly with the other's performance of its constitutionally assigned function. . . . Alternatively, the doctrine may be violated when one branch assumes a function that more properly is entrusted to another. . . . This case presents the latter situation. . . .

On its face, the House's action appears clearly adjudicatory. The House did not enact a general rule; rather it made its own determination that six specific persons did not comply with certain statutory criteria. It thus undertook the type of decision that traditionally has been left to other branches. Even if the House did not make a _de novo_ determination, but simply reviewed the Immigration and Naturalization Service's findings, it still assumed a function ordinarily entrusted to the federal courts. . . .

The impropriety of the House's assumption of this function is confirmed by the fact that its action raises the very danger the Framers sought to avoid--the exercise of unchecked power. In deciding whether Chadha deserves to be deported, Congress is not subject to any internal constraints that prevent it from arbitrarily depriving him of the right to remain in this country. Unlike the judiciary or an administrative agency, Congress is not bound by established substantive rules. Nor is it subject to the procedural safeguards, such as the right to counsel and a hearing before an impartial tribunal, that are present when a court or an agency adjudicates individual rights. The only effective constraint on Congress' power is political, but Congress is most accountable politically when it prescribes rules of general applicability. When it decides rights of specific persons, those rights are subject to "the tyranny of a shifting majority" . . . .

In my view, when Congress undertook to apply its rules to Chadha, it exceeded the scope of its constitutionally prescribed authority. I would not reach the broader question whether legislative vetoes are invalid under the Presentment Clauses.

[From Justice White's dissent:]

Today the Court not only invalidates S 244(c)(2) of the Immigration and Nationality Act, but also sounds the death knell for nearly 200 other statutory provisions in which Congress has reserved a "legislative veto." For this reason, the Court's decision is of surpassing importance. And it is for this reason that the Court would have been well-advised to decide the case, if possible, on the narrower grounds of separation of powers, leaving for full consideration the constitutionality of other congressional review statutes operating on such varied matters as war powers and agency rulemaking, some of which concern the independent regulatory agencies.

The prominence of the legislative veto mechanism in our contemporary political system and its importance to Congress can hardly be overstated. It has become a central means by which Congress secures the accountability of executive and independent agencies. Without the legislative veto, Congress is faced with a Hobson's choice: either to refrain from delegating the necessary authority, leaving itself with a hopeless task of writing laws with the requisite specificity to cover endless special circumstances across the entire policy landscape, or in the alternative, to abdicate its lawmaking function to the executive branch and independent agencies. To choose the former leaves major national problems unresolved; to opt for the latter risks unaccountable policymaking by those not elected to fill that role. Accordingly, over the past five decades, the legislative veto has been placed in nearly 200 statutes. The device is known in every field of governmental concern: reorganization, budgets, foreign affairs, war powers, and regulation of trade, safety, energy, the environment and the economy. . . .

. . . [T]he legislative veto is more than "efficient, convenient, and useful." It is an important if not indispensable political invention that allows the President and Congress to resolve major constitutional and policy differences, assures the accountability of independent regulatory agencies, and preserves Congress' control over lawmaking. Perhaps there are other means of accommodation and accountability, but the increasing reliance of Congress upon the legislative veto suggests that the alternatives to which Congress must now turn are not entirely satisfactory. . . .

. . . [T]he apparent sweep of the Court's decision today is regrettable. The Court's Article I analysis appears to invalidate all legislative vetoes irrespective of form or subject. Because the legislative veto is commonly found as a check upon rulemaking by administrative agencies and upon broad-based policy decisions of the Executive Branch, it is particularly unfortunate that the Court reaches its decisions regarding particular individuals. Courts should always be wary of striking statutes as unconstitutional; to strike an entire class of statutes based on consideration of a somewhat atypical and more-readily indictable exemplar of the class is irresponsible. It was for cases such as this one that Justice Brandeis wrote:

> "The Court has frequently called attention to the 'great gravity and delicacy' of its function in passing upon the validity of an act of Congress. . . . The Court will not 'formulate a rule of constitutional law broader than is required by the precise facts to which it is to be applied.'"

Unfortunately, today's holding is not so limited.

If the legislative veto were as plainly unconstitutional as the Court strives to suggest, its broad ruling today would be more comprehensible. But the constitutionality of the legislative veto is anything but clear cut. The issue divides scholars, courts, attorneys general, and the two other branches of the National Government. If the veto devices so flagrantly disregarded the requirements of Article I as the Court today suggests, I find it incomprehensible that Congress, whose members are bound by oath to uphold the Constitution, would have placed these mechanisms in nearly 200 separate laws over a period of 50 years.

The reality of the situation is that the constitutional question posed today is one of immense difficulty over which the executive and legislative branches--as well as scholars and judges--have understandably disagreed. That disagreement stems from the silence of the Constitution on the precise question: The Constitution does not directly authorize or prohibit the legislative veto. Thus, our task should be to determine whether the legislative veto is consistent with the purposes of Art. I and the principles of Separation of Powers which are reflected in that Article and throughout the Constitution. . . .

This is the perspective from which we should approach the novel constitutional questions presented by the legislative veto. In my view, neither Article I of the Constitution nor the doctrines of separation of powers is violated by this mechanism by which our elected representatives preserve their voice in the governance of the nation. . . .

The power to exercise a legislative veto is not the power to write new law without bicameral approval or presidential consideration. The veto must be authorized by statute and may only negate what an Executive department

or independent agency has proposed. On its face, the
legislative veto no more allows one House of Congress to
make law than does the presidential veto confer such power
upon the President. Accordingly, the Court properly
recognizes that it "must establish that the challenged
action under S 244(c)(2) is of the kind to which the
procedural requirements of Art. I, S 7 apply" and admits
that "not every action taken by either House is subject to
the bicameralism and presentation requirements of
Art. I" . . . .

Although the [Presentment] Clause does not specify the
actions for which the concurrence of both Houses is
"necessary," the proceedings at the Philadelphia
Convention suggest its purpose was to prevent Congress from
circumventing the presentation requirement in the making of
new legislation. . . . There is no record that the
Convention contemplated, let alone intended that these
Article I requirements would some day be invoked to restrain
the scope of Congressional authority pursuant to duly-
enacted law. . . .

It is long settled that Congress may "exercise its best
judgment in the selection of measures, to carry into
execution the constitutional powers of the government," and
"avail itself of experience, to exercise its reason, and to
accommodate its legislation to circumstances."

The Court heeded this counsel in approving the modern
administrative state. The Court's holding today that all
legislative-type action must be enacted through the
lawmaking process ignores that legislative authority is
routinely delegated to the Executive branch, to the
independent regulatory agencies, and to private
individuals and groups.

This Court's decisions sanctioning such delegations
make clear that Article I does not require all action with
the effect of legislation to be passed as a law.

The wisdom and the constitutionality of these broad
delegations are matters that still have not been put to
rest. But for present purposes, these cases establish that
by virtue of congressional delegation, legislative power
can be exercised by independent agencies and Executive
departments without the passage of new legislation. For
some time, the sheer amount of law--the substantive rules
that regulate private conduct and direct the operation of
government--made by the agencies has far outnumbered the
lawmaking engaged in by Congress through the traditional
process. There is no question but that agency rulemaking
is lawmaking in any functional or realistic sense of the
term . . . they [administrative rules] have the force of the
law.

If Congress may delegate lawmaking power to
independent and executive agencies, it is most difficult to
understand Article I as forbidding Congress from also
reserving a check on legislative power for itself. Absent
the veto, the agencies receiving delegations of legislative

or quasi-legislative power may issue regulations having the force of law without bicameral approval and without the President's signature. It is thus not apparent why the reservation of a veto over the exercise of that legislative power must be subject to a more exacting test. In both cases, it is enough that the initial statutory authorizations comply with the Article I requirements.

The Court's opinion in the present case comes closest to facing the reality of administrative lawmaking in considering the contention that the Attorney General's action in suspending deportation under S 244 is itself a legislative act. . . .

. . . [T]he Court concedes that certain administrative agency action, such as rulemaking, "may resemble lawmaking" and recognizes that "[t]his Court has referred to agency activity as being 'quasi-legislative' in character. . . ." Such rules and adjudications by the agencies meet the Court's own definition of legislative action for they "alter the legal rights, duties, and relations of persons . . . outside the legislative branch" . . . and involve "determinations of policy". . . . Under the Court's analysis, the Executive Branch and the independent agencies may make rules with the effect of law when Congress, in whom the Framers confided the legislative power, Art. I, S 1, may not exercise a veto which precludes such rules from having operative force. If the effective functioning of a complex modern government requires the delegation of vast authority which, by virtue of its breadth, is legislative or "quasi-legislative" in character, I cannot accept that Article I--which is, after all, the source of the nondelegation doctrine--should forbid Congress from qualifying that grant with a legislative veto.

Until 1917, Congress had never established laws concerning the deportation of aliens. The Immigration Act of 1924 enlarged the categories of aliens subject to mandatory deportation, and substantially increased the likelihood of hardships to individuals by abolishing in most cases the previous time limitation of three years within which deportation proceedings had to be commenced. . . . Thousands of persons, who either had entered the country in more lenient times or had been smuggled in as children, or had overstayed their permits, faced the prospect of deportation. Enforcement of the Act grew more rigorous over the years with the deportation of thousands of aliens without regard to the mitigating circumstances of particular cases. . . . Congress provided relief in certain cases through the passage of private bills.

In 1933 when deportations reached their zenith, the Secretary of Labor temporarily suspended numerous deportations on grounds of hardship, and proposed legislation to allow certain deportable aliens to remain in the country. The Labor Department bill was opposed,

however, as "grant[ing] too much discretionary authority". . . .

The following year, the administration proposed bills
to authorize an inter-Departmental committee to grant
permanent residence to deportable aliens who had lived in
the United States for 10 years or who had close relatives
here. . . . These bills were also attacked as an
"abandonment of congressional control over the deportation
of undesirable aliens". . . and were not enacted. . . .

The succeeding Congress again attempted to find a
legislative solution to the deportation problem. The
initial House bill required congressional action to cancel
individual deportations, but the Senate amended the
legislation to provide that deportable aliens should not be
deported unless the Congress by Act or resolution rejected
the recommendation of the Secretary.

The compromise solution . . . allowed the Attorney
General to suspend the deportation of qualified aliens.
Their deportation would be canceled and permanent residence
granted if the House and Senate did not adopt a concurrent
resolution of disapproval. . . . The Executive Branch
played a major role in fashioning this compromise, . . . and
President Roosevelt approved the legislation which became
the Alien Registration Act of 1940. . . .

In 1947, the Department of Justice requested
legislation authorizing the Attorney General to cancel
deportations without congressional review. . . . The
purpose of the proposal was to "save time and energy of
everyone concerned. . . ." The Senate Judiciary Committee
objected, stating that "affirmative action by the Congress
in all suspension cases should be required before
deportation proceedings may be canceled". . . . Congress
not only rejected the Department's request for final
authority but amended the Immigration Act to require that
cancellation of deportation be approved by a concurrent
resolution of the Congress. President Truman signed the
bill without objection.

Practice over the ensuing several years convinced
Congress that the requirement of affirmative approval was
"not workable . . . and would, in time, interfere with the
legislative work of the House". . . . In preparing the
comprehensive Immigration and Nationality Act of 1952, the
Senate Judiciary Committee recommended that for certain
classes of aliens the adjustment of status be subject to the
disapproval of either House; but deportation of an alien
"who is of the criminal, subversive, or immoral classes or
who overstays his period of admission" would be canceled
only upon a concurrent resolution disapproving the
deportation. . . . Legislation reflecting this change was
passed by both Houses, and enacted into law as part of the
Immigration and Nationality Act of 1952 over President
Truman's veto, which was not predicated on the presence of a
legislative veto. . . . In subsequent years, the Congress
refused further requests that the Attorney General be given

final authority to grant discretionary relief for specified categories of aliens, and S 244 remained intact to the present.

Section 244(A)(1) authorizes the Attorney General, in his discretion, to suspend the deportation of certain aliens who are otherwise deportable and, upon Congress' approval, to adjust their status to that of aliens lawfully admitted for permanent residence. . . . Thus, the suspension proceeding "has two phases: a determination whether the statutory conditions have been met, which generally involves a question of law, and a determination whether relief shall be granted, which [ultimately] . . . is confined to the sound discretion of the Attorney General [and his delegates]" . . . .

There is also a third phase to the process. . . . [T]he Attorney General must report all such suspensions, with a detailed statement of facts and reasons, to the Congress. Either House may then act, in that session or the next, to block the suspension of deportation by passing a resolution of disapproval. . . . Upon Congressional approval of suspension--by its silence--the alien's permanent status is adjusted to that of a lawful resident alien.

The history of the Immigration Act makes clear that [it] did not alter the division of actual authority between Congress and the Executive. At all times, whether through private bills, or through affirmative concurrent resolutions, or through the present one-House veto, a permanent change in a deportable alien's status could be accomplished only with the agreement of the Attorney General, the House and the Senate.

The central concern of the presentation and bicameralism requirements of Article I is that when a departure from the legal status quo is undertaken, it is done with the approval of the President and both Houses of Congress--or, in the event of a presidential veto, a two-thirds majority in both Houses. This interest is fully satisfied by the operation of S 244(c)(2). The President's approval is found in the Attorney General's action in recommending to Congress that the deportation order for a given alien be suspended. The House and the Senate indicate their approval of the Executive's action by not passing a resolution of disapproval within the statutory period. Thus, a change in the legal status quo--the deportability of the alien--is consummated only with the approval of each of the three relevant actors. . . . "The President and the two Houses enjoy exactly the same say in what the law is to be as would have been true for each without the presence of the concurrence of the President, and a majority in each House."

This very construction of the Presentment Clauses which the Executive Branch now rejects was the basis upon which the Executive Branch defended the constitutionality of the Reorganization Act, which provides that the President's proposed reorganization plans take effect only if not vetoed by either House. . . .

I now briefly consider possible objections to this analysis.

First, it may be asserted that Chadha's status before legislative disapproval is one of nondeportation and that the exercise of the veto, unlike the failure of a private bill works a change in the status quo. This position plainly ignores the statutory language. . . . A grant of "suspension" does not cancel the alien's deportation or adjust the alien's status to that of a permanent resident alien. A suspension order is merely a "deferment of deportation."

Second, it may be said that this approach leads to the incongruity that the two-House veto is more suspect than its one-House brother. Although the idea may be initially counter-intuitive, on close analysis, it is not at all unusual that the one-House veto is of more certain constitutionality than the two-House version. If the Attorney General's action is a proposal for legislation, then the disapproval of but a single House is all that is required to prevent its passage. Because approval is indicated by the failure to veto, the one-House veto satisfies the requirement of bicameral approval. . . .

Third, it may be objected that Congress cannot indicate its approval of legislative change by inaction. In the Court of Appeals' view, inaction by Congress "could equally imply endorsement, acquiescence, passivity, indecision or indifference." This objection appears more properly directed at the wisdom of the legislative veto than its constitutionality. The Constitution does not and cannot guarantee that legislators will carefully scrutinize legislation and deliberate before acting. In a democracy it is the electorate that holds the legislators accountable for the wisdom of their choices. It is hard to maintain that a private bill receives any greater individualized scrutiny than a resolution of disapproval under S 244(c)(2). . . .

The Court of Appeals struck S 244(c)(2) as violative of the constitutional principle of separation of powers. It is true that the purpose of separating the authority of government is to prevent unnecessary and dangerous concentration of power in one branch. For that reason, the Framers saw fit to divide and balance the powers of government so that each branch would be checked by the others. Virtually every part of our constitutional system bears the mark of this judgment.

But the history of the separation of powers doctrine is also a history of accommodation and practicality. Apprehensions of an overly powerful branch have not led to undue prophylactic measures that handicap the effective working of the national government as a whole. The Constitution does not contemplate total separation of the three branches of Government. . . .

The legislative veto provision does not "prevent the Executive Branch from accomplishing its constitutionally assigned functions." First, it is clear that the Executive Branch has no "constitutionally assigned" function of suspending the deportation of aliens. "Over no conceivable subject is the legislative power of Congress more complete than it is over the admission of aliens". . . . Nor can it be said that the inherent function of the Executive Branch in executing the law is involved. The Steel Seizure Case resolved that the Article II mandate for the President to execute the law is a directive to enforce the law which Congress has written. "The duty of the President to see that the laws be executed is a duty that does not go beyond the laws or require him to achieve more than Congress sees fit to leave within his power." Here, S 244 grants the executive only a qualified suspension authority and it is only that authority which the President is constitutionally authorized to execute.

Moreover, the Court believes that the legislative veto we consider today is best characterized as an exercise of legislative or quasi-legislative authority. Under this characterization, the practice does not, even on the surface, constitute an infringement of executive or judicial prerogative. The Attorney General's suspension of deportation is equivalent to a proposal for legislation. The nature of the Attorney General's role as recommendatory is not altered because S 244 provides for congressional action through disapproval rather than by ratification. In comparison to private bills, which must be initiated in the Congress and which allow a Presidential veto to be overridden by a two-thirds majority in both Houses of Congress, S 244 augments rather than reduces the executive branch's authority. So understood, congressional review does not undermine, as the Court of Appeals thought, the "weight and dignity" that attends the decisions of the Executive Branch.

Nor does S 244 infringe on the judicial power, as JUSTICE POWELL would hold. Section 244 makes clear that Congress has reserved its own judgment as part of the statutory process. Congressional action does not substitute for judicial review of the Attorney General's decisions. The Act provides for judicial review of the refusal of the Attorney General to suspend a deportation and to transmit a recommendation to Congress. . . . But the courts have not been given the authority to review whether an alien should be given permanent status; review is limited to whether the Attorney General has properly applied the statutory standards for essentially denying the alien a recommendation that his deportable status be changed by the Congress. Moreover, there is no constitutional obligation to provide any judicial review whatever for a failure to suspend deportation. "The power of Congress, therefore, to expel like the power to exclude aliens, or any specified class of aliens, from the country, may be exercised entirely through executive officers; or Congress may call in the aid of the judiciary to ascertain any uncontested facts on which an alien's right to be in the country has been made by Congress to depend". . . .

I do not suggest that all legislative vetoes are necessarily consistent with separation of powers principles. A legislative check on an inherently executive function, for example that of initiating prosecutions, poses an entirely different question. But the legislative veto device here--and in many other settings--is far from an instance of legislative tyranny over the Executive. It is a necessary check on the unavoidably expanding power of the agencies, both executive and independent, as they engage in exercising authority delegated by Congress.

I regret that I am in disagreement with my colleagues on the fundamental questions that this case presents. But even more I regret the destructive scope of the Court's holding. It reflects a profoundly different conception of the Constitution than that held by the Courts which sanctioned the modern administrative state. Today's decision strikes down in one fell swoop provisions in more laws enacted by Congress than the Court has cumulatively invalidated in its history. I fear it will now be more difficult "to insure that the fundamental policy decisions in our society will be made not by an appointed official but the body immediately responsible to the people. I must dissent.

[From Justice Rehnquist's Dissent:]

A severability clause creates a presumption that Congress intended the valid portion of the statute to remain in force when one part is found to be invalid. . . . A severability clause does not, however, conclusively resolve the issue. "[T]he determination, in the end, is reached by" asking "[w]hat was the intent of the lawmakers". . . . Because I believe that Congress did not intend the one-House veto provision of S 244(c)(2) to be severable, I dissent.

By severing S 244(c)(2), the Court permits suspension of deportation in a class of cases where Congress never stated that suspension was appropriate. I do not believe we should expand the statute in this way without some clear indication that Congress intended such an expansion. . . .

The Court finds that the legislative history of S 244 shows that Congress intended S 244(c)(2) to be severable because Congress wanted to relieve itself of the burden of private bills. But the history elucidated by the Court shows that Congress was unwilling to give the Executive Branch permission to suspend deportation on its own. Over the years, Congress consistently rejected requests from the Executive for complete discretion in this area. Congress always insisted on retaining ultimate control, whether by concurrent resolution, as in the 1948 Act, or by one-House veto, as in the present Act. Congress has never indicated that it would be willing to permit suspensions of deportation unless it could retain some sort of veto.

It is doubtless true that Congress has the power to provide for suspensions of deportation without a one-House veto. But the Court has failed to identify any evidence that Congress intended to exercise that power. On the contrary, Congress' continued insistence on retaining control of the suspension process indicates that it has never been disposed to give the Executive Branch a free hand. By severing S 244(c)(2) the Court has "confounded" Congress' "intention" to permit suspension of deportation "with their power to carry that intention into effect". . . .

Because I do not believe that S 244(c)(2) is severable, I would reverse the judgment of the Court of Appeals.

Index

Act to Promote Defense of U.S., 53
Adams, Brock, 141
Administrative Law and Government Relations Subcommittee, Senate, 51, 56
Administrative Procedure Act, 13, 95, 110, 113, 118, 126, 138, 155, 160
Advance notification, 8 17
Air bags. See Passive restraints
Akerman, Robert, 5
Alien Registration Act of 1940, 29, 169
American Automobile Association, 142
American Federation of Teachers, 87
American Motors, 142
Amolsh, Arthur L., 166, 167
Amtrak Improvement Act of 1975, 53
Anderson, John B., 14
Appointments Clause, 45
Appropriations riders, 159-60
Arenas of power, 11-12, 15
  administrative, 11, 13, 15
  distributive, 11, 12, 15, 150-51, 163-64
  pluralistic arenas, 11-13, 15
  See also Subsystem politics
Arieff, Irwin, B., 21
Armed Services Committee, Senate, 35
Ashbrook, John, 106
Ashley, Thomas, 65, 70
Atkins v. U.S., 45-46

Bailey, Patricia P., 158, 167
Baker, Stewart A., 117
Balance of powers, 42
Banking, Finance, and Urban Affairs Committee, House, 16, 57-58, 64, 67, 72, 162
Banking, Housing, and Urban Affairs Committee, Senate, 16, 57, 72
Baruch, Morton S., 69, 70, 80
Basic Educational Opportunity Grants Program, 83, 90
Beilenson, Anthony C., 51
Bell, Griffin B., 54-55, 108-9
Berry, Mary, 96-97, 100, 103, 117
Bicameralism, 47
Bickel, Alexander, M., 41
Blissett, Marlan, 79
Bolling, Richard, 44-45
Bolton, John R., 42, 55
Boren, David L., 73, 175
Boyer, Ernie, 96
Brandeis, Louis D., 173
Brademas, John, 94
Brown, Clarence J., 132
Brown, Garry, 57, 63
Bruff, Harold, 17, 52, 56, 61, 67, 73, 79, 80, 81, 84, 92, 93-94, 116, 117, 154, 161, 166, 167
Buchanan, John, 99, 104
Buckley v. Valeo, 45
Burger, Warren, 1, 171-73, 183-91
Byrnes, James, 43

Califano, Joseph A., 94-95, 116

Cannon's Precedents of the
House of Representatives,
44
Carter, Jimmy, 9, 36-37,
49-50, 54-55, 56, 61, 76,
86-88, 96, 108, 109,
122-26, 141, 145
Cater, Douglas, 21
Chadha, Jagdish Rai, 169-74
Chadha v. Immigration and Nat-
uralization Service, 29,
46-47, 169-74, 183-201
Chrysler v. Department of
Transportation, 141
Civiletti, Benjamin, R., 93,
107, 111, 113, 118, 119
Civil Rights Act of 1965,
Title VI, 68
Clark v. Valeo, 45
Cleveland, Frederick N., 79
Coastal Zone Management Act
of 1980, 36
Cohen, Richard E., 118
Coleman, William, 141
Come into agreement, 20, 29,
44
Commerce, Science, and Trans-
portation Committee,
Senate, 12
Common Cause, 12
Comprehensive Environmental
Response, Compensation
and Liability Act, 54
Congressional Budget and
Impoundment Control Act
of 1974, 30
Congressional Research
Service, 9, 30, 42, 149,
174
Congressional staff, 3, 15,
52, 71, 83, 92, 97, 113,
150, 152-55
Congressional Watch, 12
Consumer Energy Council of
America et al. v. Federal
Energy Regulatory
Commission, 47-49, 136,
167
Consumer Product Safety
Act of 1972, 139
Consumer Product Safety
Commission, 7, 174-75

Consumer's Union of U.S., Inc.
v. Federal Trade Commission,
47
Cooper, Ann, 19, 40, 55
Cooper, Joseph, 19, 40, 55
Corcoran, Tom, 132
Craig, Barbara Hinkson, 181
Curtis, Charles, 86
Curtis, Charles B., 131

Dahl, Robert, 21
Danforth, John C., 178
Department of Agriculture, 29
Department of Defense Authoriza-
tion Act of 1980, 35
Department of Education, 7, 9,
16, 17, 30, 78, 83-115, 150,
160-61
Department of Energy, 64, 80
Department of Housing and Urban
Development, 3, 16, 17,
57-78, 115, 151-52, 154,
160-62
Department of Interior, 29, 86
Department of Interior and
Related Agencies Appropria-
tions for FY 1979, 53
Department of Justice, 16, 39,
47, 138
Department of Transportation,
17, 121, 139-44
Deportation suspensions,
169-74, 183-201
Deregulation, 122-38 passim,
144
Dingell, John D., 124, 126, 129,
131-32, 134-35, 174-75
Dirksen, Everett, 43-44
Dixon, Jr., Robert G., 10, 21,
43, 55, 113, 119
Dunlop v. Bachowski, 14

Eaton Yale and Towne, Inc., 141
Eckhardt, Bob, 45
Edson, Charles L., 71
Education Amendments of 1972
9, 30, 85, 90
Education Amendments of 1974,
20, 84, 89, 98, 114
Education Amendments Act of
1978, 89, 96, 101, 104, 155
Education and Labor Committee,
House, 17, 84-85, 91,
94-97, 101-2, 106, 162

Eilberg, Joshua, 170
Eizenstat, Stuart E., 108
Elementary and Secondary
    School Act, 88
Emergency Energy Conservation
    Act of 1979, 54
Emergency Homeowners Relief
    Act of 1975, 61
Emergency Price Control Act
    of 1942, 53
Emergency Unemployment Com-
    pensation Act of 1975,
    54
Energy Interim Consumer
    Product Safety Standard
    Act of 1978, 20
Energy Policy and Conserva-
    tion Act of 1975, 20, 54,
    64
Energy Research and Develop-
    ment Administration
    Authorization Act of
    1975, 20
Energy Security Act of 1980,
    136
Environmental Defense Fund v.
    Ruckelshaus, 14
Epilepsy Foundation, 142
Ervin, Sam, 44
Executive Order 12044, 76
Ex parte contracts, 13

Fair housing, 3, 68-73
Federal Communications
    Commission, 12
Federal Elections Commis-
    sion, 45, 52, 68
Federal Energy Regulatory
    Commission, 16, 18,
    47-49, 115, 121, 144,
    150-52, 153
Federal Insecticide, Fungi-
    cide and Rodenticide
    Act, 36
Federal Register, 17, 58, 64,
    68, 69, 70, 75, 83-85,
    90, 97, 103, 105, 110,
    178
Federal Salary Act of 1967,
    46
Federal Trade Commission, 3,
    7, 13, 47, 55, 156-60

Federal Trade Commission
    Amendments of 1980, 13, 18,
    47
Federal Trade Commission Im-
    provements Act of 1980, 2, 3
Fenwick, Millicent, 70, 78
Fisher, Louis, 42, 55, 79, 115
    149, 153, 159-60, 166
Florida East Coast Railway Co.
    v. U.S., 22
Ford, Gerald, 60, 179
Ford, Wendell, 142
Ford, William D., 84, 92-93, 94,
    95, 111
Ford Motor Company, 139, 140,
    141
Foreign affairs, 26, 27-28, 35,
    37, 48, 53
Foreign Assistance Act of 1961,
    28
    of 1974, 28
Foreign Relations Committee,
    Senate, 35
Forestry Service, 29
Framers, 38, 154, 172
Franklin, Grace, 21-22
Freeman, J. Leiper, 21
Funeral rule, 157

Gasch, Oliver, 66
Gelfand, Mark I., 79
Gelhorn, Ernest, 17, 52, 56, 61,
    67, 73, 79, 80, 81, 84, 92,
    93-94, 116, 117, 154, 161,
    166, 167
General Education Provisions
    Act, 84, 92
General Motors, 141, 142
General Services Administration,
    29
Gilmour, Robert S., 21, 163, 167
Ginnane, Robert W., 39-40, 54,
    55
Goldman, Leslie, J., 145
Goodling, William, 97, 105-6
Gore, Jr., Albert, 132
Granat, Diane, 166
Grassley, Charles, 175
Griffin, Robert P., 142

Hall, George, 131
Harmon, John, 111
Harris, Patricia, 61-62, 64-66,
    68, 72, 78, 80

Hills, Carla, 60
Holden, Jr., Matthew, 131
Holt, Robert T., 21
Home Box Office v. FCC, 13
Hoover, Herbert, 25
Hopi and Navajo Tribe Act,
    1974, 53
Housing and Community Develop-
    ment Act of 1974, 62, 79
    of 1978, 16, 57, 63, 78, 79
    of 1980, 58, 67
Housing programs, Section 8,
    60, 68
    Model Cities, 60
    Community Development Block
    Grants, 60, 61
    Urban Development Action
    Grants, 60
    See also Fair housing
Hufstedler, Shirley M., 88,
    101, 107-113, 118

Immigration and Naturaliza-
    tion Act of 1952, 29,
    169, 173
Immigration and Naturaliza-
    tion Service, 170
Immigration and Naturaliza-
    tion Service v. Chadha,
    1, 3, 46-47, 169-74, 179,
    183-201
Incremental gas-pricing rule,
    47, 121, 126-135
Insurance Institute for High-
    way Safety, 142
Interior and Insular Affairs
    Committee, Senate, 20
International Security
    Assistance Act of 1978,
    28
    of 1979, 35
Interstate and Foreign Com-
    merce Committee, House,
    12, 124
Iron triangle. See Subsystem
    politics

Jackson, Henry, 125
Jackson, Robert H., 54
Jacobs, Jr., Andrew, 176
Javits, Jacob, 45
Jefferson's Manual of Parlia-
    mentary Procedure, 44

Johnson, Lyndon B., 58, 88
Jordan, F. Forbis, 116
Judiciary Committee, House, 72
    170

Kaplan, Abraham, 11, 21
Kelly, Richard, 65
Kennedy, John F., 58
Kramer, Ken, 111-12
Kramer v. Hufstedler, 111-12

Labor and Human Resources Com-
    mittee, Senate, 17, 84,
    90-91
Landrieu, Moon, 72
Lasswell, Harold, 11, 21
League of Nations, 24
Legislative Appropriations Act
    of 1932, 9, 25, 53
Legislative veto, arts in
    education, 97-100
    constitutionality, 1, 10-11,
    38-50, 57, 111, 137-38
    educational appeals board,
    100-2, 110-11
    education, 96-107, 131
    expansion in use, 26-37
    form: committee, 20, 29, 40,
    41-42, 45; concurrent
    resolution, 17, 20, 70;
    generic, 3, 36, 51, 56;
    joint resolution, 1, 57-58,
    178; one-house, 9, 30,
    44-49, 125, 130-36, 157,
    171-74; simple resolution,
    19-20, 25-26, 38-40; two-
    house, 8, 25, 44, 96-113,
    134, 157
    functional consequences, 2-3,
    9, 49-52, 75-79, 83-84,
    90-95, 112-14, 134-35, 144,
    149-50, 152-55, 159-64
    gym equipment, 104-7, 110
    incremental gas pricing,
    130-38, 152, 164, 174, 178
    pocket (games-of-chance rule),
    161
    thermal standards, 64-68, 73
    78, 79, 150-51
    spatial deconcentration,
    68-73, 77, 78, 151-52
    used-cars rule, 158-59, 164,
    174

Lend Lease Act, 54
Leventhal, Harold, 50
Levin, Betsy, 107
Levin, Carl, 52, 61, 73, 81, 175
Levitas, Elliott H., 2, 9, 21, 36, 174, 175, 178
Lowi, Theodore, 11, 21, 22
Lugar-Stevenson bill, 130
Lynn, James, 60

Maass, Arthur A. 41-42
MacAvoy, Paul W., 145
Madden, Mimi, 166, 167
Madison, Christopher, 147
Magnuson-Moss Act, 156-58
Malbin, Michael J., 145
Martin, Dave, 44
McCorkle v. U.S., 46, 173
McFarland, M. Carter, 79
McGrew, Jane, 75, 81
McKinney, Stewart, 65
McMurty, Virginia A., 55-56
Melsheimer, John T., 54
Merton, Robert K., 11, 21
Military and Naval Construction Act of 1952, 53
Miller, George, 101-2
Miller, III, James C., 157
Millett, John, 39, 55
Mitchell, William D., 25, 44
Moakley, J. Joseph, 175, 179, 181
Moe, Ronald, 42, 55
Moffett, Toby, 133, 145
Morrill Act of 1862, 86
Morrison, Alan B., 138, 147, 170
Mortgage Bankers Association, 77-78
Motor Vehicle and School Bus Safety Amendments of 1974, 17, 140
Muris, Timothy I., 157-58

Nader, Ralph, 12
National Aeronautics and Space Administration, 29, 53
National Association of Home Builders, 59
National Association of Housing and Redevelopment Officials, block grant study, 62

National Association of Student Financial Aid Administrators, 90
National Bureau of Standards, 65-67
National Consumer Law Center, 131
National Education Association, 86-87, 95
National Energy Conservation Policy Act of 1978, 64, 80
National Highway and Traffic Safety Administration, 16, 115, 139, 141
National Traffic and Motor Vehicle Safety Act of 1966, 139
Natural Gas Policy Act, 2, 18, 47, 48, 122-26, 129, 135 139
Navy Public Works Construction Authorizations of 1944, 29
Nicola, Thomas J., 54
Nixon, Richard M., 30, 60, 61, 179
Norton, Clark F., 10, 19, 20, 53, 54

Occupational Safety and Health Act of 1970, 139
Office of Education. See Department of Education
Office of Management and Budget, 11, 16, 86, 179
O'Hara, James, 91
O'Neill, Thomas P., 94, 123
Ornstein, Norman, 5

Packwood, Robert, 158
Parliament, 23-24
Pashayan, Jr., Charles, 176, 178
Passive-restraint standard, 3, 17-18, 121, 138-41, 177
Pearson-Bentsen substitute, 124
Peck, Raymond A., 144
Pell, Claiborne, 17, 90, 97, 105
Pendyck, Robert S., 145
Percy, Charles, 125
Perkins, Carl, 17, 97-115 passim
Pertschuk, Michael, 55, 166
Petrini, Edward, 131

111257

Petroleum Marketing Practices Act of 1978, 20
Phillips Petroleum Company v. Wisconsin, 122
Political Action Committees, 51–52
Powell, Jr., Lewis, 172, 190–92
Presentment Clause, 38–40, 44, 172
Presidential Recording and Materials Preservation Act of 1974, 30
Presidential veto, 25, 38, 47
Preyer, Richardson, 130–31
Preyer-Stockman bill, 130
Proxmire, William, 82
Pryor, Tim, 81
Public Building Act of 1949, 43–44
Public Building Purchase Contract Act of 1954, 53
Public Utility Regulatory Policies Act of 1978, 20
Public Works Committee, Senate, 43

Reagan, Ronald, 157, 164
Redford, Emmette S., 79
Reed, Daniel, 86
Rehnquist, William H., 173, 200–201
Reorganization, 25–26, 36, 43
Reorganization Act of 1932, 37 of 1939, 25, 39, 53
Report and wait, 8, 17, 44
Reuss, Henry S., 64–65, 71, 80
Riddle, Wayne, 116
Ripley, Randall, 21
Roberts, Steven V., 166
Rodgers, Lindsay, 39, 55
Romney, George, 60
Roosevelt, Franklin D., 36, 54
Rosenberg, Morton, 174, 181
Rosenthal, Benjamin S., 87
Rousselot, John, 100

Sarosohn, Judy, 147, 166
Schattschneider, E. E., 73, 81
Schmitt, Harrison, 36
Schuster, Bud, 142
Schwartz, Bernard, 5, 42–43, 55

Science and Technology Committee, House, 20
Seacoast Anti-Pollution League v. Costle, 14
Seat-belt interlock system, 139
Seidman, Harold, 10, 19, 21, 50, 56, 114, 119
Separation of powers, 2, 16, 41, 42, 46, 47, 172
Severability, 46, 173
Shalala, Donna E., 74
Shanker, Albert, 87
Sharp, Philip R., 131–33
Sheldon, Georgiana, 131
Sierra Club, 12
Simons, Lawrence B., 71
Singer, James W., 166
Skelton amendment, 87
Small Reclamation Projects Act, 53
Smith, Mike, 96–97, 100, 103, 118
Southern Regional Council, 62
Special Subcommittee on Separation of Powers, Senate, 41, 55
State Farm Mutual Automobile Insurance Co. v. DOT, 147
Stevenson, Adlai, E., 145
Stockman, David, 133–34
Subsystem politics, 2–3, 11–13, 15, 50, 60, 150–54. See also Arenas of power, distributive
Sundquist, James L., 5, 150, 153, 166
Symms, Steven, 99

Un-American Activities Committee, House, 41
United Auto Workers, 142
Used-cars rule, 3, 18, 47, 158–59, 164, 174

Vermont Yankee Nuclear Power Corp. v. Natural Resources Defense Council, Inc., 22
Volkswagen, 140

War Labor Disputes Act of 1943, 53
War Powers Resolution of 1973, 28, 44, 174

Watershed Protection and Flood
      Prevention Act of 1954, 53
Watkins v. U.S., 41
Watson, H. Lee, 19, 24, 53, 166
Waxman, Henry A., 174
White, Byron, 1, 45, 172-73,
      192-200

Wilkey, Malcolm R., 163
Willmann, John B., 79
Wilson, Woodrow, 25
Wines, Michael, 147
Wright, James, 94